P9-BBP-566

$2

"We're taking fire!" Hollister yelled ___ ___ w his rifle onto the chopper deck and hauled him___ in just as another short burst of enemy fire sliced past.

Hollister counted heads and yelled to the pilot, "Go! Go! Go!"

Moody jerked some pitch into the blades and rolled the chopper forward just before its skids cleared the ground completely.

But before they even got a few feet off the ground they heard an awful thunking sound up front. The chopper jerked first left then right as a few enemy tracer rounds passed between the pilots.

As they lost momentum and altitude, the thought of going down in another chopper flashed through Hollister's mind and he instinctively began to look for somewhere to jump. . . .

By Dennis Foley
Published by Ivy Books:

LONG RANGE PATROL
NIGHT WORK
SPECIAL MEN: A LRP's Recollections
TAKE BACK THE NIGHT

Books published by The Ballantine Publishing Group
are available at quantity discounts on bulk purchases for
premium, educational, fund-raising, and special sales
use. For details, please call 1-800-733-3000.

TAKE BACK
THE NIGHT

Dennis Foley

IVY BOOKS • NEW YORK

Sale of this book without a front cover may be unauthorized. If this book is coverless, it may have been reported to the publisher as "unsold or destroyed" and neither the author nor the publisher may have received payment for it.

Ivy Books
Published by Ballantine Books
Copyright © 1996 by Dennis Foley

All rights reserved under International and Pan-American Copyright Conventions. Published in the United States by Ballantine Books, a division of Random House, Inc., New York, and simultaneously in Canada by Random House of Canada Limited, Toronto.

http://www.randomhouse.com

Library of Congress Catalog Card Number: 96-94667

ISBN 0-8041-0725-4

Printed in Canada

First Edition: October 1996

10 9 8 7 6 5 4 3

Dedicated to
Joe T. Stroud
who would fly anywhere, anytime—
to help a Ranger in harm's way.

PROLOGUE

1993—The Pentagon

Vice Chairman of the Joint Chiefs of Staff General T. P. Terry stood at the window in his Pentagon office. Rain fell in sheets on the northern Virginia countryside.

"General, I'm just the wrong guy for this job."

Terry turned and looked at Lieutenant General Grady Michaelson. "Guess it won't be the first time you and the chain of command have differed on the best place to put you."

Michaelson smiled at his old friend. "Seems like this calls for more of a political animal than I am. I have to be honest with you—I want to weasel my way out of this."

"Grady, the Chairman personally picked you by name. He'll be back from Belgium next week and you can take it up with him. Until then, you are our new man at the White House."

Michaelson waved his arm toward the concentric rings of the five-sided building. "I've got to believe that there's someone here far more qualified to do this than I am. Hell, you've known me for more than twenty years. I'm a field rat. A mud soldier. I'm liable to step on my crank and really piss someone off over there."

"The Chairman's attitude is that you know everything about what the man in the Oval Office knows absolutely nothing about—wars and warriors."

"Doesn't make me any happier to hear that." Michaelson made a disapproving face. "Jesus, doesn't this business ever get any easier?"

"Farther up the flagpole you climb the more your ass is in the breeze. You know that."

1

"And I was just a ballpoint pen away from signing the papers to hang up my green suit after thirty-one years."

"Why didn't you?"

"I got a call from the Chairman. He said he needed me for one more tough job. Hell, I figured after the jobs I've had—how tough could it be? But I didn't figure on this."

Terry took a more sober tone. "If soldierin' was easy, everybody'd be doing it, Grady. He needs you to do this. Things are about as bad as they can get. You can't even measure the distance between here and the Oval Office."

"Okay. What's the Chairman want me to do?"

"Get over there and see if you can tactfully guide the president and his amateur staff through anything that involves the Chairman's and the DoD's business."

"Anyone over there have any idea what we do?"

"Not until you get there."

Michaelson's sedan pulled out of the rain to a stop at the covered north entrance to the White House. He tried to put the miles he had traveled as a Green Beret–Ranger infantryman in perspective as he looked out across Pennsylvania Avenue from inside the fence.

"Have a good meeting, sir," the driver said as he held the door open for his three-star passenger.

"Thank you, son," Michaelson said as he got out and pulled down on the skirt of his blouse to straighten it out.

A young stallion of a polished Marine stood by the doorway, ready to open it for the general. "Good morning, sir," he said as he made opening the door look like something he was proud to do.

"Thank you, Corporal," Michaelson said as he acknowledged the Marine's ceremonial function.

But as he began to cross the threshold an attractive young woman staffer, arms loaded with a sheaf of papers, juggling an umbrella, flattened herself against the door frame as if to avoid any chance of touching Michaelson on her way out.

The umbrella caught in the jamb and she lost her grip on the paperwork, which spilled out onto the ground.

As fast as it happened, the general and the Marine stooped to pick up the papers before the wind caught them.

"Get away. Let them alone!" the woman spat out. "I don't need any help from *you* people."

Michaelson hadn't heard her tone since the sixties.

She gathered the papers, stood quickly, and walked briskly down the driveway without so much as an appreciative nod for their efforts.

Michaelson watched her walk away, her disdain clear in her attitude. "So, that's the way it is around here?"

" 'Fraid so, sir. Semper Fi," the corporal said.

CHAPTER 1

1972

The worn bearing inside the left hub on the wheelchair squeaked. At the top of each revolution, the chair crossed over a floor joist under the covered ramps connecting the hospital wards.

Hollister first became aware of the precise placement of the aged joists the night he was admitted to Letterman Army Hospital. They sent him there after six weeks in a hospital in Vietnam, five more in Guam, and a long medevac flight to San Francisco.

Each time they wheeled him from one ward to another—and to and from the operating room—he heard the hollows, then the joists, then the hollows again. That and the smells of disinfectant and hospital alcohol formed his mental picture of what the hospital looked like. He wondered if he would still notice the sounds when the bandages came off his eyes. Or if he would even care.

A medic pushed him through the swinging doors, into the conference room, spun his chair, and set the brakes.

"Thank you, young man," a voice said to the medic. "We'll call you when we're finished. You can go now."

Someone in the room reeked of Aqua Velva.

"Captain Hollister, I'm Colonel Nickerson."

Hollister could only imagine what he looked like. He wouldn't be surprised to find the man to be balding, thick around the middle, and void of even the slightest evidence of combat experience on his uniform.

"Yes, sir," Hollister said.

"With me—here in the room—are Specialist Peterson, who

will be recording our words, and Captain Sharpe from the Staff Judge Advocate's office."

Hollister didn't respond. He just listened to the soft pressure of Peterson's fingers against the plastic keys on the court recorder's transcriber.

"I have been appointed as the Article 32b investigating officer in the matters and events surrounding the actions of Brigadier General Jarrold T. Valentine on or about 11 June, last.

"Before we begin it is my duty to inform you of your rights under the Uniform Code of Military Justice. . . . "

Hollister tried to listen as the uncomfortable colonel stumbled over the words from the red book that explained his rights before being questioned. But all Hollister could hear was the sound of the keys on the recorder's machine.

He thought of how many times he had read the same words to soldiers facing courts-martial and nonjudicial punishment. He didn't need to hear them again.

"I know my rights. What is it you want to know, Colonel?"

1969

The headlights of Hollister's car splashed onto the curb stop next to the large Fort Benning cinder-block building that housed Charlie Company. The concrete stop had been hand-lettered in Fort Benning's trademark blue paint. It read: COMMANDING OFFICER HONOR GUARD COMPANY.

"Sir—let me help you with that stuff," said a soldier's voice from the dark.

Hollister recognized Private First Class Lewis, his driver. "Mornin', Lewis. No problem. I got it," Hollister said. He hung the coat hangers through his upturned fingers and grabbed his boots with his free hand. He nudged his car door closed with his knee, and the two walked up the sidewalk to the yellow pool thrown by the bug-repelling fire light over the double doors.

"You takin' a burial detail out, sir?" Lewis asked as they stepped onto the gleaming surface of the brown-speckled asphalt tile in the hallway outside Hollister's office.

"Yeah, I think we've got one that needs a little mothering."

In the orderly room, the first sergeant and the company clerk snapped to attention. They gave Hollister his customary first salute of the day.

"Good mornin', Cap'n," First Sergeant Perry Mann said. Not waiting for a returned salute, he followed Hollister into his office.

"Mornin', Top. How bad is it today?"

Mann handed Hollister a list on a clipboard. "No better, no worse than yesterday or the day before. For my money—they're all only a bit better than a sharp stick in the eye."

Hollister hooked his uniform on the coatrack and set his parade boots on top of his desk. He took the list and scanned it. "I never thought there were shittier jobs in the States than in Vietnam, but this is no goddamn contest."

The page contained the destinations of five burial details and the names of the NCOs and officers in charge.

"I'm happy to say that your ol' first sergeant here has to go to a meeting with the brigade command sergeant major. I'm much happier facin' that old bear than goin' with you to bury another fine American boy."

Hollister looked up from the page to see Mann walking back to his desk in the outer office. It struck Hollister that Mann, a black soldier with two wars under his belt and twenty-six years of service stripes on his sleeve, would use the word *boy* without it registering on him as a word offensive to the blacks demonstrating in the streets for greater civil rights.

Hollister pulled his chair away from his desk and became conscious of the pain in his head and his hip. He knew the throbbing in his head would go away before the morning was over, but the burning in his hip, from a wound he picked up in a chopper crash in Vietnam, would only get worse as the day went on. He pulled the center drawer of his desk open a few inches and let his fingers search for a small tin.

Inside it was a handful of aspirin. He threw three into his mouth and swallowed them, dry. "Well, First Sergeant, I'd rather be beaten with a pipe than do this one more time. I don't know what ties my gut up tighter—getting shot at or trying to console a mother at another military funeral," Hollister said to an unseen Mann in the outer office.

"You can heal from a bullet wound."

Hollister nodded in agreement, unlaced his boots, and slipped out of them.

He took off his fatigues and hung them in his closet. He then pulled his service cap off the shelf and inspected the large officer's eagle and the condition of the spit shine on the black leather visor. He blew on the visor to scatter any unseen dust.

Satisfied, he put the hat back and pulled his trousers out from under his blouse and stepped into the legs without creasing them.

He sat down with his fly open, allowing him to bend enough to put on his fresh set of boots without wrinkling his trousers.

The peach-colored glow on the horizon promised a clear day. Hollister put his coffee cup down and headed out of the mess hall to the adjacent parking lot.

" 'Tench-hut!" a voice yelled in the poorly lit concrete apron, designed for trucks to unload foodstuffs.

"As you were," Hollister replied, allowing the five fifteen-man burial details to finish last-minute preparations.

Lieutenant Sandy Garland slipped to a point in front of the assembled details and saluted. "Mornin', sir."

Hollister returned the salute. "We on time?"

"Yes, sir." Garland fell in step with Hollister and followed him to the start of the first rank.

The NCO in charge of the first burial detail called his men to attention. "Sir, detail ready for inspection," he said, looking straight ahead.

Hollister returned the sergeant's salute and began his inspection at the soldier's headgear.

The sergeant, a boy no more than twenty, wore his uniform proudly. He demonstrated how seriously he took his duties by the attention he'd paid to every little detail. His metal insignia gleamed. His blouse and trousers were perfectly pressed. Nowhere on his uniform was there so much as a loose thread or a worn item.

Hollister looked down. The soldier's boots gleamed from hours of spit shining. "Outstanding, Sergeant Elliott. Follow me. Let's see how your folks look."

Elliott stepped into place to the left of Lieutenant Garland and followed the two officers.

It was Hollister's policy that every funeral detail would be inspected as if it were the most important thing they would do all year. At first, the troops in C Company thought it was just chickenshit, but they quickly realized it was Hollister's way of showing respect to the soldiers they would bury. Every man in C Company knew the fastest way to get on the wrong side of James Hollister was to take one of the burials lightly.

Hollister moved down the line, found two ties that needed attention and one insignia with polishing cloth lint stuck to it.

The other four details were in about the same shape. While Hollister would consider them a shade below the standards he had mastered while going through the Seventh Army Noncommissioned Officers' Academy in Bad Tolz, Germany, almost six years earlier—they were perfect by contemporary standards. Almost every man in his company had been to Vietnam and was serving out his remaining months of service at Fort Benning. Even the least motivated among them was better than most of the others at Fort Benning.

"They look good, Sandy," Hollister said. "Have they eaten yet?"

"Yes, sir, those that wanted to."

"All right, let 'em grab a smoke, and then let's get 'em on the road.

"I'll be going with Sergeant Elliott's detail."

"Where to, sir?"

"Calumet—on the road to Savannah."

"I'm headed for Mobile."

"Okay then, have the mess hall put some coffee on your bus. You got a long ride. And you'll let me know if you run into trouble in Mobile?"

"Yes, sir. But how much trouble can I get into in Mobile?"

They both looked at each other, knowing almost anything could go badly on a funeral detail.

Back at his desk, Hollister unfastened the four large brass buttons on his blouse to avoid creasing it. First Sergeant Mann handed him more papers to sign, flipping the pages and pointing at the signature blocks for him to initial or sign. While speaking to Hollister, he still carried on the business of running the headquarters by firing off instructions to the company clerk who was relaying phone calls and trying to organize the sick call roster for three soldiers headed to the medics.

"What the fuck's their problem?" Mann asked.

"Got one with swollen tonsils, one with a twisted ankle from PT this morning, and the other one says it's personal," the clerk typist said.

"Personal? Personal my fucking ass! Get that sick, lame, and lazy som'bitch in here. I'll tell him what *personal* is." He then turned his attention back to Hollister and changed his tone. "Ah, sir, that needs to be dated the day before yesterday—in your hand-writing."

Hollister knew they were late submitting the document and hated fudging dates, but he also knew it was absolutely impossible for an infantry company commander to accomplish all of the duties assigned to him, counsel all the soldiers he was required to counsel, read all he had to read, write all he had to write, and make all the suspense dates that were on his back. He wrinkled his brow and looked at Mann. "So, what was the date, the day before yesterday?"

"February thirteenth, sir," Mann replied. "Far too late for you to do your Christmas shopping."

Hollister looked back up at Mann. "You really know how to remind a guy when he is backed up, Top."

Mann smiled broadly. "For us folks, every day's a picnic. Hell, we get three squares a day, spiffy uniforms, and high-top correc-tive shoes. Yes, sir, Captain, every day's a holiday, and every meal's a banquet."

A soldier appeared in the doorway in front of the first sergeant's desk. "Private First Class Rameriz, reporting to the first sergeant."

Mann looked up from the paperwork and hollered out into his office, "Stay right fucking there, you sorry excuse for an infantry fighting machine." He then dropped his tone again. " 'Scuse me a minute, sir, while I take care'a this boy."

Mann straightened up and pushed his chest out before stepping back into his own office. Hollister raised his pen and watched Mann work.

"Boy! It is my understanding you have a problem that you want to take to the medics but you can't share it with your own first sergeant. Is that right?"

The private looked nervously around the office and then back to the first sergeant. "Yes, Top. It's sorta personal."

Hollister watched the expression on Mann's face turn from mock surprise to mock anger. He had spent so much of his life around soldiers like Mann. Soldiers who had it down pat, were solid, predictable, and reliable to a fault.

"Sorta personal?" Mann bellowed.

"Yes, First Sergeant. I don't have to tell everyone, do I?"

Sergeant Mann leaned forward. "No, mister, you don't have to tell *everyone* your problem. You just have to tell your kind, old first sergeant."

"I don't wanna be disrespectful. But how does it help things if you know, Top?"

"You think that I'm not concerned about your welfare, young soldier? Don't you think it's important for *me* to know if you have a problem that might affect the others?"

"Yes, First Sergeant, I'm sure you're plenty concerned, but—"

"You got yourself a sneezin' peter, don't you now, boy?"

The soldier tried to absorb the question and reply, but Mann interrupted him again. "It's much the same as if you had yourself leprosy or food poisonin' or something. I'd have to make sure the other troops don't get into the same mess. Now tell me, did you go on over to Phenix City and get yourself some of that rotten civilian poontang?"

"No, First Sergeant. I don't have the clap or nothin' like that."

"Well, what the hell is your problem?"

"I got them hemorrhoids, Top."

"Piles? You have *piles*?" Mann asked, his eyes bulging.

The soldier dropped his voice and mumbled, "Yes, First Sergeant."

"Hell, boy. That's an infantryman's occupational hazard," Mann said as he stepped closer to the soldier and patted him on the back. "Means that you are doin' the hard work, lifting the big loads, making the morning PT runs, and soldiering through it all.

"Now you don't need no sick call, and I don't need to send you over to waste the time of some important doctor. You just get yourself up to your latrine and fill the mop sink with all the hot water you can stand. Then you drop your trousers and soak your ass."

Mann looked at his GI wristwatch. "You got twenty minutes, boy. Now get to it."

All fifteen of them stood, holding on to the overhead handrail in the small bus. No one in the honor guard sat down on the way to a funeral. To do so would guarantee a wrinkled uniform.

The rural Georgia countryside flew by the bus windows. Some on board talked about girls and cars. Hollister gazed out the windows, not really seeing anything—thinking about his wife, Susan.

"Kudzu," Sergeant Elliott said.

"Huh?"

"Never seen anyplace that had as much of this stuff as Georgia. Look. Look there, sir," Elliott said. "It's eating up that telephone pole."

It was completely covered with the native vine. Hollister chuckled. "I remember Ranger School. I've walked through, slept in, and untangled enough kudzu to cover two states."

"Bet you don't miss that."

Hollister paused. "Actually, I kind of feel like I'm ghosting here in C Company. We pull so little field duty, we ought to be backing up to the pay table."

"I'd say that's lucky. At least we're back from Vietnam. I haven't even been back long enough to get completely unpacked. 'S gonna take me a while to get used to all the comforts of home."

"You like being back, huh?"

"Like it? Sir, how long since you been back here?"

Hollister thought for a few seconds. "Goin' on a year now."

"It's bad, sir. I don't mean the combat 'n' stuff. I mean the other shit . . ."

"Like?"

"Like them starting to pull the troops out."

"That's not good?"

"It's good for them goin' home. It's real bad for them still there. Everybody's spooked. Nobody wants to be the last American wasted over there. And the drugs and the race shit."

A black soldier standing next to Hollister and Elliott, a combat veteran himself, heard the comment. "I hear that shit, man. Nobody needs it—nobody."

"What do you think we should do?" Hollister asked Elliott.

"We either got to do the job and get it done or pack up and get out in a New York minute. This *drawdown* and *Vietnamization* shit is bad news."

Hollister let Elliott's words sink in. He had always found the line soldier's take on things to be somewhat exaggerated or oversimplified, but almost always solidly based in the reality that the soldiers felt. They never came up short of opinions when asked. "Well, maybe we can still come out of there having done some good."

"Not as I can see, sir."

Hollister flipped the pages in his small army-green notebook and refreshed his memory—the name of the deceased, next of kin, and the name of the church. He didn't want anyone at the funeral or the cemetery seeing him checking his notes. He wanted them to think that he was almost as familiar with the key names at the funeral as the family was. But he knew better. He had been to almost seventy-five such funerals since he had assumed command of C Company, and every one tugged at his heart and his gut. He knew *Sands, George A, E-5, 4th Infantry Division, Vietnam,* wasn't going to be any easier to bury than the others had been.

"We're 'bout there," the bus driver said.

The signs on the roadside signaled the approach to Calumet. One indicated the miles, another advertised the Rotary Club, and another sign read: POPULATION 488.

Every man on the bus groaned. Someone in the back offered, "Don't be holdin' yer breath waitin' for no local lovelies to be comin' by to see us. Be surprised if this town even has electricity."

"Check this out," another soldier said.

Suddenly the bus went silent. On a side of an abandoned outbuilding, a poster had been stapled up announcing a Ku Klux Klan meeting in Calumet for that very evening.

The silence was finally broken by a black soldier's voice. "Hope we beat feet out here before dark, Cap'n."

"Count on it," Hollister said.

Hollister had dropped off the firing squad at the cemetery to find a good spot not too near the mourners, while he, Elliott, and the pallbearers went on to the church to wait for the hearse. Since a light rain had started to fall, Hollister had instructed Elliott to keep the pallbearers on the bus until they were needed.

He slipped into the church and found it filled with nearly a hundred local people and what looked like relatives who had come to town for the funeral.

An elderly man introduced himself. "I'm Fest, *Mister* Fest, with the funeral home."

Hollister quickly slipped off his white cotton glove and took the old man's frail hand. He wasn't sure why the man would want to make a point out of being known as *Mister* Fest, but he went along with it. "Mister Fest, I'm Captain Jim Hollister. Are things on schedule?"

"Oh, yes. Things are *exactly* on time, Captain." He lifted his watch from his vest pocket and held it in his palm. "The deceased will be here in six minutes. We're always *exactly* on time."

Hollister looked into the church. "Can you point out the family? I understand that Sergeant Sands wasn't married."

Fest pointed his long slender finger as discreetly as only an undertaker could. "The lady with the lavender hankie is Mrs. Sands, and the gentleman next to her is the deceased's father."

Hollister leaned a little closer to Mr. Fest. "I'll be outside getting my people ready to bring the casket in."

The rain continued to fall—a little heavier than before, but Hollister and the others didn't put on the ugly brown raincoats that the army had issued them. Each man stood at a rigid position of attention—to the rear of the ten-year-old white hearse carrying Sergeant Sands's remains.

Hollister opened the huge rear door, and the first two soldiers leaned in to grasp the casket and pull it out.

Hollister took up his position behind the casket and was about to give the command to move the pallbearers up the stairs when he noticed Mrs. Sands standing in the door of the church, her hand to her face, tears streaming down her cheeks. "No . . ." she said. "No, I won't allow it. No sir."

Her words were not directed at anyone, but Hollister waited for a second to see if she would say something else that would help him understand. Under his breath he spoke to the pallbearers. "Steady. Hold what you've got."

He stepped around them and moved toward Mrs. Sands. Mr. Sands and Mr. Fest tried to console Mrs. Sands, who was alternately sobbing and complaining.

"You can't do this, young man," she said.

"Can't do what, ma'am?" Hollister asked.

"I'll let 'em carry my boy's body to the door, but those coloreds can't come into my church. No sir, I will not allow those coloreds into this tabernacle of God. My boy had to serve with nigras over there, but he wouldn't want them in his church."

"Ma'am. I realize how much pain you're in, and I'm sure you don't mean what you're saying. These are soldiers. They have come to pay the highest respect to your son. I'm sure you know how sorry they are for your loss."

The woman snatched the balled-up handkerchief from her face. "Boy . . . I'm not gonna tell you again. That box with my son in it is coming into the church my family has prayed in for three generations, but those black faces will not be carrying it."

Mourners had gathered behind Mrs. Sands, waiting for Hollister to respond. She put him in a no-win situation. The last thing he wanted to do was lash out at her on the day she was burying her son.

Hollister raised his finger to wipe the rain off the leather brim of his service cap. "Madam, this detail is here for you and your son. I will not *weed out* the black soldiers for you or anyone else. You must accept my burial detail as is or I'll be forced to take them back to Fort Benning right now."

Mrs. Sands became hysterical and told Hollister he'd regret that.

The bus ride back to Fort Benning was no easier for Hollister than it had been to Calumet. He knew he would be faced with criticism from the chain of command for not staying, for not finding another solution to the problem. Certainly someone would blame him for not separating the soldiers by color, or for just arguing with the next of kin.

It was dark again by the time he pulled into his parking space at the BOQ. He fumbled with his keys and finally got the sticking door to open. As if on autopilot, he flipped on the TV and the light switch, and dumped his hat and keys on the quartermaster-issue coffee table.

While the television warmed up, he poured himself a drink from the ever-present bottle that stood on the sideboard of the kitchenette.

He stood by the sink, drinking the warm bourbon, and only turned to watch the news. He knew that as soon as he sat down on the couch, he'd just have to get up to refill his glass.

He never missed the Vietnam casualty reports and the news pieces filed by only a handful of competent newsmen. He had little use for the crowd that spent most of its time at the Caravelle Hotel or the ones who rewrote the press releases handed out by the Joint Public Affairs Office in Saigon's Rex Hotel. He only trusted the reporters whom he had personally seen in the field, collecting information to file themselves.

Sometime during the news he dozed off. The station signed off after midnight, and the hissing noise that replaced programming woke Hollister.

He looked at the clock on the nightstand next to his bed, where he had propped himself up to watch the small black-and-white TV and finish another drink. Next to the clock was a framed photograph of Susan.

Her smile tugged at his gut. He missed her. He hated living without her. And he didn't know if he could ever get her back.

He lit a cigarette, turned off the television, and poured himself another drink.

Standing at the small kitchenette sink, he looked out the window at the circling C-130 aircraft loaded with paratroopers. They were lining up to drop pass after pass of student parachutists on their first night jump.

No soldier ever forgot his first night jump. Hollister was no different. Being an Airborne-Ranger was a life unlike any other. One that so often came between soldiers and the ones they loved.

She'd never come back as long as he was a soldier. He was sure of that. He poured himself another drink and lit another cigarette.

CHAPTER 2

Vietnam

In a travel magazine Yoon Dlei village would look interesting, filled with the textures of a people who fabricated all of their needs from the Vietnamese tropical rain forest.

But only at a distance was the village romantic and exotic. Up close, the rain leaked through the matted palm fronds, once tight and well sealed. It had been a long time since there had been enough men in the small Montagnard village to keep all the structures repaired and comfortable for their families.

Krong, the aging chief of the small band of Montagnards who had slash-and-burn farmed the hills in western Binh Long Province for hundreds of years, tried to patch the hole in the roof. He wouldn't let himself remember when such tasks were never done by a man of authority in what was once a large tribe.

His granddaughter, Jrae, held her infant child to her breast and huddled in the corner of the longhouse. All she had to squat on was a pallet made of salvaged cardboard, swollen from being wet, then dry, then wet again over the months since it was pressed into service.

Jrae was fairer, less stocky, and taller than the other women in the tribe. It was a matter of no small embarrassment to her that she was not full Montagnard. Her mother had befriended and then was seduced by a French anthropologist who had studied their tribe after World War II. They lived as man and wife until the French-Indochina War heated up, and he was called back to Paris. He had promised to return, but never did. Jrae's mother went back to her tribal village and lived in shame until her death from tuberculosis.

Jrae's childhood had made her different from the other girls in the village. By the time she and her mother returned from the city of Da Lat, where they had lived with her father, she had been exposed to Vietnamese and French cultures, had learned their languages and even conversational English from the missionaries who ran the clinic in her neighborhood. But no matter what she had learned—she was still an outcast in the Vietnamese community. She was the daughter of a Montagnard—a spurned ethnic minority for centuries.

For Jrae the cardboard eased the discomfort of the skinny saplings that made up the flooring of the longhouse. The scrap of woven blanket she used to cover her half-naked body and that of her son flaked dried mud each time she moved it.

The rain plopped onto the floor. Children whimpered and coughed. And their mothers rocked and soothed them. One of the women walked to the fireplace, sculpted out of a large termite's nest, and put some charcoal on the waning fire. She took a large scrap of aluminum that had once been a can and fanned the glowing embers to spread the fire to the new charcoal. Sparks leaped out of the fireplace and popped at the top of their arcs.

The woman pulled her head away but couldn't avoid the smoke. There was no provision to let the smoke out of the long-houses, except letting it filter out through the roof. Smoke always filled the dwelling, burning everyone's eyes.

An elder ran into the longhouse. "They come again."

Krong looked at him, puzzled but worried by Toong's tone. "Who?"

"Republicans."

One of the children, old enough to understand, began crying and scurried to put her mother between her and the door to the open village.

Krong closed his eyes for a moment as if to endure some pain or brace for it. He remained silent, summoning up strength from a reservoir of his own making.

He put down the thatch he had been using to repair the roof, brushed back his platinum-threaded hair, and patted the chignon on the back of his head. "I will talk to them."

He picked up his ratty wool blanket he had once traded a French soldier a hand ax for and wrapped it around his bare shoulders. At the door he turned and spoke to the women. "Stay inside. Do not show yourself."

*   *   *

The two Montagnard men and two skinny dogs waited in the center of the circle of longhouses for the South Vietnamese soldiers to arrive. The old men stood proudly and defiantly, each trying to remember when they were stronger. When they were warriors, providers, and the defenders of their people.

The Vietnamese burst into the village. Six soldiers in various states of drunkenness stumbled across the rain-swept village. Their sergeant stepped up to Krong. "Rice wine—where is it?"

Krong didn't answer.

The soldier grabbed the old man's withered arm and shook him. "What is it that makes you *moi* act stupid?" he asked, using the term for the savages they believed the nomads to be. "We will make trouble. Act now. Be smart, old man."

Krong wouldn't look away from the Vietnamese soldier's eyes. It was an insult to make direct eye contact with them, and he wanted to show his contempt. He yelled out to an unseen villager in one of the other longhouses. "Bring the wine."

"Hurry!" the Vietnamese soldier added.

While they all waited for two old women who carried a large crock of fermented rice wine to the center of the village, the soldiers made insulting remarks about the Montagnards and laughed at the women as they carried the jug.

In the darkened doorway of the chief's longhouse Jrae stood and listened—her baby half-asleep, clinging to her. She knew what the soldiers were saying. They wanted women. They urged their sergeant not to stop at demanding only wine. He should ask for all the women, too. They would then pick the ones they wanted from the group.

Krong heard the talk, too, but pretended not to.

The sergeant laughed at his comrades and agreed. "Your women are good for pleasuring us," he said, lustfully rubbing the crotch of his wet uniform trousers.

"You have your wine. Now go. Leave us. We are only hill people. Leave us to suffer through this night. Go be with your own kind."

"We spend these same nights at the outpost down near the river guarding your people. There is a real threat to our people. Still we protect your skinny old men and your stupid women because the puppets in Saigon say we must. Your women—they can warm us tonight. We want women."

"No. Now go away and leave us," Krong said, growing more angry with the soldiers.

The Vietnamese sergeant shoved him with the heels of his hands. "Shut up! Be grateful that we don't just kill you and tell Saigon that the Communist VC did it."

The sergeant spat out encouragement to the others, already dipping cups into the crock and slopping wine on themselves as they drank. He gave them permission to find the women they wanted and just take them.

Krong protested again, but the soldiers didn't stop. They ran to the longhouses and looked for young girls.

One of them entered Jrae's longhouse and looked at her standing in the doorway—her baby at one of her swollen breasts. He laughed at her fearful expression but didn't resist the temptation to reach out to fondle her free breast. She recoiled from his grasp and threw herself off balance. She staggered and the soldier laughed at her clumsiness.

She screamed out for him to leave them. But the soldier walked to the far end of the longhouse and found another girl, Sraang— only thirteen. He grabbed her by the wrist, held her out so he could look at her body, and grunted in approval. She was tall and dark skinned. Her hair was jet black, long and straight to her waist. The soldier looked at her naked chest and yelled out to the others that he had found a young one who was not as disgusting as the rest of them. He laughed and then dragged her out into the night.

Sraang was Jrae's sister. Her only sister—ten years her junior. She was born to her mother and her mother's second husband—a Montagnard who was killed by the Viet Cong not long after Sraang was born.

Jrae's younger brother, Pek, had been taken a year earlier. That time they came with a recruiting pitch—explaining to the Montagnards that the Republican puppets in Saigon would eventually kill them all. Their only hope was to join the Viet Cong to fight Saigon. When the recruiting plea failed, they just took Pek. That was the first of the roundups that eventually took all the men under forty from their village.

After the soldiers left, Jrae collapsed on the cardboard pallet and cried, remembering just such a night when other soldiers had dragged her off. She held the baby who was a memory of the soldiers who used her—drunken and insulting. They had taken turns with her and then left her on the pathway near her village for her tribe to find her. Just remembering the night brought back the pain and the embarrassment of the men handling her small body, sweating on her, grunting, pushing, and hurting her.

She was ashamed. Though none of the elders in the village accused her of any wrongdoing, she felt as though she had betrayed her tribe by having sex with Vietnamese soldiers. But the ultimate pain came when she found that she was pregnant. Every day since the birth of her son, she had been reminded of that night.

By dawn there was still no sign of Sraang.

Jrae alternated between the unavoidable duties of her day and moments of fear when her mind wandered to the things that could be happening to her sister.

She hoped that Sraang would return before the small tribe moved.

Two weeks earlier, the South Vietnamese sent a province officer into the village to tell them that they could be relocated to a resettlement camp near Tay Ninh. They would have to give up their nomadic lifestyle and move to a government resettlement camp if they wanted to survive.

The older men knew whatever fading authority they held in their small group would disappear the moment they arrived at a resettlement camp. Younger men and stronger men at the camp would insist that they be given the power to make decisions for Krong's people.

CHAPTER 3

Hollister sat quietly at the bar in the basement of the main officers club. The Infantry Bar was filled with the after-work crowd. He sat alone and made circles on the bar top with the water on the bottom of his beer mug. At the corner of the bar, the evening news was on TV. Cronkite mixed reading the news from Saigon with lecturing his viewers about America's inability to extract itself from the Vietnam War.

Angered, but not sure why Cronkite angered him, Hollister signaled the bartender for a refill.

A loud Transportation Corps captain was telling some story on the stool next to Hollister, waving his arms all around as he talked to his friend on the third stool over. Hollister was slightly bothered by the loudmouth but decided just to let it pass. All he wanted was just a quiet drink and some time to think.

"Hey, you fuckin' sorry-ass Ranger!"

Hollister looked up into the bar mirror and saw the smiling face of Major Jack Stanton, his old helicopter gunship platoon leader from Hollister's second tour in Vietnam.

"Shit," Hollister said without turning around. "Isn't there anywhere on post where a guy can go to get a drink without the place filling up with assholes?"

"This place filled up with assholes when you walked in," Stanton said playfully.

Stanton pulled up a stool next to Hollister and mounted it like a horse. "You buyin'?"

"Me?" Hollister shook his head. "Seems to me that I've been buyin' since the day I met you."

"You drinkin' solo, pardner?"

The animated captain next to Hollister made a wide gesture with his hand while telling his story and slammed his fist on the bar. Hollister watched his glass jump, almost spilling its contents. He waved for the bartender to bring Stanton a drink.

"Oh, I get it. The wife?"

"Don't know what to do about her, Jack."

"She still home? In New Jersey?"

"New York."

"She comin' back?"

"We been at this a couple a years now. She wants me out of the army, out of Benning, and God knows what else."

"So?"

"So what am I gonna do? Can you see me on some campus with a bunch of long-hair hippies?"

They both laughed at the picture of Airborne-Ranger Hollister without his close-cropped haircut.

"I'd pay real money to see that," Stanton said.

"Well, wish in one hand and shit in the other, and see which one fills up first."

"That what you told her?"

"In so many words."

"So she walked?"

"She knew I was a soldier when she met me and when we got married."

"She's tired of it, Jim."

"We're all tired of it."

"You oughta be gettin' short, huh?"

The aggravating captain next to Hollister laughed loudly at something his friend had said. Hollister looked at the captain and then back to Stanton.

"I'm real ripe for reassignment. If I don't put in my papers to get out, and I get alerted for movement to Vietnam—I'm stuck."

"Yeah," Stanton said. "I know. They'll send your request back and tell you to reapply after you return."

Hollister gently tapped his glass on the counter and got the bartender's attention. "Wanna do it again?"

"Susan know how ripe you are?"

"Nope. What are *you* gonna do, Jack?"

"Hey. Sam's got me. I'm in for the long haul. Five more years, and it's rockin' chair time. I just can't walk away from fifteen years," Stanton said.

"I can't walk away either, and I don't know how to explain it to Susan."

"You better figure it out, man. She's really gonna be pissed if she gets a letter saying, 'Oh, by the way, I'm going back to Vietnam for my third tour.'"

Before Hollister could reply, the bellowing captain next to him stepped off his stool, tripped on the footrail, and bounced off Hollister. With whiplike speed, Hollister reached out and grabbed the captain by the throat, his fingers on either side of his windpipe, and pulled his face close. "You're not only a pain in the ass, but you're a clumsy pain in the ass. Now get a grip on yourself or I'll *help* you to the fuckin' door. You got me?"

The captain's eyes bugged out—he was surprised at Hollister's hostility. He nodded and tried to straighten up to avoid the pain Hollister's grip was causing.

"Hey, Jim. Lighten up," Stanton said.

Hollister let go of the captain but reinforced his words with a cold stare.

The captain grabbed his change off the bar and headed for the door—encouraged to leave by his buddy.

Neither Hollister nor Stanton said anything for quite a long time.

"Shit," Hollister said. "I just don't know what's gotten into me. I'm short fused—"

"And a real joy to be around," Stanton said.

"I'm sorry, man. I'm just tired."

"How long I been knowin' you?"

"Couple a years now."

"I've watched you get froggy. When we get this in aviation units, we put guys behind a desk to take some of the weight off of them. Maybe getting out and heading for some campus somewhere will help."

Hollister looked up at Stanton. "You think I'm that fucked up, huh?"

"Nope. But I think that you've carried your share of the war." He jerked his thumb toward the doorway. "Give someone else like that clown a chance to prove something. Ease off."

Stanton left the bar around nine. Hollister stayed and had more to drink. He looked at the clock on the dash of his MG roadster. It was after eleven.

The military policeman's flashing red lights hardly reflected off Hollister's rearview mirror before he checked his speedometer and started to pull over to the side of the road.

There were few things less forgivable than getting a DUI on an army post. Hollister ran through a list of possible excuses he might be able to use on the MP. None of them seemed worthwhile, so he resigned himself to getting out his wallet and registration.

A tall black soldier approached his car. In the backlight of the MP sedan's headlights, all that Hollister could make out in his mirror was the sergeant's bright sleeve chevrons.

"Evenin', sir," the sergeant said.

"Good evening," Hollister said, trying to sound as sober as he could.

"It'd be a damn shame to have to write a DUI on an old platoon leader of mine," the sergeant said.

Hollister, not sure what he was talking about, scooted down in his seat to look out and up under the low-cut canvas top on his roadster. It was then that he saw the smiling face of former Private First Class Tyrone T. Thibideaux, an MP turned long-range-patrol member in the Airborne brigade in Vietnam. "Damn you, Three-T, I thought I recognized that voice," Hollister said, happy to see his friendly face.

"You think you'd recognize it better if I whispered?" he said, referring to the way they normally talked in the field.

They both laughed. Hollister remembered Thibideaux as a good soldier who went on several patrols with Hollister's platoon until he was injured in a freak accident and evacuated to the States. "What are you doing back in an MP suit?"

"When I screwed up my back and got bounced from the infantry, they let me fall back on my MP time."

"And a staff sergeant in just four years?" Hollister asked, only a little surprised.

"Sometimes you get lucky, sir."

"It's good to see you."

"Speaking of getting lucky, Captain, you know why I pulled you over, don't you?"

Hollister nodded affirmatively.

"Well, you 'bout the luckiest captain on Fort Benning tonight 'cause the post chief of staff is on our ass to be on folk's asses about DUIs. Now, if you just head on over to your BOQ, I'm going to follow you. You know, in case you need any help. And we'll just call it a wash. What d'ya think, Cap'n?"

"I think that's a lot more slack than I got coming to me. Thank you, Sergeant T."

"My pleasure, Cap'n."

Hollister pulled into his parking space in front of the BOQ. Thibideaux turned on the interior lights in his sedan and gave Hollister another abbreviated salute before he drove off.

Hollister sat in his car, his head still spinning from all the booze. He let it sink in—how close he had come to very real trouble. It was almost impossible to keep a DUI from ruining any career aspirations an officer might have. Once the delinquency report was submitted, wheels began to roll that ended up with at least a negative comment about drinking on an officer's efficiency report. That alone was enough to miss the next promotion list. Miss two lists and an officer was *invited* to leave the service. A chill went through him as he thought of how close he had come to having his future decided for him.

"I've got an appointment with the chief of staff," Hollister said.

"Mornin', Captain," the post command sergeant major said from behind his polished oak desk. "Let me see if Colonel Valentine's free."

The sergeant major put his large cigar in the ashtray and stood to step across the headquarters reception area to the colonel's office.

The new post chief of staff had only been in the job for five weeks. Hollister had not yet met him—not face-to-face.

Hollister's name had first come to Valentine's attention when the grieving mother in Calumet had called her senator. It was less than an hour later when the phone lines burned all the way down to Hollister's level. Valentine had made it clear how unhappy he was to have received a call from the Senate Office Building on his first week in his new job. He especially didn't like having to call his boss, the commanding general, with the news of the incident.

Hollister stepped smartly to a point in front of Colonel Jarrold T. Valentine's desk, stopped, and saluted. "Sir, Captain Hollister reports."

Colonel Valentine returned Hollister's salute. "Pull up a chair, Hollister. We have some talking to do."

Hollister had heard nothing good about Valentine. His reputation was that of a hard-ass who was widely known throughout the infantry for handing out punishment like candy for the most minor infractions of military discipline. He had an especially dark reputation for being hell on company-grade officers.

"You don't know much about drugs, do you, Hollister?"

The question took Hollister by surprise. "Pardon me, sir?"

"I've looked at your personnel file. Doesn't look to me that you've been around the kind of units that have drug problems."

"Well, sir. I know about them. I was an enlisted man in Germany when marijuana was getting to be a problem. I've seen my share of soldiers nuked by drugs.

"And I've served on courts-martial. I've been a trial counsel on a couple of possession cases. But as far as being in units with drug problems? No, sir. I can't say I have."

"Well, I've got a very *big* problem. I've got soldiers with serious drug problems."

"Sorry to hear that. I don't see much of it in my company—"

Valentine interrupted. "I know that, but your brigade has the most drug cases of any unit on post."

"Why's that, sir?"

Valentine pointed to an acetate-covered chart near his desk and scanned the information grease-penciled in. The chart showed rising numbers in AWOLs and courts-martial convictions. He squinted as if the chart hurt his eyes and then turned back to Hollister.

"For one, you're too far down in the pecking order. They arrive, and someone at main post decides that a soldier looks like he might be a problem child, and he gets turned down for assignment to the School Brigade or the Infantry School."

"So we get them out at the brigade," Hollister said.

"Right. Benning's getting trash, and your brigade is getting the bulk of them."

Hollister had no idea why the chief of staff—ranking colonel at Fort Benning—would be telling him the problems that he shared with the colonel commanding his brigade.

But it didn't seem to apply to Hollister because all of the troops in the honor guard were not only volunteers, they were also handpicked. He didn't have one serious problem with drugs.

"I know what you're thinking, *not in your company*. Well, that's why I want to talk to you. I can take these dopers and dump them in the stockade with very little effort. It'll clear up my drug problems, and they'll become someone else's problem."

Colonel Valentine stood and walked to the narrow window in

the cinder-block post headquarters. He absentmindedly straightened his tie and looked out across the parade field in front of the Infantry School. "You see, I don't work that way, Hollister."

He turned back around and picked up a set of notes from his desk. "I want you to take a look at these. I'm interested in giving these guys a chance—just one, but a chance."

The comment didn't make much sense coming from a hard-ass colonel, and it showed on Hollister's face.

"I understand that you have the space. I want you to take a free platoon bay you have in your company and turn it into a holding tank."

"Holding tank?"

"Here it is. When a battalion commander comes up on a drug user, we only have one option right now—that's throw the book at him. To let them get by is a very bad precedent. I need another option. What I want you to do is set up a remedial training program for drug users. When we find them, I want them sent to your company. I want them stripped of every damn thing they own so they can't possibly bring drugs into the barracks. I want someone with them during training, while they eat, sleep, and even crap."

"And what kind of training are you talking about, sir?"

"Soldiering. You can see in my notes. Take them with you and let's talk in a few days. You'll have everything you need. I want you to keep these guys busier than they have ever been with the toughest training you can set up. Hopefully, we can break them of the drugs and give them a chance to clean up their act."

"And then what?"

"If they clean up their act, they go back to their units with no stain on their records."

"And if they don't?" Hollister asked.

"Then I throw their worthless asses in the stockade."

There was a long pause. Neither man said anything as Hollister looked down at the notes. What he saw, he didn't like. "Colonel, I'm not sure I'm the man for this job—"

The colonel's tone changed to a harsh, clipped delivery. "I didn't ask for your opinion on my selection. Now don't give me any grief on this. Just do it, *Captain*!"

Hollister quickly stood and came to attention. He knew he didn't like Valentine, but there was no sense arguing with him. "Yes, sir. Will that be all?"

"I want to see what you've got for me in five days. You're dismissed."

Lieutenant Garland, Hollister, Colonel Valentine, and Sergeant Major Sawyer entered the 5th Platoon bay, on C Company's second floor. It wasn't like a normal platoon bay. The double swinging doors had been replaced by a wire mesh that filled the hole and had its own smaller, locking door.

From the long hallway, anyone could see the entire length of the platoon bay. It contained only two doorless wall lockers, a dozen red butt cans, and two fire extinguishers.

Garland led the others through the locked cage door to the wall lockers. "Colonel, this is the basic issue for each of the— *trainees*," he said, stumbling over what they would call the new, special charges.

There, laid out on the shelves in the locker, was one sleeping bag, an aluminum GI mess kit with only a single large spoon, a canteen and cup, a double-edged safety razor, a toothbrush, and a bar of GI soap.

"We're thinking the less they have, the less likely they'll be to conceal drugs—not to mention the fact that they'll be miserable," Garland said.

"Add a New Testament," Colonel Valentine said.

The lieutenant wrote a reminder in a small spiral notebook. "They'll be stripped down to their boxer shorts at the door, and nothing will be allowed in the room but their basic issue of equipment and the trainees themselves."

"Uniforms for training?" Valentine asked.

"Each morning they will be issued fatigues, socks, boots, and clean underwear. They'll turn in everything but the boxer shorts when they return to the platoon bay in the evenings."

"Okay," Valentine said. "You get your first batch of *trainees* this week."

The late news was more of the same. Casualties were mounting, opposition to the war in the streets in America was always good copy for Cronkite, and the Paris peace talks droned on. Hollister opened the refrigerator door for another beer and then checked his watch. It would be easy to have another beer, but he passed.

Putting on his field jacket over his fatigues, Hollister picked up his car keys and stepped back to the door. He stopped long enough to look around his empty BOQ room before he turned the light out.

He decided to park across the street from the company and walk over rather than pull into his reserved parking space. He knew from experience the only way to find out what is really going on at night in your own company is to arrive unannounced.

The Charge of Quarters almost turned over the first sergeant's chair trying to get his feet off the desk and onto the floor. He stood at attention and reported to Captain Hollister, the boot he was polishing still encasing his left hand and forearm.

"Evening," Hollister said.

"Good evening, sir. I'm just trying to—"

"I'm sure you were trying to do something you felt needed to be done."

"I just finished checking the fire lights and posted the KP roster for tomorrow morning, and I—"

"As you were," Hollister said, trying to get the soldier to relax.

"Thank you, sir. Is there anything I can help you with?"

"Nope, just want to walk through and make sure you guys haven't got every hooker from Phenix City up here tonight."

The soldier looked at Hollister for some sign and then smiled when he noticed that Hollister had. He stepped out from behind the desk and grabbed the large wire loop holding the keys to every lock in the company area.

"Stay here. I can find my way around," Hollister said.

The hallways were empty and there was little movement in the barracks. Midweek, there was usually some late-night gabfest going in one of the cadre rooms, but Hollister noticed the lack of such get-togethers in the past weeks. It was a bad sign—a sign of sagging morale.

As he climbed the stairs and walked down the hallway to the 5th Platoon bay, he thought of the troubles in his brigade—increased drug and racial problems, plenty of disputes over petty arguments, and fights—lots of fights. It all meant morale. He'd been a soldier long enough to be sure about that.

"Good evening, sir," Sergeant Reid, a squad leader from the 1st Platoon, said as he stood from the chair he had been balancing on its back legs.

Hollister reached out and grabbed the folding metal chair

before it tipped back against the cinder-block wall—making a racket. "Evening, Sergeant Reid. How's it going tonight?"

The acting security guard gestured toward the darkened platoon bay. " 'S been real quiet, sir. Had a little trouble earlier when some assholes from the fifth of the thirty-first rolled by outside and started yelling crap up at these people."

"What did they do?"

"They yelled shit back at them."

Hollister smiled. "At least they haven't completely lost their spirit. Let's take a look."

Reid stuck the key in the lock to open the wire-mesh door to the darkened bay. Hollister could hear the sounds of one of his charges sleeping heavily, punctuating the dark with pumplike breathing.

Suddenly, both Hollister and Reid spotted a dim flicker of light behind a single wall locker. It had been moved away from a wall and butted up against the support beam at the far end of the bay.

Reid and Hollister walked toward the light. They were careful to avoid the dozen soldiers who slept cocoonlike in their sleeping bags on the hard tile floor.

At the locker, Hollister took the flashlight from Reid. Its beam found the naked body of a young soldier, faceup on the floor. Next to him, a short candle burned—throwing eerie light patterns across his face.

The boy was still, the color drained from his face—his eyes wide open.

Then Hollister saw it—a hypodermic needle still dangling from the soldier's forearm.

Not waiting to figure it all out, Hollister immediately checked the boy for any signs of breathing or a heartbeat. Training—army training—ran through his head. *Clear the airway. Stop the bleeding. Protect the wound. Treat or prevent shock.*

"Get to the phone. Get an ambulance here—now!"

Before Reid had made it to the end of the bay, Hollister had popped the soldier's neck back, opened his mouth, and begun mouth-to-mouth breathing.

There was no response. But Hollister wouldn't quit. He gave the soldier four quick, forceful breaths and then found the spot just above the bottom of his sternum and began chest massage.

*   *   *

Reid quickly returned, bringing the company's senior medic with him. Together, they continued CPR for fifteen more minutes—until the ambulance arrived.

Even though the medics kept up the heart massage and the mouth-to-mouth all the way out of the building, Hollister knew. He had seen enough dead soldiers to know. This one would never recover.

With the lights on and everyone in the bay awake, Hollister stood them all up and made them come to the spot behind the wall locker to see what was there.

"You fuckers think this is all a joke—this drug shit. Huh?"

None of them replied.

"You see this? You know what this is?" Hollister held up a mess-kit spoon with a greasy residue in it and the hypodermic needle. In the other hand he held up the bottom half of a Kiwi shoe-polish can. "He shot the oil out of this shoe polish in his fucking veins! Shoe polish."

The twelve trainees, all still wearing only their boxer shorts, looked away from Hollister to avoid making eye contact.

"How fucking stupid do you have to be to shoot this shit into your body?" Hollister screamed. He didn't wait for an answer and didn't expect one. Frustrated, he threw the can across the room and walked toward the exit.

At the doorway, Reid locked the lock and looked at Hollister—fearfully.

"I don't want you to tell me how this happened. But by tomorrow afternoon, I want you in my office with your take on how we can stop this from ever happening again. We fucked up. Let's see if we can make something right come of it."

It was nearly two A.M. when Hollister started to leave his orderly room. On the way out, he ran into four MPs and a medic who were carrying a soldier up the stairs to the 5th Platoon bay.

"Mornin', Cap'n," the medic said.

"What's this?" Hollister asked.

"Got a new customer for you. He's real fucked up on LSD."

"From?"

"The day room over at Headquarters Company," the medic said, trying to keep a grip on the wriggling soldier, wrapped tightly in two wet sheets.

Hollister could tell the temperature was starting to get to the soldier—his lips were turning a gray-blue. The first time he saw a drug user wrapped up that way, the medic had explained it. The evaporating water caused the soldier's body temperature to drop to the point where he was more concerned with how cold he was and less of a threat to anyone or himself. And the wet sheets served as a body handcuff. It was almost impossible to break free of the wrap if it was done right.

"We're gonna take him upstairs and put him to bed," the medic said.

Hollister put on his hat and continued down the stairs. "I don't particularly care what you do with him. You can leave him in those sheets all night—as far as I'm concerned."

It took two more hours to fill out the paperwork at the hospital and a half hour collecting the few personal items the dead soldier had—a Saint Christopher medal, a high-school class ring, and a wedding band.

Hollister would have to write yet another letter to another widow.

CHAPTER 4

It had been four days since they had seen Sraang. Krong put on his finest clothes and, accompanied by two of the other elders, walked down the mountain to the South Vietnamese Army outpost.

Sergeant Thoang, in charge of the tiny outpost guarding the bridge over the small river flowing out of the hills, acted surprised that the Montagnard headman would accuse South Vietnamese soldiers of carrying off one of his young girls. He laughed. "Maybe she just felt it was time for her to find a man on her own."

Krong's Vietnamese was not that good, but he understood the games and the insults. He looked at the faces of the Vietnamese soldiers lounging around in hammocks, eating pineapple slices, and listening to a radio. They giggled like children. Krong recognized two of the faces. They had come to his village the night they took Sraang away. He pointed them out. "They know where she is. They took her from us," he said in broken French and Vietnamese.

Sergeant Thoang leaped to his feet. "What? You accuse my men? Are you stupid, old man? I can have you thrown in prison for collaborating with the Viet Cong." He thrust his hand out and wagged his fingers in Krong's face—a serious insult in both cultures. He then swung his arm around and pointed at the lazy soldiers. "Apologize—now! Now, old man."

Krong was too proud to apologize. He just shook his head and acted as if he was confused by the language problems. Then, without excuse, he turned and walked back up the road toward his village. Behind him, the South Vietnamese soldiers laughed at the old man and the little girl who was missing. The parts he could understand were painful.

*   *   *

Krong, Jrae, Jrae's son, and one of the dogs sat together in Krong's longhouse. Since his wife had died, three years earlier, Krong had often asked his grandchildren in to be with him in the evenings. But this night it was particularly awkward because Sraang was not in her place.

"We go to the new camp?" Jrae asked.

"I have seen the camps. They are no place for our kind. They are pens no better than pigs are kept in."

"If we stay?"

"If we stay here, we will die."

"And if we go?" she asked.

"And if we go, our kind will die out."

She said nothing while the old man closed his eyes and listened to his own words.

After a long time, she put her son down on her blanket and walked back to the cooking area to get some food for her grandfather. It was only then that she let herself cry for him and for all of them. She didn't want him to see her cry.

Krong waited outside the team house for Sergeant Jackie Beck. The sun beat down on the old man, and the dust blew in swirls along the roadway paralleling the Special Forces compound on the outskirts of Da Lat. He watched the trucks and motorbikes as they raced by on the other side of the chain-link fence. There were fences everywhere he looked.

In his life, he had thought fences were only built to keep pigs out of the crops but never to keep men in or out of a place. He knew when his people were moved down from the hills to the relocation camp, they would suffer the confinement of the fences. The thought caused him to feel pain in his chest. For him, their spirit would forever be damaged by limiting their freedom to move about their rain forest.

The aging village chief also knew they couldn't continue to suffer the late-night raids by the Vietnamese on both sides of the war. He had to move his people to where they would be safe, or he would see them all die or be carried off in the night.

Sergeant Jackie Beck was one of the new breed of Special Forces soldiers. Vietnam was his first Green Beret assignment. He had hoped to go to a detachment somewhere on the Cambodian or Lao border, but found himself on temporary duty in Da Lat helping the South Vietnamese relocate the Montagnards. He was promised a better job as soon as the *Yards* were all moved.

He exited the office with Captain Nguyen in trail. Nguyen was a South Vietnamese captain, tasked with providing the vehicles to move the Montagnards. Beck had quickly learned that there was no love lost between the Montagnards and the Vietnamese. And Nguyen was in no hurry to get anything done. He had promised Beck they would make the arrangements to have Krong's people moved, soon. But soon had dragged on too long for Beck and for Krong's people.

Krong and Nguyen stood mute while Beck did all the talking. "We will come today to make the final survey of your village so *Dai Uy* Nguyen can draw the right vehicles to get your folks and their things moved all at once."

Krong liked Beck. He didn't know Beck was somewhat of a mountain man himself. Beck grew up in the north Georgia mountains. Though they were separated by half a globe, Krong knew he could trust the twenty-four-year-old soldier with the big grin and freckles on his forearms.

That day Krong went back to his village and announced the decision to move. He was met with little resistance. The others too were drained and heartsick at the losses and the repeated toll exacted from them.

Some days later Beck found Krong, again squatting outside his office. He tried to apologize for the week's delay, but to do so would have been to blame Captain Nguyen for the holdup. So Beck simply lied and said they were having trouble in the motor pool and the jeep he had drawn needed some work before they could use it to drive up to Krong's village.

Beck knew Krong had walked alone the twenty-five miles to see him. He offered to feed him and then to drive him back to Yoon Dlei village.

Krong appreciated Beck's gesture. And even though the American food was strange to his taste, it was still filling.

It was dark by the time Sergeant Beck and Krong turned off the hard-top road in the valley onto the red-dirt trail leading to Krong's village.

Beck was a little anxious about driving into the highlands at night, but wanted not to give the old man the idea that he was afraid. Still, he strained to look out at the limits of the headlights painting the trees along the roadway.

After an hour, the roadway became increasingly difficult for the jeep. There would be no way Captain Nguyen's trucks could make it up the road to the village. They would need choppers.

Watching the road and deep in thought, Beck didn't notice the look of alarm that came over Krong's face. Krong reached out and grabbed Beck's arm for him to stop the jeep and shut off the engine.

The sounds of the rain forest were silenced by the presence of the jeep. Wildlife stood mute, and only a whisper of the wind moved through the treetops. Beck killed the lights and looked over to Krong, who strained to hear something.

Beck heard it, too. Up ahead of them there seemed to be a woman's voice—crying, then silent, then crying again.

Beck and Krong stepped cautiously from a tree line surrounding the stilted, tribal longhouses. Unsure of what they were about to find, neither man wanted to walk down the road directly into the front gate of the village. They could see the flames of the burning longhouses.

Just inside the tree line perimeter, Krong spotted a body. It was Toong—his lifelong friend. The man's body was on its side. A large circle of blood pooled underneath him, and his matted hair was pulled from its perpetual tight knot—falling across his face.

Beck saw the body, too, but said nothing. Instead, he stepped toward it, bent down, and gently turned it over, confirming the elder's death. He looked at Krong, who was fixed on something across the compound near the smoking remains of two of the longhouses. It was Jrae, wearing only a tattered loincloth. Near her was the body of her baby—motionless.

She stood in horror, tied to the base of a large mahogany tree, her face contorted by pain. Spittle threaded from the corner of her open mouth down across her nearly naked body as she sobbed in convulsive heaves.

Her eyes searched for the impossible—some sign in Beck's eyes that would tell her her son was still alive.

Beck looked around at the starburst, scorch-marked depressions on the ground around her son's body, then at the boy, and then to Krong. His expression told Krong there was no hope for the little boy.

Jrae caught Krong's expression, let out a shriek of pain, and collapsed in her agony.

Beck guessed the Viet Cong made the mother watch while they tossed hand grenades at the terrified little boy. He closed his eyes for just a moment to absorb the horror of it and then motioned for Krong to work his way over to Jrae—to be careful, knowing the mother was ripe to be booby-trapped.

Krong did as he was told.

Beck looked back down at the lifeless form of the little boy. Finding a puddle of muddy water next to his knee, Beck scooped up a palmful and slowly dripped it onto the child's forehead and whispered a blessing in awkward altar-boy Latin. Then, with his thumb, he made the sign of the cross on the boy's tiny forehead—baptizing him.

CHAPTER 5

It was still well before sunrise when Hollister arrived at his company. The winter morning was cold and damp—characteristic of all Fort Benning winters. He entered the building through the mess hall and picked up his first cup of coffee on the way to his office. The scalding black fluid had lost some of its taste in the making. Still, he needed the coffee to clear his head. It was another morning begun with a pounding head and a sour taste in his mouth.

He swallowed several aspirin and returned the bottle to his desk drawer. His in-box was filled with a pile of what to him were make-work tasks that the overblown headquarters between him and the Secretary of Defense had created over the course of the Vietnam War expansion. He pulled the pile out of the box and put it on one side of his desk.

Hollister looked at the five inches of paperwork and decided to pass. He pushed his chair back and walked out into the outer office where the company clerk was sorting out still more paperwork.

"I'll be out with the special training platoon, if anyone's looking for me," Hollister said, unbuttoning his fatigue shirt.

The troops running in front of Hollister in the small formation were not like any troops he had ever served with. They were crippled up by their addictions or their poor attitudes or both. There was no spirit in their step and no enthusiasm in their voices as they repeated the Jody cadence Garland led.

It was just as well that it wasn't a spirited run. Hollister was still suffering from the pounding in his head. It was another in a long series of such mornings. As he shuffled down the street, also conscious of the sourness in his stomach, he made a small resolution to cut down on his drinking and smoking and to try to get more exercise to purge his system of the residue of his bad habits. That, too, was a repetition of so many similar promises.

They reached the top of the hill, adjacent to the parade field. At the end of a company street, Hollister spotted a lone figure, silhouetted by a barracks fire light, watching the runners approach.

Hollister recognized Colonel Valentine, wearing his fatigues and a sweatshirt with his name stenciled on the front.

"Morning, Captain," Valentine said as he fell into step with Hollister.

"Good morning, sir. You going to join us?"

"I want to see what's happening with your special training here."

Hollister was glad he had picked that morning to go out with his troops to inspect training. Being there would keep any of Valentine's critical remarks from being directed at Garland, who neither created the special training nor should be blamed for any failure.

"What's the score now?"

"We've accepted forty-two into the training, graduated twenty-two and sent them back to their units, and have a dozen right now—not counting the one who died. That means we've only had seven who have ended up in the stockade," Hollister said with a note of pride in his voice.

"Not good enough," Colonel Valentine said.

"Sir, without this training platoon you'd be facing forty-one courts-martial."

"It's not how many didn't face military punishment—it's how many *did* I'm concerned with. Starting today, anyone who doesn't look like he'll be safe to send back to his unit—recycle him. Keep him here a couple more weeks."

"But sir—"

"No buts, Hollister. I want the court-martial numbers down, and we'll sweat this damn crap out of their systems or kill them trying."

Hollister let Valentine's words sink in. His orientation on the numbers and not on the troops bothered him.

They covered the best part of another block of barracks before Valentine spoke again. "You have some problem with my plan?"

Hollister knew better than to argue. "No, sir. I'll take care of it."

*   *   *

Hollister tried to cool down while watching the troops as they found their grounded headgear and shirts. Some of them looked tired, not from the PT but from the drugs and the booze that had brought them to his training platoon.

"You been here how long?" Hollister asked the boy who had been brought in wrapped in a wet sheet.

"Be nine days tomorrow, sir," he replied, tucking his shirttail in.

Hollister recognized the name over his pocket. "What's the story, Greenwood? You gonna clean up your act or get a stay in the post stockade?"

"I'm not going to the gray-bar hotel, sir."

"How'd this happen? Your paperwork says you're a Ranger, Airborne, and made sergeant in Vietnam. How the hell do you get from there to here?"

"I wanted to go to an Airborne unit and ended up in a fucked-up mechanized infantry battalion for nine months. We thrashed around in Three Corps and damn near knocked down everything standing. I got malaria, and they evac'd me to Camp Zama in Japan. I spent a little time in the hospital, and then they put me in the casual company waiting for reassignment. I fucked around there for almost three more months, pulling shitty details for some fat-ass acting first sergeant who kept screwing with my papers to keep me from going back to Vietnam."

"You didn't say anything to anyone?"

"Sir, I wasn't gonna complain about not going back to that lame-ass mech company."

"You didn't want to go back to Vietnam, huh?" Hollister asked.

"I don't think Vietnam was the problem. I just didn't want anything to do with sitting on my ass on a track hull or at that god-forsaken firebase getting rocketed and pulling details. I'da much rather pulled details in Japan, and time off was terrific. But it's what got me in trouble. Some of the guys who'd been there a while were into drugs, and I, ah . . ." He shuffled his feet and rolled his cap around in his hands. "I got into it, too."

"A mistake?"

"Biggest mistake I ever made."

"You seem to be shaping up here. Your training record says you are keeping your nose clean."

"Sir, I'll do anything to make up for this. I'm not real proud of getting myself so fucked up."

"What do you want to do when you get out of here?"

"I want to get a decent job in an Airborne battalion and see if I can soldier my way out of the hole I got myself in."

"You finish this two weeks, you got a chance."

"Yes, sir," the boy said. "I know that."

The next six weeks were only more of the same for Hollister. At work, things were not improving. More dead American soldiers were returning to the Southeast, and more of Hollister's burial details were dispatched to provide military funerals.

Then, one morning's activities were interrupted by First Sergeant Mann, who stuck his head in the door of Hollister's office. "Sir, call for you—Infantry Branch."

Hollister had dreaded the call. "Captain Hollister, sir."

"Hollister, this is Colonel Marchand in captain's assignments. You ready for movement orders, son?"

Accepting his new assignment was sure to go badly with Susan. Hollister had tried to make her understand that it wasn't a job like working for a bank. He couldn't just quit, just walk away, just forget it all. He would have to call her and tell her and listen to her repeat the same complaints and make the same promises to leave him for good.

Circling back to main post, he pulled his car in at the corner of Eubanks Field—the Airborne School's tower training area—and parked. Getting out, he looked across the several dozen acres of open, manicured grassy fields at the three 250-foot jump towers. The training area brought back memories of an easier time. He remembered the hours on the asphalt track—running in formation with the three hundred other trainees in his jump school class. He wondered how many of them had survived the first years of Vietnam. But he knew the answer. He was burying soldiers like them every day.

He lit a cigarette and looked back over his shoulder at the Officer Candidate School barracks. They, too, held many memories. He remembered Kerry French, his old OCS roommate, killed in Vietnam. Kerry was only one of so many of his friends who had died over there. The thought of all of their sacrifices being pissed away to suit a political sway made him feel a twinge of nausea.

He missed the days before the war. The days when he was young and excited about becoming a paratrooper-Ranger.

How could he ever make her understand?

The morning dew cast a dulling drape over the normally shiny tops of the soldiers' black helmets. For Hollister, it was just another predawn inspection of still another burial detail readying itself to load the buses and head out into the Georgia countryside.

"Sir, Lieutenant Garland just called from the hospital," First Sergeant Mann said from the top of the landing leading into the barracks.

Hollister stopped his inspection and turned to his first soldier. "What's the problem?"

"No problem, sir. Seems like the lieutenant's baby won't wait until he gets back from the burial detail. His wife is in the delivery room right now. He wants to know if you want him to get back here."

Knowing Garland would even consider his job so important made Hollister feel good about picking him as his executive officer. He shook his head and waved his hand for the first sergeant. "No. Tell him to take care of mama, and we'll get along."

"Roger that, sir," the first sergeant said and he turned to step back inside.

"Oh, Top," he yelled. "Look at my schedule and see what can be rearranged. I'm going out with Lieutenant Garland's detail."

The drive was pleasant enough for Hollister. A couple of aspirin and more coffee dulled the ache in his head, and a piece of dry toast from the mess hall eased the sourness in his stomach.

The Georgia countryside was separated from Alabama's by the coffee-colored stripe of the Chattahoochee River. Once they passed into Phenix City, it was an unending string of used car dealerships, small bars, and roadhouses.

He remembered the nights when he was in Airborne School and they used to go to Phenix City for the girls, the booze, and the bars. He allowed himself a moment to remember the fun—but only a moment.

The names were written in his notebook in his first sergeant's handwriting. He had entered them for Hollister while Hollister was changing uniforms. Eleanor DeWitt was the widow of a lieutenant killed in Phu Yen Province. She was the mother of their three-year-old, born during their four-year marriage.

Hollister appreciated having the information the first sergeant was able to get from the Survivor's Assistance Officer who had been helping Mrs. DeWitt with the administrative details of settling things between her and the army.

The burial detail was to meet the funeral party at graveside and not the church. Pallbearers from the family had taken the casket from the church to the hearse, and the widow wanted the interment to be with military honors.

Checking his watch, Hollister saw they still had enough time to set up before the family arrived at the cemetery.

A representative from the funeral home rushed up to meet Hollister as his detail got off the small army bus. "Captain, I'm Renaldo," the nervous little man said. Hollister didn't know if it was the man's first or last name—but didn't really care.

"Yes?"

"You are here for the DeWitts?" he asked, looking over toward the ground crew securing the tie-downs on the canopy stretched over the folding chairs for the mourners.

"Yes—you weren't expecting another military burial detail, were you?" Hollister asked, concerned there might have been two funerals scheduled and he only got the word about one. It had happened to him before.

"No—no, you are the only people I am expecting."

"Okay, then. Where are we?"

Renaldo pointed to the sharp, red-clay edges of the gaping hole in the Alabama grass. "The graveside services will be held here, and you can place your firing squad anywhere in the cemetery."

Hollister walked away—up the gentle rise behind the grave site. He looked around for the crest of the hill. He wanted the firing squad to be silhouetted against the skyline if at all possible. It was the last thing a man with a rifle wanted to do in a war zone—stand out on the horizon.

From the top of the rise, he could see the size of the cemetery. It must have held twelve hundred graves, and there was room for at least three times that number. How many of the tenants had arrived at their final rest through wars? He wondered how many more would come there from this war. He suddenly felt tired of thoughts of the war, of days like the one ahead of him, and of widows like the one he would soon meet.

Hollister's soldiers stood at a rigid and respectful position of attention behind the dark blue Cadillac hearse backed up to their parallel rows. He gave the near-silent commands to open the hearse, remove the casket, and turn to begin carrying it to the grave site.

Every man in C Company spent hours practicing all of the jobs required of them on funeral details. While they practiced, they became expert at hearing the very muffled snap of the detail commander's fingers. Each pair of snaps, muted by the white cotton gloves he wore, would prepare them for the next motion and then tell them when to execute the move.

Hollister followed the casket and pallbearers from the hearse to the lowering apparatus over the freshly dug grave and caught sight of Eleanor DeWitt.

She was midtwenties, blonde, tall, and slight. Her son was dressed in his Sunday best and held her hand—walking with her from the limousine to the rows of canopy-covered chairs.

The pallbearers placed the gleaming mahogany casket onto the lowering apparatus. Hollister took his position at the foot of the casket, while the priest took his at the head. The round and balding clergyman wore a crisp, starched surplice over his black wool cassock. The stark colors were offset by the narrow purple band of satin draped around his neck.

Hollister stole a look up the hill at the firing squad. The soldiers stood abreast, rifles at parade rest, their heads and eyes fixed to the front—motionless. Off to their flank and a bit higher on the gentle slope, Hollister had posted the bugler, who stood alone and still.

After Mrs. DeWitt, her son, and her parents were seated, the priest began his final words.

"God did not tell this young woman and mother she would be here today. He did not warn her that her contribution to her country would cost her so dearly. His plans for her—"

Hollister's mind drifted from the priest's words to the faces in the crowd of mourners. They were all ashen, every eye swollen and red.

He thought of the widow. He would have to tell her how sorry he was, and he would have to tell—*her name*? He couldn't remember her name. His notebook was inside his blouse, and he would draw too much attention to himself if he pulled it out to look again.

Sweat beaded on his upper lip, and a trickle of it ran down the channel formed in the small of his back. He had to remember. Think, Hollister! He tried to focus. He could see the page in his notebook as if it were in his hand. He had checked her name before he got off the bus, and Renaldo even mentioned her name. Christ! He could remember Renaldo's name. Why not hers?

The priest finished. Hollister felt a shock of panic running up his spine. He had to do something. He just had to remember her name.

The priest nodded to Hollister, which gave him a chance to move. He knew he couldn't reach in his pocket, but looking around might jog his memory. Suddenly, a hundred funerals ran through his mind, and he began to feel weak in the knees. He scolded himself to straighten up and get the job done.

He turned his head toward the firing squad and nodded—officially. The light wind kept the funeral party from hearing the whispered command up on the hill. The soldiers were precise and in unison as they aimed, fired, aimed, fired, and aimed and fired for the last time. The bugler began the slow mournful sounds of Taps, and a few under the canopy broke out in great sobs and sniffling.

The rifle volleys, the bugle call, and the flag folding over, Hollister turned to accept the trifolded American flag that had draped the casket during the ceremony. Holding it high and respectfully, he walked directly to the widow. He still hadn't pulled her name from his head and considered just trying to get by without even addressing her by name when she, unsure of what to do, leaned forward to stand.

As she did, the tape on the chair back was revealed for just a split second. Hollister caught the words MRS DEWITT before an older man next to her stopped her and told her just to stay seated and wait for Hollister to come to her.

Reaching the widow, Hollister was careful not to look her son in the eyes. He knew if he did there was either a chance the boy would feel like speaking to him, throwing the ceremony out of its formal tone, or he would simply break out in tears for the boy's loss.

He kept his eyes focused on Mrs. DeWitt's and bent stiffly at the waist as he held the flag out to her. He hoped his voice wouldn't crack as he spoke. "Mrs. DeWitt, the president of the United States and a grateful nation extend their deepest sympathy for your grievous loss and wish you to accept this flag as a token of their appreciation and respect for your sacrifice."

The woman's gloved hands shook as she accepted the flag. She took it to her breast and held it tightly for a moment, while Hollister stood erect and executed the smartest, most perfect salute he could give her.

She cried.

He swallowed hard to keep from doing the same. He dropped his salute; she reached out and touched his hand. "Thank you, Captain," she whispered.

All he could muster was, "Yes, ma'am," before he turned smartly to keep her from seeing the tears in his eyes.

He had counted the steps from the casket to her chair, and he retraced them as he tried to clear the blurriness from his flooded eyes.

First Sergeant Mann went to the admissions desk while Hollister hurried down the hall to the emergency room. An army nurse started to make a move like she was going to stop Hollister from going into the treatment area and then had a second thought when she looked at the expression on his face. He was clearly in no mood to be messed with.

"My name's Hollister. There's a man in here assigned to my company," he said to the backs of four lime-clad hospital staffers who hovered over a naked, shaking body on a paper-topped examining table.

"Wait outside!" a voice said, no one bothering to turn around to give Hollister the courtesy of knowing just who spoke.

"You talking to me?"

Finally, a doctor, graying—thin on the top—turned. "Weren't you talking to *me*, Captain?"

"Listen, I'm not here for an argument. I just want to find out about my man."

"Well, just wait outside, and we'll have something to tell you," the doctor said sarcastically. He quickly turned back to the soldier who had progressed from shaking to strong convulsions.

Hollister knew the doctor was right. He had no place there. Still, he wanted to make sure the soldier was being treated and someone was looking out for him.

He stepped back toward the door he had entered and watched

while the soldier struggled against the large tube they were forcing up his nose and down into his stomach.

Hollister met First Sergeant Mann in the waiting room. They decided there was no use in both of them waiting. There was plenty to be done back at the company area and most of it was on the first sergeant's desk. He left and promised to send back Hollister's driver and jeep.

The floor-model ashtray had a little trapdoor in it. Each time Hollister finished a cigarette, he dropped it into the chrome clamshell-like jaws and then pushed down on the plunger. The jaws opened; the butt fell into some dark tube where it disappeared into the base of the ashtray.

Hollister tried to use the time in the waiting room to think. His head was so crammed with things all competing for his time and attention. He was still undecided about going back to Vietnam. In the back of his head, he knew it would happen. He just fooled himself into thinking he could still stop the wheels from grinding him out of Fort Benning, to Fort Bragg for the Special Forces qualification course, and then on to Vietnam to a Green Beret assignment.

And there was Susan. Nothing short of quitting would satisfy her. He couldn't accept her ultimatum. He loved her. He missed her. But one way or the other—they were in very real trouble, and he knew it.

"You the boy's CO?"

Looking up, Hollister saw the doctor who had run him out of the treatment area. He had taken his scrubs off and was wearing his uniform—complete with lieutenant colonel's leaves.

"Yes, sir," Hollister said, getting to his feet. "How is he? Is he going to make it?"

The doctor pulled his glasses off and rubbed the bridge of his nose. "Yeah, he'll live—but he won't be good for much."

Hollister was confused by the comment. "You mean he isn't okay?"

"I mean that kid had enough pills in him to make him the next American on the moon. He fucked himself up pretty good. His heart stopped for several minutes, and it looks like there's enough brain damage to keep him in another world than ours the rest of his days."

The news just cut through Hollister. He shook his head and absentmindedly looked for his cigarettes.

"You know anything about him?"

"Yes, sir. He was sent to me for some remedial training for being involved in drugs in the first place. He's from a mining town in West Virginia. He served a year in Vietnam with an engineer company. He wanted to get a job as a heavy equipment operator when he got out of the army."

There was nothing Hollister could do for the soldier. He resigned himself to the fact that even seeing him would not make the soldier's life any better. He walked down the corridor and found himself face-to-face with Colonel Valentine. It was obvious to Hollister the man was unhappy from the color of his face.

He stuck his finger out and poked it at Hollister. "What the hell is going on? I give you these people to shape up, and every goddamn time I turn around, another one is putting more poison in his system? You better have a goddamn good explanation for this, Hollister."

Hollister's immediate impulse was to hit the colonel right in the face. He surprised himself with the urge, but Valentine had definitely picked the wrong time to screw with Hollister.

"Colonel, I'm no expert in this drug thing—"

"You can damn sure say that again. Not only are you screwing up this job—I have to find out you were stopped recently by the MPs for drinking."

"I don't understand, sir. An MP who used to work for me in Vietnam stopped me to say hello. I was never cited for anything."

"Because he was your friend, I'm sure. And that's another thing that irritates me about you, Hollister. I think you are just too damn familiar with enlisted men."

Hollister got even angrier at the way Valentine said *enlisted men*, like they were some kind of bugs. "I'm proud to call many of them my friends, Colonel. If we can stand shoulder-to-shoulder together in combat, I don't see how it is ever possible to be too familiar with them later."

"Damn it, Hollister, I was told you were a water walker and you were the man to take on this job and what did I get? I got unsatisfactory performance out of you, *Captain*."

Hollister could feel the blood pulsing in his neck. He clenched his fists and released them to dissipate the anger rising in him.

"Well, maybe you did pick the wrong man, Colonel. I'm a troop commander, not a fucking nurse."

The colonel's face flushed. "At ease, mister. You are on the edge of pissing me off, and *I* am very close to relieving your ass."

Hollister realized the colonel hadn't even asked about the soldier. "Maybe you should do that, Colonel. It's obvious to me your visit here has nothing to do with finding out how that boy is in there," Hollister said, thrusting his thumb toward the emergency room.

Before the colonel could respond, the post sergeant major walked up behind him and excused himself. "Colonel, I don't mean to interrupt, but I need to speak with you."

Hollister caught the look in the old sergeant's eyes. He realized Sergeant Major Sawyer was trying to keep the colonel and Hollister from having a showdown where the colonel would have to prove to Hollister how much more power he had.

"Colonel, I've talked with the medical officer of the day, and he said you can get in to see the young soldier before they move him to a ward, but we have to go now," Sawyer said.

"Right, right, Sergeant Major," the colonel said, and then he turned back to Hollister. "You and I will finish this later. You are dismissed, Captain," the colonel said, not waiting for an answer before he stepped off toward the emergency ward with Sawyer.

Hollister stood there, seething in anger at the colonel. He was aware of his own behavior and a little surprised—it just wasn't like him.

"Captain," a voice said behind him.

Hollister spun around and almost screamed, "What?" only to find a young private first class standing in the doorway with a set of keys and a vehicle logbook under his arm.

"I'm sorry, sir. First Sergeant Mann sent me to pick you up—if you're ready to go."

"Yes, yes I am. Sorry, I didn't mean to snap at you."

CHAPTER 6

Somewhere in the night, Jrae packed up what she could carry on her back and readied herself to move to Da Lat. She fought the urge to cry, knowing her home would be a memory by the end of the day. After taking a last look around inside, she clutched her few possessions and helped Krong down the steps of their long-house. He had grown increasingly feeble in the recent weeks—never fully recovering from the loss of Sraang.

Jrae stood next to Krong and watched the near chaos in the center of the village. The children were divided in their reactions to it all. Some of them screamed in terror at the sounds of the helicopters, while others were curious and unsure of them. The line appeared to split at an age where a child could have had enough bad experiences with choppers flown by both the Americans and the South Vietnamese. Many of them had been the targets or near the targets of gunships. The distinction that these were troop-lift ships was lost on them. For all of them it was the first time they had seen choppers on the ground and in their village.

For the adults it was purely a matter of loss. What remained of their longhouses burned furiously, fanned by the rotor wash of the choppers. Jrae's was the last to be ignited. A South Vietnamese soldier pulled the pin on an incendiary grenade and lobbed it up onto the thatch shading the porch and steps. The white flame spread to the dry thatch with a pop—involving the entire roof in less than a minute.

The flying cinders from their own longhouse rained down on Jrae and Krong. She looked at the flames and then at Krong. As the longhouse timbers began to collapse, he forced himself to stand erect and straight, as if he refused to be broken by the sight.

Someone pushed Jrae from behind, and she stumbled toward one of the choppers, ashes blurring her vision, smoke choking her and burning her throat.

The last moments in her village were crowded with the memories of her childhood there and in carbon-copy villages along her tribe's nomadic path. She thought of her dead baby, of Sraang, and other tribal brothers and sisters. She remembered her mother and the days she had spent at her side learning women's work. She knew she would never see Yoon Dlei again.

The pilots took up a common orbit over the burning village as they waited for the last ship to lift off and join the flight. Jrae clutched the metal seat frame in the chopper and looked out and down at her village. The sensation of flying was overshadowed by the enormity of what she saw below.

All that remained of the structures were burning stumps, once the sturdy upright skeletons of the longhouses. The white ashes outlined the ground the dwellings once shaded from the hot Vietnamese sun.

The smell of burning thatch, rats that had lived in it, and the sweet smell of mahogany smoke filled Jrae's nostrils. She looked to Krong for some sign and saw him weeping silently at the other side of the open doorway.

The words of the South Vietnamese government were little help to Jrae. They promised safer and more comfortable living conditions at the relocation camp. But they couldn't promise Jrae she would be forgiven for leaving the grave sites of her ancestors and her child.

As the choppers turned eastward and began to fly down the side of the mountains, Jrae left the old Montagnard world forever.

Lewis pulled Hollister's jeep to a stop in the circular driveway in front of Building 4—the Infantry School building. Hollister looked over at the towering statue of the infantryman standing watch over York Field.

He remembered the first day he entered the building. It seemed so many years had gone by since then. He didn't know why, but it made him feel sad. "Lewis, why don't you find yourself a cup of coffee?" Hollister looked at his watch. "I'm sure I won't be finished inside an hour."

*　　*　　*

Major General George I. Parrish was the ranking man at Fort Benning. He had the tough job of setting the standards for infantrymen armywide and training thousands of soldiers, NCOs, and officers to go to Vietnam.

Hollister was ushered into Parrish's office by his aide, a tall lieutenant who had been a student of Hollister's when he taught at the Ranger School. "Good morning, sir, the general will be right with you," he said, pointing to a chair for Hollister, who declined, preferring to stand.

Hollister had liked the general from the moment he met him. Parrish had just returned from commanding the 25th Infantry Division in Vietnam when Hollister was being considered for the job of honor guard commander. General Parrish had to approve Hollister's selection since Hollister would be representing Fort Benning at almost every important civic and military event.

The day they met, General Parrish spent an hour with Hollister asking him about Vietnam, training, and leadership. He never asked him any questions about drill and ceremonies or any of the functions he would be required to perform as the honor guard commander.

The general hung up the phone and spun around in his large leather chair. "Hollister, good morning, son. How are things?" the general asked, sticking out his hand to shake Hollister's.

Hollister leaned over the large desk to shake the general's hand. "Good, sir. Things are good," he said—it being bad form to complain to someone several echelons up the chain of command.

"Good. Sit."

Surrendering to the uncomfortably low-cushioned chair, Hollister sat and placed his helmet on the floor next to the chair so he could take notes on his knee.

"We have a visitor coming tomorrow afternoon—and I want you to turn out your troops and show him just how terrific we are here at Benning."

Hollister gave a puzzled look because the general normally didn't talk to him directly about a routine honor guard review for a visiting VIP.

"It's Westmoreland," the general added.

"Oh," Hollister said, understanding the importance.

"He hasn't been down here since he became chief of staff. And I want him to go away knowing we have things under control."

"Is there something special about this—other than it being the army chief of staff, sir?" Hollister asked, unsure why they were talking unless there would be a change to the usual routine.

"No, I want you to do your usual bang-up job. I've been pleased with your performance, and I want you to just do it the same way."

"Well, thank you, sir. You can count on my people to get it done right," Hollister said, still thinking the general had something else in mind.

The general reached over and pushed down a toggle switch on a small intercom.

The voice of his aide on the other end crackled, "Yes, sir?"

"Bring that paperwork in here."

"Yes, sir," the aide said before his voice was clipped off by the intercom.

The general let a smile creep across his face. He looked back at Hollister. "You know, Jim, there are lots of tough things a general has to do, spared occasionally by an enjoyable task."

The aide entered and handed the general a folder and stepped back to wait for any other instructions.

Hollister wasn't sure what the general was getting at, but he knew he was uncomfortable.

"There are almost eight hundred captains here at Fort Benning—going to school, teaching, and assigned to the garrison?"

"Yes, sir," Hollister replied.

The general opened up the folder and took out a photocopied set of orders and held them up. "But there are only two names on this promotion list to major for captains who are as junior as you are—and yours is one of them."

Hollister didn't believe what he was hearing. *He had been deep selected for promotion to major?* "Sir? Me? Major?" His brain rattled at the seeming contradiction between his own performance and the announcement. Only officers with the highest efficiency report ratings and an impressive list of tough assignments made the list.

He had never much thought about making major because he didn't feel he was anywhere near the zone of consideration. He also put off thinking about it because he knew college would be a part of the selection board, and he still hadn't assembled enough college credits to post to his records.

He had no idea what his efficiency reports looked like since there was no requirement for commanders to show them to the rated officers. He had only seen one. It was the max report that

Major Sangean had given him when he was a Long Range Patrol company operations officer on his second tour in Vietnam. He had considered it a fluke or a gift. He surely didn't think his other OERs were equally glowing in their assessment of his performance. But the proof was there. He would be a major well before his OCS classmates.

The general stood up and stuck out his hand again to congratulate Hollister. "That's right, son. You've been picked very early to be a new major." He then made a face of mock frustration. "But since you're on the bottom of the list, it'll probably be more than a year before your sequence number comes up. But as of yesterday—you are now a *captain, promotable*. You'll be able to take on jobs and responsibilities of a major, even though we aren't paying you for it yet."

They both laughed. Only the army could figure out how to get more out of a soldier without paying him for it.

"Sir, I don't know what to say."

"Well, just know this promotion is a reflection of how your previous commanders have felt about your performance in peacetime and combat assignments. You have a good record, and you're a respected soldier. And I'm glad to have you in my command. I know you deserve this promotion, and the army has made a wise choice picking you over so many other captains senior to you."

The words embarrassed Hollister. He was so surprised by the announcement and the praise from the general, he just stood there mute.

The general laughed. "I understand. It's a lot to swallow— isn't it?"

"Yes, sir!"

"You realize this means things are going to change for you? Assignments will be better. You'll probably be offered a regular army commission, and you'll, no doubt, find civilian schooling falling into your lap."

The fringe benefits took a moment to sink in for Hollister. A regular commission was an officer's version of tenure, and civil schooling meant the army would send him to college on the army's time.

The morning brought with it all the last-minute checking of details before putting on an honors ceremony complete with the band and an artillery salute battery.

While there was never enough time to check all that needed checking, Hollister hoped that what he did overlook might still be acceptable to the army chief of staff.

He looked at the ranks of soldiers and bandsmen lined up perfectly on imaginary lines on the clipped grass of the parade field. They stood proudly, waiting for the welcoming ceremony to begin.

As soon as the general's chopper arrived, Westmoreland moved with dispatch to the reviewing stand where General Parrish waited. The two then stepped down from the stand and marched to Hollister's post in front of the assembled honor guard.

Not knowing firsthand that everything was ready nagged at Hollister while he greeted the general and then trooped the line. If anything did catch General Parrish's eye, he chose not to mention it to Hollister as he thanked him and returned to his post at the reviewing stand for the pass in review.

Hollister marched his company, the color guard, and the band past the reviewing stand, did a sharp right, and moved to the base of its steps. There, he stopped, turned around, and saluted the colors as they passed.

Once the last of his honor guard had passed the stand, Hollister turned to General Westmoreland and saluted. "Sir, this concludes the ceremony."

Westmoreland returned Hollister's salute and stepped down from the stand to shake his hand. "Thank you, Hollister. Fine job. I always love coming back to Benning because you all do a wonderful job here."

Before Hollister could respond, General Parrish and Colonel Valentine stepped up next to Westmoreland. Westmoreland turned and caught sight of Valentine. "Hollister here has a fine-looking honor guard."

Valentine puffed his chest a bit and smiled. "Yes, General. He's a good man."

Hollister was stunned at the hypocrisy of Valentine's words. He was tempted to show some sign of surprise but was interrupted by Valentine's bombast.

"And you know, General, young Hollister here's the kind of soldier I like to point out to the young lieutenants—as an example. He's been deep selected for early promotion. And I'm very proud to have been part of putting him there."

Since he'd been in the army, Hollister had met and worked for only a few officers he thought were complete assholes. Valentine was one of them. For Valentine to take any credit for Hollister's promotion was to Hollister a cold, hard lie. Valentine had not even been in his job long enough to influence the major's selection board.

Hollister remembered how much time, energy, and emphasis had been placed on an officer's word in OCS. He still believed it was very important. And watching a colonel lie to somehow take credit in front of the chief of staff of the army sickened Hollister. There wasn't much he could do about it but promise himself he would never become a Valentine, and promise himself he would never turn his back to Valentine. He couldn't be trusted.

Jrae sat in the only piece of shade she could find under the metal roof of their structure. Aluminum sheeting covered the open timber frame of what the South Vietnamese called refugee housing. The floors were hard-packed earth, but the shelters contained nothing else in the way of living accommodations. The ground was adequate to sleep on in the dry season, but many sought the comfort of hammocks.

Jrae was forced to sleep among the other Montagnard women. Women she didn't even know. From her place, Jrae could see the hundreds of mountain people going through their daily routines. Some wove bamboo into baskets, while others carried square five-gallon cans of water balanced on the ends of carry poles. Old people sat near their few possessions and watched the others suspiciously.

She was able to recognize the differences in the features and the clothing worn by members of other Montagnard tribes. So she knew they were not of her people. Her people and these were as alien to one another as if they had come from different sides of the globe. Some were able to communicate in French, and others had enough in common in their dialects to get along. But most of them were unsure of the others and wary.

Jrae looked at Krong. "Where do you go? Can I get some water for you?" Jrae asked.

"No. I am only going to wash the filth from my hair," Krong said. "Don't worry for me. I am well."

She watched as he turned away. He walked, hunched over, to a government-built latrine. It was designed to accommodate as many as fifty people at a time. And in its efficiency came a complete loss of privacy and dignity. Jrae was worried. She had seen him scuff to the latrine far too many times over the past several days.

She had tried to talk to him about it before, but he changed the subject and made it clear to her he would neither be fussed over nor be a burden to his people. Instead, he told her it was time for her to think about her survival. He would be gone soon, and she would be alone. She was the last in her family line, and the few others from their village were all having their own problems. She should not expect them to look out for her.

The thought of being without Krong was painful for Jrae. He had been her family's heart her whole life. What they did, what they were, and where they traveled were all decided by Krong. There was never a question about his wisdom or his authority. But since they had been put out of the choppers in Da Lat, his power and influence had disappeared.

"Have you ever used one of these?" Sergeant Jackie Beck asked Jrae.

She shook her head—no. She had seen one once in a clinic run by the nuns, but she wasn't sure how it operated.

"Okay. Here is a copy of the *Stars and Stripes*, an American newspaper. I want you to pick out an article and copy it using this old gal," he said, patting the worn-out, upright Remington as if it had a personality.

Jrae watched as Beck rolled a piece of paper into the typewriter and tapped on a few of the keys.

"See here? You match the letters on these keys to the letters on the page, and you'll type a copy of the news article. That's how you practice. Can do?"

Jrae nodded even though she wasn't completely sure what he had her doing.

The days in Jackie Beck's office began to make some sense to Jrae, and she soon became quite skilled at copying things on the typewriter. And working around Americans helped to improve the English she had learned from the nuns when she was a young girl.

But along with the growing comfort she felt among the more Western world came alienation from her own people and a new problem for her. She recognized there was little she could do about the distancing. There was a notion among some of the Montagnards that it was somehow disloyal to their kind to befriend

Viets or Americans. But those same Montagnards were dying with their insistence that they cling to the old ways and the old ties. Their spirits faded before they did, but Jrae saw it in their eyes long before their bodies gave out.

She was determined not to give up just because she had been separated from her cultural homeland and village life. She would adapt, and she would survive.

Her other problem was the American and the South Vietnamese men. Working in an office, she came into contact with them daily. Some of them would treat her with indifference, some were friendly, others would show open contempt. And still others would treat her like a common prostitute.

She was occasionally approached with propositions she tried to refuse without creating friction. She quickly became aware of the high priority placed on maintaining face. It was no different among the South Vietnamese men and the Americans. They were equally crushed when she refused them. The South Viets tended to react with insults about her heritage and her limited worth. They often covered her rejection by finding fault with her work. She responded to this by redoubling her efforts to become a better clerk and interpreter. Though many of the South Vietnamese had been assigned to work with the Montagnards for years, none of them had bothered to learn their language. Jrae worked at English, Vietnamese, and several dialects of Montagnard. As her proficiency grew, so did her usefulness to the South Vietnamese.

The Americans tended to laugh off her rejections as if they had only been kidding her all along. But privately they resented her lack of enthusiasm for their advances. Sometimes she would feel as if she were being punished by the Americans, disguised as extra work. This, too, she accepted. She would not be broken. She would not let her spirit be damaged by the insults and the punitive actions of her employers. She took strength from her own discipline. While other women wasted time sitting around the camp watching the days pass by, she practiced her typing and improved her grasp of the many languages spoken there.

CHAPTER 7

He walked through the main waiting area of San Francisco International Airport, and people stared at Hollister. He just assumed there was no one in that place who was undecided about Vietnam, and he was certainly a symbol of the war.

He wore his starched khakis with highly polished paratrooper boots, rows of combat ribbons, his master parachutist's and combat infantryman's badges on his chest. On his head—his new green beret, having finished the training en route to Vietnam. He felt like he was in some people's crosshairs and others' prayers. But he held his head high, carried his B-4 bag and small carry-on bag as if the weight was nothing, and tried to take in the people around him without seeming to care.

He was amazed at how things had changed in the six years since his first departure for Vietnam. Then there were no hippies, no draft dodgers, no antiwar demonstrators, no draft-card burners, and no one in the airport to even care who he was or where he was going.

But things had changed so much; hardly a head remained unturned as he walked the length of the concourse to get to his gate.

He was ready. He had heard all, of the horror stories about people spitting on soldiers. He had considered wearing civvies but then got angry that he even considered it. He was going off to serve his country, and he would not do it like a thief in the night.

The flight from the West Coast to Vietnam was always awful. It was not just long, it was filled with the finality of going off to war, with the uncertainty of war, and with the depression of knowing there was at least a year ahead of you before you were eligible to return.

Hollister had drawn a commercial ticket. He was traveling with other soldiers, civilians of all walks of life, and tourists on their way to Honolulu. The stewardess was a cute little redhead named Pammy, who had spotted Hollister's uniform and kept him in tiny bottles of bourbon from the time they lifted off at San Francisco International until they orbited Saigon.

The second leg of the trip stopped in Guam for refueling, and then straight into Saigon.

For Hollister, the approach into Saigon was not much different from his first time. The city was a blur of headlights, and the countryside was spotted with parachute flares and hundreds of navigation lights on the aircraft he could see on the descent into Tan Son Nhut Airport.

It was three in the morning when they landed. A sergeant was waiting at the ramp to start in-processing for the 131 new arrivals.

As always, it started with a formation—lining everyone up. Hollister found a spot and dropped his bags while the sergeant went through the most critical initial instructions.

"If during this in-processing, you hear sirens located on the corners of the building behind me or you detect incoming enemy rockets, artillery, or mortar fire, you will immediately break ranks and head for the large bunkers located one hundred meters to my rear—adjacent to the parking area. Is that understood?"

Hollister looked around at the airport area. He hadn't been there since his first tour, when he had stood in roughly the same place to get his first glimpse of Vietnam. Everywhere he looked there were signs. More and more buildings had been built to hold more and more people and cargo going through the airport. He had read in a news magazine in the States that Tan Son Nhut had become the busiest airport in the world.

He shook his head. Soldiers, MPs, civilian employees, military vehicles, and aircraft filled every possible space in his field of view. Still, it was a shabby little airfield with too much happening and only one reason for being—the war.

"Those of you who are scheduled for Fifth Special Forces Group assignments will be met inside the ATCO terminal by someone from the SF liaison team. You can fall out now and head on over there."

*   *   *

The air traffic control terminal was one of the oldest buildings at Tan Son Nhut. Many thousands of soldiers had waited there for word on a flight to some place in Vietnam—most of the time those waits were very long.

Hollister entered; not much had changed. There were soldiers waiting to go home, some new arrivals, soldiers waiting to go to other parts of Vietnam, and a large group waiting on a flight to Singapore—for R & R.

Hollister found a mail drop cut in the plywood wall next to one of the counters taking up two walls inside the building. He pulled the letter he had written Susan out of his bag and looked at it before he dropped it into the slot marked "MaiL" in uneven, hand-written letters of mixed case.

He realized there was not much in the letter. At best, it would do nothing to raise his hopes that it would help patch things up between him and Susan.

"Captain Hollister?"

Hollister turned around, expecting to find someone from the Special Forces processing detachment. Instead he found a staff sergeant wearing a baseball cap and a II Field Force shoulder patch. "Yes. What can I do for you?"

"Sir, I'm Sergeant Kent from Two Field." He jerked his thumb toward the doorway. "I've got a vehicle outside, and I'm supposed to pick you up."

"You aren't from the SF liaison team, are you?"

"No, sir. I'm not. All I was told by the duty officer was to get down here and pick you up."

Hollister knew the sergeant didn't have a clue and wasn't responsible for the change in his travel plans. He also knew it wasn't even worth arguing with him. He remembered what a soldier had once said about a similar situation on his first tour: *What the hell. It all goes toward a year.*

Hollister shrugged, nodded, and pointed toward the door. "After you."

The streets of Saigon were the biggest change. They had always been crowded with Americans, Vietnamese, refugees, and carpet-baggers from all over Asia. But Hollister was surprised at how much it had all grown. Next to the numbers of people scurrying to work, the numbers of black-market stands going up for the day were mind-boggling.

He looked at the wide array of American products for sale. It was obvious the problem was completely out of control. Air conditioners, GI-issue American combat gear, folding cots, helmets, fatigues, and several boxes of Tide soap were on display on one corner. Only a few feet away, a vendor had a display of C rations stacked chest high. Hollister thought of the nights out in the bush when he would have given a month's pay to have a can of C rations.

The II Field Force Vietnam headquarters complex had only expanded since he had been there last. They had added more and more barracks, offices, and warehouses. Sergeant Kent turned into one of the first gates they reached and waited for the guard to raise the red-and-white metal barrier pole stretched across the road.

Hollister was immediately struck by the sight of a sloppy-looking soldier leaning against the guard shack, talking on a field phone, oblivious to Hollister and Kent.

Kent tapped the horn on the jeep and got no response from the soldier. He reached down to throw the jeep out of gear and Hollister stopped him. "No, you stay here. I'll take care of this."

Hollister got out of the jeep and straightened his beret. He walked around the front of the jeep and up to the soldier's back. "You suppose we could bother you to open the gate, soldier?"

The soldier slowly looked over his shoulder, the phone still pressed to his ear. Seeing Hollister standing there, his hands on his hips, a scowl on his face, he quickly mumbled some good-byes into the phone and dropped it.

The soldier spun around and saluted, leaving the phone dangling from its cord against the guard shack. "Oh, sorry, sir. I was on the phone."

Hollister decided to let the weak excuse go and just let the soldier do the talking instead of getting into an argument. The soldier awkwardly stepped over to the counterweight on the barrier and leaned on it to raise the gate. "I'm really sorry to hold you up, sir. You, can, ah . . . go ahead now."

Hollister stared at the soldier for an uncomfortably long time for the soldier and then thanked him, a clear trace of sarcasm in his voice.

"Sorry 'bout that, sir," Sergeant Kent said, using the well-worn saying often repeated throughout Vietnam. "We been getting some pretty lame actors over here in the last year. They just drag ass and give you some sorry-ass excuses and slow everything down. It's like they don't care there's a war on and time is important to the kids out there," Kent said, pointing toward the tree line to the northwest of the roadway.

"You been *out there*?"

"Yes, sir. I was a recon NCO in an artillery battalion for eight months. Then they sent my battery home, and I got reassigned here. I'm pretty happy. Being a forward observer was what I was trained for, and now I get to work at the field force artillery headquarters. Good chow and a real cot and, well, I like it."

Hollister was happy to see the combat veterans were still being sent to the headquarters to work rather than filling it up with people who had no appreciation for what the field rats were going through.

He'd been in the same headquarters section many times before. But on this trip, it looked more crowded with desks, more handiwork adorned the walls, and more phones seemed to be ringing. Sergeant Kent had led him to the operations sergeant major's desk—but the sergeant major wasn't there.

Hollister checked his watch. It was only a few minutes after seven, and the headquarters was already humming. "Sergeant Kent, I can take it from here. Why don't you go get yourself some coffee or breakfast?"

"Oh, okay, sir. I'll do that. I don't know where the sergeant major is, but I'm sure someone will be able to help you out pretty quick here. I'll drop back by here to make sure you're okay."

Hollister stuck out his hand and shook Kent's, thanking him for the ride. He looked around for someplace to wait and found a chair. He dropped his gear next to it.

"You just sit around on your ass when there are things to be done, dragons to be slayed, and virgins to be deflowered?"

Hollister recognized the voice and broke into a broad smile. He stood and turned toward the voice. Lieutenant Colonel Grady Michaelson had been Hollister's Long Range Patrol detachment commander on his first tour in Vietnam. They didn't come much better than Grady Michaelson. "Goddamn it. If you aren't a sight for sore eyes, sir."

They shook hands and grabbed each other's upper arms—glad to see each other.

"I had no idea you were here," Hollister said.

"Been in country about two weeks. Just left the War College, and they decided I had to pull a staff tour or turn in my suit," Michaelson said, making a face at his assignment.

"What's the job?"

"Operations."

"Hell, at least it's an operations job, sir. I've met folks on the way over assigned to civic actions and worse. So what you have up your sleeve, sir?"

Michaelson slapped Hollister on the shoulder and looked at his watch. "Listen, I've made arrangements to get you up to Nha Trang this afternoon, but wondered if you had a little time to help me out with a problem."

"Sure. If you're buyin' the coffee, I've got the time."

They crossed the small open area in front of the headquarters building. Hollister realized just how good it was to see Michaelson again. He had taught him plenty about combat and more about himself and soldiers. It was a small reassurance to Hollister that all of the stories of doom and gloom about Vietnam going to hell were not completely true. They couldn't be, with Michaelson making some of the decisions.

The officers club was deserted that time of the day. Michaelson waved one of the waitresses over and ordered coffee.

Hollister selected a table near the window partially covered by rows of sandbags. He liked being able to look out at the hot Vietnamese morning while enjoying the noisy air-conditioning inside the club.

"It's not the same place out there," Michaelson said, dropping his cap on the empty chair next to him and pulling out his cigarettes.

"I've heard. But just how bad is it?"

"Start with the understanding no man wants to be the last one to die here. They all know we're going home, and they all want to be around to see the lights turned out. On top of that, we're up to our asses in press criticism, racial troubles, drug problems, Viet corruption, discipline problems, and worst of all—we have run out of leaders."

"How so?"

"Remember the platoon sergeants and lieutenants we had in sixty-five and sixty-six?"

"Yes, sir."

"They were good at what they did, and all of them had some experience. Some had even served in World War Two and Korea. We brought most of them back for a second tour, burned them out or ran them off.

"Now we're getting NCOs who have been in the army less than two years, and the lieutenants have been in less than a year. They have no skills, no experience, and they get no respect. Soldiers are fragging leaders who do their jobs, and leaders are trying to court-martial problem children. They just have no persuasive tricks other than throwing the book at the troublemakers. Lieutenants are afraid of being fragged and try to become buddies with their troops. It's bad soldiering."

"Whew. I heard it was bad, but never imagined all of this," Hollister said.

"The bottom line is that units have pulled back to handle all of their problems. They run fewer operations in a month than they used to in a week."

"And that means—"

"The bad guys have filled in the void. We need to get out of the base camps and mix it up with the VC."

Hollister took a sip of the coffee and then lit a cigarette. He waited for Michaelson to continue.

"It's bad, but not hopeless. We've got to get this shitty attitude out of the troop units and get them back on their feet. They need successes out there to breed successes."

"How can I help?" Hollister asked.

"You've got a history with Juliet Company."

"I've been trying to follow them back in the World." He dropped his head. "I was sure sorry to hear about Captain Vance getting killed."

"They were doing a damn good job when Vance was CO, but after his death, the job somehow passed to a pissant major named Simonson. He took J Company and drove it into the ground like a tent stake."

"Worked them too hard?" Hollister asked.

"No," Michaelson said, sipping his coffee. "The fucker has no idea what he's doing. He's never been a troop commander, never spent a day in the field over here, but somehow sweet-talked himself into command of Juliet Company. He went down there and turned them into a bunch of prima donnas who hardly ever go to the field. They gobble up rotor time and never seem to find a single zip in the bushes. They got their cranks in a few squeezes and field force had to divert resources to bail them out more than once. He got a few folks dead doing stupid stuff and wouldn't listen to anyone.

"The NCOs tried to tell him he was making a mistake, but he just got rid of the NCOs who spoke up. He's a disaster of a field commander."

"I hate to hear it. J Company was a good company, and we came a long way that first year I was with it."

Michaelson crushed out his cigarette in the cheap ashtray on the table. "Why don't we take a run over there and look around?"

Hollister looked at his watch. "Do I have time before my ride to Nha Trang?"

"Sure," Michaelson said. "Anyway, if you miss that flight, I'll set you up with another. I have some pull around here now."

Hollister caught a glimpse of a rare smile on Michaelson's face.

The roadway linking the Bien Hoa Army and Air Force Base complex to Long Binh's field force headquarters was built up with paper-thin shopfronts and more vendors. When Hollister had last driven down the road, it was devoid of any merchants or stores. "Jesus, things have changed around here. Everything looks so worn-out, dirty, run-down, and overcrowded."

Michaelson drove and pointed out some other changes. "Look up there at the ARVN watchtower."

The raised platform was surrounded with sandbags, holding a machine gun, two ARVN soldiers, and a large spotlight. It was their job to keep a watch over the broad fields, which stood empty behind the thin ribbon of roadside stands. Both of the soldiers were asleep in hammocks strung across the uprights supporting the tin roof.

"They're like this night and day. We tell the ARVNs their troops are flat on their asses, and they tell us they need more equipment and money. And Nixon tells everyone the Viets are ready to take over the war."

CHAPTER 8

Michaelson pulled over across the road from the Juliet Company compound. "How's it look?"

Hollister immediately felt the tug in his gut. He remembered the days when he served with the former Juliet Company (Long Range Patrol), 51st Infantry, (Airborne). Since he had left, the company had been redesignated as a Ranger company, dropping the LRP designation. The job was the same, the risk was as great, and he had hoped the soldiers would be the same.

"Looks a little worse for wear," Hollister said. The fading black and red paint on the huge Ranger scroll arced over the entrance to the compound was peeling and cracking.

But he was most surprised at the troops. He saw sad-looking excuses for Airborne-Rangers casually crossing the compound. Their uniforms were dirty and uncared for. They needed haircuts and sported mustaches and long sideburns. What weapons they carried were carried with little regard for safety.

He could tell from across the compound something was wrong. They had no life in their step. He remembered that all of the LRPs he had ever worked with in Vietnam took every moment back in the rear to recharge their batteries and enjoy the precious moments of relative security. The men he watched were down.

And there were other signs of sagging morale. The compound was dirty—unpoliced. Scraps of paper, tufts of weeds, and piles of garbage were everywhere. Then there were the choppers. He was shocked to see the choppers tied down and buttoned up in the middle of the day. No one was standing by to crank if a team made contact. "Don't they have teams on the ground?" Hollister asked.

"Yeah, a couple out in War Zone D," Michaelson said. "See what I mean?"

Hollister nodded. "This is really sad."

"Gonna get sadder."

"How's that?" Hollister asked.

"The general wants to shut down J Company, unless . . ."

"Unless what?"

"Unless we can come up with a plan to shape their asses up," Michaelson said.

Hollister smiled at Michaelson. "So this is what this trip is all about?"

Michaelson smiled back. "I really need you, Jim. This is a good company gone to shit. If I can't talk you into it—it's gone. So, did you bring a black beret with you?"

Hollister took off his green beret and looked at it. "I was kinda looking forward to a tour with SF."

"It'll be there long after we turn the lights out here."

"So what about the guy who's commanding Juliet Company right now?"

"You're the guy commanding J Company. We relieved Simonson last night. He left on the milk run this morning for a desk job in Da Nang while you were coming into Tan Son Nhut."

Hollister looked at Michaelson, puzzled. "What if I hadn't taken the job?"

"We'd be making arrangements to break up the company and send the troops to other assignments." He made a stern face. "I'm not shitting you when I tell you the general wants this company back in shape fast, or we're both going to be looking for jobs."

Hollister took a big, deep breath and let it out. "Okay, sir. I'll do it. But some folks aren't going to be very happy about it."

Michaelson only nodded, stepped on the starter, and fired the jeep up.

The rest of the day was filled with briefings at the field force headquarters, in-processing, some quick shopping at the PX, dinner with Michaelson, and meeting his boss, Colonel T. P. Terry—the G-3.

They ate at the officers club at Long Binh and then lingered over coffee. Terry was a no-nonsense veteran of two tours with battalion and brigade command experience.

"It's changed since you left here, Jim," Colonel Terry said, stirring his coffee with the handle end of his greasy dinner knife.

"That's what I've been hearing," Hollister said, as he shot a glance at Michaelson, who leaned back and lit a cheap cigar—his trademark.

"Don't get me wrong. There's nothing wrong with these kids that leadership and a little ass kicking won't fix. They're the same kids this army has been fielding ever since we were fighting redcoats."

"What's the difference now, sir?" Hollister asked.

"Oh, there's no problem here. It's home. It's back on the streets in the World."

Hollister absentmindedly unclasped the catch on his Rolex and rubbed the skin underneath. "How's that?"

"They've had their head filled full of shit about how wrong the war is, what fools they are for coming over here, how rich white kids aren't doing their share, and how we're just going to pull the plug anyway—so why should they bust their humps?"

"Hard to blame them if they believe what they hear," Hollister said.

Michaelson blew smoke toward the ceiling fan and leaned back in his chair. "Let them wallow in that, and they'll be convinced all the horseshit is absolutely true. Then, take the shabby treatment they've gotten since they were drafted, and you can see why every problem we have is of our own doing."

Terry picked it up. "So while the country is self-destructing, we have to make these folks as effective as we can while they're here." He raised his hand, anticipating Hollister's comment. "I know ... *no* we don't have to do anything superhuman—just smart enough to get as many Americans home as we can. It means the more the U.S. forces pull back into firebases and base camps while the fucking peace talks are jerking around, the more they need Ranger patrols out there keeping an eye on Charles."

"You don't have to sell me. We're on the same side here," Hollister said.

The colonel smiled. "We didn't say this for you. We said it for us. We need to hear it now and then."

They all laughed, and the colonel leaned back in his chair. "Let's get a beer and then check into the office and see if peace has broken out."

"What's first?" Hollister asked.

Michaelson slapped Hollister on the shoulder. "Well, young

promotable captain—it's about time you really find out about a
field-grader's life. We start with the paperwork."

It was well after midnight when Hollister looked at the equal
stacks of after-action reports and operations summaries flanking
the center of a field desk.

"I'm calling it a night. I'm just a sorry-ass staff officer, and
unlike you, I don't have the burden of command," Michaelson
said, jabbing Hollister playfully.

Hollister tapped one of the stacks. "This is fucking criminal. I
know how puffed up these reports are. So when they still read as
bad as they do, things must be pitiful in J company."

"That's right. You surprised?"

"No sir. Just heartbroken over how far down they are." He
picked up one document and then another. "Stupid accidents. Poor
coordination. A lack of training. Leadership problems down at
patrol level. Equipment failures and commo problems. Hell, it's
like everyone in that company just got off the goddamn boat."

"Yep. You got your work cut out for you. *And* if you don't
do it—they're gonna shut you down. How's that for a little
pressure?"

"Thanks," Hollister said.

"Hey, I never promised you anything but hard work."

Hollister smiled at his old friend. He remembered what a prick
Michaelson had been as a Ranger School instructor when Hollister was his student. He was right. He never promised him anything but what he was looking at at that very moment.

"Thanks. Is there anything else, sir?"

"Yeah. Try not to make my life more miserable than it
already is."

"I'll also need the leeway to chuck some of the deadwood. That
means I need your support and some help getting replacements."

"I understand. Do what you have to do. I'm already working
on some replacements I know you'll be needing."

Hollister took his notes back to the thinned-out crowd at the officers club and looked them over while he nursed a cup of coffee
and a tumbler of straight bourbon. His mind was running at top
speed while he tried to figure out where to start.

It occurred to him he had never been in a unit in real trouble
before. He had lived some kind of charmed life, where the

troops were terrific, and the units enjoyed a better than average reputation. He had only seen the symptoms of problems—like the druggies back at Fort Benning that he was charged with sobering up.

He ordered another bourbon and more coffee, made more notes, and tried to put together a plan. He knew he'd have to hit the street running and that he would certainly be one unpopular son of a bitch in J Company. But that's what it would take.

It was almost two-thirty when he finally sat down on the cot in the transient BOQ room at Long Binh. But sleep didn't come. He tossed and turned and worried about the task ahead of him. Around four, he decided that he was wasting his time. A courier was happy to have him hitch a ride over to the Bien Hoa where the Ranger company was billeted.

He reached the door leading into what had been the small officers club end of the BOQ and found the door open and half off its hinges. He quietly stepped inside the large room, painted by the blue-pink wash that would soon give way to another hot Vietnam dawn.

In the hallway flanked by officers' rooms he heard someone giggling—a woman. He stopped, and one of the doors opened. A tiny Vietnamese woman, wearing only an olive drab towel wrapped around her, stepped through the door and walked away from him—toward the other exit that led out to the latrines.

Hollister continued down the short hallway and looked into the other rooms. Half had the doors open, and there was no one in them. He wondered if the officers assigned to the empty rooms were already up and over at the mess hall.

From one of the rooms with the door closed, a light painted the outline of the door frame as its occupant turned on a light. Hollister decided to avoid the surprise and continued down and out the hallway by the same door that the woman had used.

Just outside the BOQ, Hollister ran into the woman coming back from the latrine. She smiled and giggled at Hollister and tried to adjust the towel to cover her tiny body. It was obvious to Hollister that she was not just a day laborer that one of the officers had convinced to stay the night. She was a bar girl or hooker.

The color changed in the compound, and Hollister could see

what he hadn't seen from the jeep the day before with Michaelson. The grounds were a mess. He realized it was Vietnam and that the place should be more tactical than decorative, but the signs of sloppiness bothered him. The water trailer was half covered with a slimy moss. The latrine was surrounded by rich green weeds for five feet in each direction—a clear sign that it was not cleaned often enough to keep the waste from seeping into the ground. He didn't need to get near it to know how it smelled. He also knew, if it looked like that on the outside, that the inside would be equally repugnant.

He continued down the company street to the hootches. Roofing was missing, steps broken and worn. Screens were torn, and piles of trash were everywhere. He stopped at one stack of cardboard boxes and picked one up. It was a C-ration box with all of the unpopular rations, like ham and lima beans, thrown away along with the fruitcake. Also in the box was a handful of corroded M-16 rounds. He dropped the box back on the pile.

He changed direction and walked toward the sandbagged bunker where all of the business of running the tactical operations took place. It was like the others, trashy, dirty, and falling apart. The sandbags were split from the sun, sand spilling out onto the ground—weakening the whole wall of bags and making it a serious safety hazard.

There didn't appear to be any life in the bunker either. Hollister just didn't have the stomach to go inside to see what shape it was in. He knew, if it was as shabby as everything else, the lives of the patrol members in the field were seriously jeopardized each time they were out.

The Charge of Quarters was asleep when Hollister entered the orderly room. He jerked awake at the sound of Hollister's paratrooper boots on the plywood floor.

"Oh, ah . . . sir," he stammered as he jumped to his feet, clad only in fatigue trousers, a T-shirt, and shower shoes. He tried to master a salute, the position of attention, and a sentence at the same time. "I'm ah . . . PFC Estlin, Captain."

"PFC?" Hollister asked.

"Yes, sir. PFC."

"You are the CQ runner?"

"No, sir," the soldier said, pushing out his chest a bit more. "I'm the CQ."

"Wait a minute. There are twenty-three NCOs on the morning report of this company, and a PFC is pulling CQ?"

"Sir, I don't know about all that. All I know is that right now, I'm CQ. And I'm probably going to be in trouble because I don't know who you are and I . . . I . . . might have dozed off a bit."

"Well, I'm Captain James Hollister. I'm the new CO around here, and you now belong to me."

The boy's eyes widened. "Oh, yes, sir. I'm glad to meet you— I think."

Hollister checked his watch. "It's now zero five ten. I'd like you to wake up every officer and NCO. Have them in the mess hall at zero seven hundred. Then go over to the mess hall and tell the mess sergeant that chow will end at zero six thirty. You got that?"

Estlin scribbled the times down and looked back at Hollister. "Yes, sir, but—"

"But what?"

"Some folks aren't going to be too happy about this. If you don't mind my sayin' so."

"I don't mind you saying so. And I can guarantee you that it's only the beginning of things that *some folks* won't like around here."

Hollister stood at the front of the room, where only moments before the cooks and KPs had cleared away breakfast trays, and watched the leadership of Juliet Company assemble.

They were a sorry-looking lot. Most were talking when they hit the doorway, but shut up once they saw Hollister standing there, hands on his hips and an unpleasant expression on his face.

Hollister tried not to react to what he saw. Some wore parts of uniforms, and others wore useless, skin-tight, tailored camouflage fatigues. There were some mustaches, long haircuts and sideburns, sunglasses, jewelry, peace symbols on dog-tag chains, and Afro haircuts. But mostly, he was upset with their attitude. They dragged ass getting into the mess hall, and with a few exceptions, most just plopped into chairs and slouched, showing contempt for what they were expecting—an ass chewing from a new hard-ass boss.

Hollister checked his watch. It was seven on the dot. He looked up and waited for the shuffling and throat clearing to die down, and then he began. "Gentlemen," he said, a slight trace of sarcasm in his tone. "My name is Hollister, James A. Effective immediately, I am the new CO of Juliet Company."

There was some mumbling and several exchanges of glances.

"That didn't require a response," Hollister added, trying to set the tone that from that moment on it would be all business. "I don't recognize many faces here, but I can tell you that I've been in the long range patrol business since it started over here. I've even served a tour here in J Company. So I'm not a new guy.

"I have to tell you that I'm here for one thing. That's to make changes around here. Most won't be pleasant. It'll come as no surprise to you that there are people in the chain of command who are starting to wonder if there is any useful purpose for J Company."

The remark brought more grumbling and several frowns.

Hollister raised his hand. "If they really thought you weren't worth keeping, why would they bother to send you a new company commander?"

A head or two nodded, but the others just listened for more.

"*I* know what this company is capable of, and I know it can be done. It takes hard work. I don't care what has happened in the past, and I don't care what kind of rep you guys used to have. Starting today—it's a new deal.

"Those of you who are interested in serving in the best Ranger company in Vietnam, stick around and roll up your sleeves because I am going to sweat your shadows to the wall. Those who don't want to put in that kind of training and don't want to live up to the new standards—I will gladly accept your request for transfer when we're finished here."

More grumbling, but a smile or two.

Suddenly, the back door to the mess hall opened and a lieutenant entered, trying to be inconspicuous. Hollister recognized him as the one whose room the hooker had left in the BOQ. He didn't let him take a second step. "Mister," Hollister said—forcefully.

The lieutenant squinted to see Hollister in the dimly lit room. "Yes, sir?"

"If you can't make it to my meetings on time, then I don't need you here. Pack up your gear and report to the field force G-1 shop for reassignment by noon today."

Hollister's words cut through the lieutenant like a knife blade. "Sir? I mean, I'm only a few minutes late."

"If you are late for this, you'll be late making a pickup, and a team can't afford your kind of punctuality. You are relieved, mister."

The lieutenant stepped back out and slammed the door.

"Let me make a point right now. Everything we do in a Ranger company depends on attention to detail. One of those details is your wristwatch. You treat time casually, and it will hand you your ass. And if I catch any of you doing it—I will show you the door."

Hollister pulled his notebook out of his pocket and flipped to a page of notes he had made the night before. "Effective immediately, there will be a PT formation every morning, which will include a run. Everyone will make it except the standby pilots, crews, the duty officer, and the duty radio operators—no other exceptions.

"Also effective immediately, we will start looking like Rangers—not palace guards and not some fucking hippies out of San Francisco. I want to see Airborne haircuts, clean uniforms, no mustaches, no jewelry, and no one in the company area in incomplete uniforms. If you expect attention to detail from the members of your platoons and teams—you have to start by setting the example, and it starts today."

He flipped through his notes and continued. "Once we're finished here, I want the troops to take the day to stand down and prepare for an inspection of the company area, all personnel, and all equipment on the property book. That includes every NCO and officer and their equipment and billets."

The comment brought more muffled groans.

"Gentlemen, I can't overemphasize that we will lead by example around here—anything else is a joke. No soldier will suffer because of sloppy leadership. And if that is too much to ask of any of you, my offer stands. I'll sign any request for transfer that comes across my desk."

He stopped and looked around the room, wanting to remember some of the attitudes obvious on a few faces. Some of the NCOs were accepting and were eagerly taking notes on his remarks. A few others had their arms crossed. He would remember the faces and deal with them later.

"I want to see the XO and operations officer in my office at zero nine hundred hours, the platoon leaders at eleven hundred, and the platoon sergeants at noon in the briefing room." He then took a long pause and waited until the room was absolutely silent. "I want it to be crystal clear that I'm not playing around here, and anyone who is, is gone. Is that understood?"

CHAPTER 9

Inside the orderly room Staff Sergeant Chastain sat hunched over a typewriter, not having much success with the keyboard.

"What's your job here?" Hollister asked.

Chastain spun around in the chair and stood with a startled look on his face. "Ah, me, sir? I'm team leader for Team 2–3. I mean I was." He poked his thumb in the direction of the typewriter and continued. "I was tryin' to type up a request for transfer, like you said we could do."

"Come into my office," Hollister said, stepping from the open room into the small office reserved for the commander.

Inside, he was immediately assaulted by the decor. The walls were decorated with captured VC equipment, and the window had an air conditioner in it. "Estlin," he yelled. "You still out there?"

Private First Class Estlin scrambled into Hollister's office. "Yes, sir?"

"What do you do when you aren't CQ?" Hollister asked.

"I'm the gofer around here. I haven't been assigned to a team."

Hollister made a sour face and shook his head. "Okay, we'll talk about that later. Right now, I want you to round up a detail and get this fucking air conditioner out of my office. I want it moved to the operations bunker. Then I want you to pull all this crap off the walls and clean this place up. This is an office, not a goddamn trophy room."

"Yes, sir." Estlin nodded. "Will do."

"Now, get over to the mess hall and get Sergeant Chastain and me a pitcher of black coffee."

He turned to Chastain. "Find a place and sit."

Chastain cleared some of the junk—Simonson's—off a chair and sat down.

"What's the problem?"

"Sir?"

"You are a second tour vet from the One Seventy-Third Airborne Brigade and a young man to be a staff sergeant. You've been here six weeks, and you're already bailing out?"

Chastain looked surprised that Hollister knew all that about him. Hollister set him at ease. "I do my homework."

"Well, sir—I don't want to whine or complain or nothing."

"You think your application for transfer is a Hallmark card telling me how happy you are? Too tough for you?"

Chastain stiffened at the suggestion and looked Hollister directly in the eyes for the first time. "No, sir. I'm no quitter. I'd rather go somewhere where I can do my job."

"What's that mean?"

"Well, the first sergeant wants to bust my hump."

"Why?"

"I'm a shake-and-bake NCO."

"I know that. What's the problem?"

"He's on my butt night and day. He promised to run me out of J Company. It took him almost four years just to make E-5, and he doesn't like me wearin' staff sergeant chevrons right out of instant NCO school."

Hollister got up and took the pitcher of coffee and the two mugs that Estlin brought into the office. "I think we can pour our own. Why don't you see if you can round up the first sergeant. I was sure that there was one on the morning report the last time I looked."

"No, sir."

"No, sir?"

"No, sir. There isn't a first sergeant on the morning report anymore."

"What are you talking about?"

"The first sergeant left the company area yesterday after Major Simonson left and said he was going to look for a new job."

"And?" Hollister asked. "What then?"

"Well, sir, he called me about nineteen hundred last night and told me that I was CQ for the night and that he wouldn't be back."

"What's the rest?"

"He said he'd found himself a good job where he didn't have to put up with some new hotshot coming to Dodge."

Hollister turned to Chastain. "Well, guess that solves your problem, doesn't it?"

Chastain smiled and stammered a bit. "I guess so, I mean, sure . . . yes, sir."

"Then get out there and tear up that 1049, and let's see if we can find some work for you to do—Sergeant."

Chastain stood and saluted. "Thank you, sir. I appreciate it."

"How old are you?"

"I'm twenty-one, sir."

"I was twenty when I made E-6, and the army survived me."

Chastain broke into a broad smile.

Captain Laurence Browning was a large man—maybe two-forty. He had played football at the military academy and had a good record—on paper.

"You've been a platoon leader in the Cav, a company commander in the Eighty-second Airborne Brigade, and an operations officer in the First Infantry Division.

"Two tours under your belt and the career course, and now you're back for more. You just got here ten days ago?"

"Yes, sir," Browning said, sitting uncomfortably on the same chair Chastain had used.

"Go easy on all that sir shit. I'm here to get the work done, not remind you that I have a few months' date of rank on you.

"Anyway, whatever went in the shitter around here, I have to assume that it was none of your doing."

Browning relaxed and shook his head. "Shitter is right. I have to tell you that when I got orders to come here, I was thrilled. But what I found was . . . well, you've seen it. It's damn near criminal. I've seen leg outfits that would put this company to shame."

"Well, at least we are on the same wavelength."

"Maybe so, but I have to tell you that I only have a passing acquaintance with how things are done in a Ranger outfit and hope that I won't step on my dick trying to figure it out."

Hollister leaned forward, pulled a cigarette out of his pack, and lit it. "I need the best executive officer I can find. Being one for a corps level Ranger company is no different from being an XO for an infantry battalion, except the tolerances are closer. When this company needs something—it needs it right then, and not when we can get it. You want to keep me happy—don't make me come looking for a body, a piece of equipment, or a piece of paper. As far as I am concerned—admin, logistics, and personnel are your three nightmares. Get with them and get serious—because I won't have time to wait on anything. You got that?'"

"Yes, sir."

"You don't have to stay, you know. That offer to let you go is open to everyone."

Browning straightened up. "Sir, this is where I wanted to be—in your kind of Ranger company, not Major Simonson's."

"Before you make up your mind, I want to tell you that, effective immediately, we change the field policy. I want to see every man in this company out in the boonies on patrol—even if it is only once. Every man has to know he's here because of those teams on the ground. So soon as I can whip up a shakedown patrol, I'm going to take it out—with staff officers and NCOs. I'll be leaving you in charge around here. I expect you to find time in your schedule to get yourself out on a patrol as soon as you can."

"Yes, sir," Browning said, nodding. "If I was on one of those teams, I'd want every staff rat to have enough field time to know what my life is like in the bush. You have my support, boss."

Estlin brought in a message from Captain Thomas: he wouldn't be able to meet with Hollister until later because he had gone to a dental appointment at the evac hospital. So Hollister met with the platoon leaders, whittled down to three after the relief earlier in the day. "How many patrols have each of you been on?"

None of the lieutenants replied.

"Are we not communicating here? How many times have you been out with a patrol—observing or leading a mission?"

"I've almost been on one," Lieutenant McIlwain said.

Hollister looked at the freckle-faced boy, a second lieutenant with a Jungle Expert patch on his pocket and a Ranger tab on his shoulder. "How did that happen?"

"I wanted to go out with my platoon, ah, Second Platoon, sir . . . and Captain Thomas caught me and told me that I was not to do that."

"The rest of you? How do you feel about it?"

Lieutenant Jerry Fass, 1st Platoon leader, spoke up. "I think that's where I belong. There's not much I can do back here. I need to be involved in the staffing of my teams and their training. It's pretty hard to train a man on patrolling techniques when he has a dozen missions under his belt and I have none."

"You feel that way?" Hollister asked First Lieutenant Nathan Hill—the 4th Platoon leader.

"Sir, I've been here three weeks. I just got back from Recondo School in Nha Trang, and I don't even know who is in my platoon yet. I mean, I know . . . I just haven't met them all yet. I only got assigned to the platoon last week."

"What were you doing until then?"

"Major Simonson had me running errands. I spent four days in Saigon scrounging the air conditioner for his office."

"And the rest of my question?"

"Yes, sir—I agree. I want to go out with my people. I couldn't face them if I were a rear echelon . . ."

"Motherfucker?" Hollister finished his sentence.

The trio of nervous lieutenants smiled.

"Okay, here's how we play this. You folks go to the field whenever you can. All I ask is that when you are out—your platoon sergeants are back and vice versa. Also, what I said this morning about leading by example applies to privileges. I don't want anything going on in that BOQ that the troops don't do. Do I make myself clear?"

The three exchanged glances, knowing that Hollister knew more about what was going on in Juliet Company than they thought he did. They all nodded affirmatively.

"If you don't set the example—I'll send your asses packing. If you stay here, I promise you that I will work you hard, and you'll sure as hell never have to apologize to anyone for your time in J Company. Understand?"

"Yes, sir!" they replied in unison.

"Okay . . . then get out of here and remember you're not a Ranger because you have the tab on your shoulder. You're a Ranger when you act like one. Now show me something."

After an hour of paperwork, which Hollister didn't know how to handle, he suddenly realized there had to be someone else familiar with the paper battle. "Estlin, don't we have a company clerk?"

"Yes, sir, we do. But he's on R and R in Singapore until the day after tomorrow."

Hollister looked at his watch; it was almost time to meet with the platoon sergeants. "How long am I going to have to wait to meet my operations officer, Estlin?"

Estlin appeared in the doorway. "He called while you were with the lieutenants. He had a chance to get a couple of teeth capped while he was up at the hospital and said he'd be a couple more hours."

It was not the answer he wanted to hear. Hollister stood, pulled his beret out of his cargo pocket, and squared it on his head. "I'll be with the platoon sergeants."

The meeting with the NCOs was not as tense as the one with the lieutenants. Three of them were older than Hollister, and one was about the same age. He knew one of them. "DeSantis, you been here since I left?"

DeSantis smiled at his old friend. "Yes, sir, and I'm real glad you're back. Been waitin' for you."

"Doesn't look like you've been letting any grass grow under your feet. Congrats on making E-7. You were a buck sergeant when I left, weren't you?"

"Yes, sir. Perfect attendance at the war."

There was a little nervous laughter among the others.

"How many of you have been patrol leaders?"

Besides DeSantis, only one, Platoon Sergeant Peterson, raised his hand. "Two years in Charlie Company up in First Field Force, sir."

"Good. Well, whether you were or weren't a team leader is not something for you to concern yourselves about right now. What I really want to know is what's the problem around here?"

They all rolled their eyes at his question.

"Problem, sir?" Platoon Sergeant Phil Seals said. "Sir, you don't have enough time for us to tell you all the problems."

Hollister took out a pack of cigarettes, lit himself one, and threw that pack on the table. "Smoke 'em if you got 'em." He yelled toward the steam table end of the mess hall, "How 'bout somebody rounding up some coffee for us?"

He then turned back to the four NCOs. "I've got enough time to hear what *you* have to say."

Immediately, the remaining tension cleared from the room as the NCOs candidly told Hollister their problems. They were precise, and he took notes, but didn't pass any judgment on the worth of their complaints. He just wanted them to get it all off their chests. They were extremely important to the running of the company, and he wanted them to know he felt they were important.

Their meeting went on for two hours. Hollister had a lengthy list of complaints, and the NCOs finally ran out of grievances. Hollister killed a last sip of cold coffee and closed his notebook.

"Okay, my turn to talk. I'm going to turn the screws. You all know that. Same deal as everyone else—you can stay or go. No questions asked. But if you stay, I'm going to bust your humps as hard as the troops. We've got one hell of a hill to climb to get back on top around here. Anyone have trouble with that?"

The four were silent.

"Okay, then. Let's get to work. I want to see your teams—inspection; full field layout tomorrow. It won't be fun."

Hollister got back to his office, and Estlin handed him seven messages scribbled on pieces of steno notebook paper, the edges raveled where they had been torn from the spiral ring.

"Sir, there has been a steady flow of people in here to see you about one thing or another. I told 'em that they'd have to wait until I could set up some kind of appointments or something."

"Okay, Estlin. Sounds like a plan to me," Hollister said. He looked at the messages. "We heard from my operations officer or the company clerk yet?"

"No, sir, but I have the names of six EMs and two NCOs who want to submit their ten-forty-nines to leave."

Hollister looked up. "Just eight? Wait until we're finished with tomorrow's fun and games."

The phone system didn't cooperate with Hollister. He made several attempts to get through to talk to Colonel Terry or Lieutenant Colonel Michaelson. Each time either they were in briefings or the lines were busy.

Finally, he got through to Michaelson and began to unload on him his preliminary situation—which included his frustration about not having a first sergeant or a company clerk.

Michaelson told him some of his problems would be solved right away because he had already been working on them.

Hollister promised to give him an update within forty-eight hours, and then went back to the paperwork. He took a sip from another cold cup of coffee on his desk and then lit still another cigarette.

He was trying to prioritize the messages Estlin had handed him when he heard the squeaky screen door open to the orderly room. He would have paid little attention to the footsteps crossing the plywood decking if they had been even. But they weren't. There was a solid step and a hollow one. Then a repeat of the uneven cadence as the steps came closer to his doorway. His mind wandered to the possibility, but he brushed it off to wishful thinking. Then he heard the gravel voice.

"Doesn't this lash-up have a fucking Airborne-Ranger first sergeant?"

Hollister didn't need to look to know that voice. It was Easy. First Sergeant Evan-Clark. Easy!

"Well, you rascal you," Hollister said, jumping to his feet to grab the old soldier around the shoulders. "What in the hell are you doing here? How did you get here? Aren't you supposed to be fishing someplace at a retirement cabin in Colorado?"

Easy laughed. "One at a time, Cap'n. I'm old, and I'm slow, and I can't answer all yer questions as fast as you can ask 'em. I never could."

Hollister stepped back and held Easy at arm's length. "How are you? That's the first question."

"I'm fine, sir. And now, you're fine," Easy said.

"What do you mean?"

"I'm your new top soldier."

"You're shitting me."

"No, sir. Colonel Michaelson and me pulled a few quick turns and twists and made it happen."

"How did you even get cleared to come over here?"

"Well, seems like the army has a problem when it comes to physical exams. If you go to any big post, they almost never have you drop your drawers beyond your privates when they give you the once-over. So I applied to come back to Vietnam, went for the physical, and the damn civilian contract doctor never even saw the top of my peg leg."

"How about your medical records?"

Easy rolled his eyes toward the ceiling and dropped his voice. "Seems like they got lost somewhere between Fitzsimmons Army Hospital and the physical exam section at Fort Carson. Don't know how things like that happen. I get really upset when I think there are NCOs out there shuffling papers with such carelessness."

They both laughed—knowing, full well, Easy made the records vaporize.

"So how did you get all this past assignments branch in Washington?"

Easy winked. "You got any idea how many of them youngsters up there in the puzzle palace were once PFCs working for me? Hell, most of them know if it hadn't been for old Easy, they'd still be spec fours someplace. Now they think they're hot because most of them are master sergeants and sergeants major. They owed me, Cap'n."

Hollister was speechless. The arrival of Evan-Clark was a gift from heaven. If there ever was a man who could help him pull Juliet Company out of its own ass—it was Easy. Hollister finally motioned to a chair. "We have lots to talk about. Are you here? I mean, do you have to go in-process somewhere yet?"

Hollister tried not to watch as Easy moved across the floor to a chair. The last time he had seen Easy standing up, he was carrying Hollister across a flooded rice paddy in II Corps. Since that day, he'd only seen him in the hospital.

With his back to Hollister, Easy cautioned him. "Don't be worryin' about how well I walk, Cap'n. I can still kick the ass of every Ranger in your company, and I'll not be holdin' you back because I have a plastic leg." He turned and gave Hollister his trademark grin.

Hollister nodded in acceptance of Easy's words, but couldn't get over how much weight Easy had lost and how much older he looked since he had last seen him. He even missed his hemp-rope mustache. "What happened to your cookie duster?"

"When the fuckin' troops started thinking hair was some symbol of manhood and defiance, I shaved it to make my point— a soldier's a soldier and not a mustache or a sideburn. Kinda hard to bust their asses for looking like hippies when I'm wearin' a mustache."

Leading by example—it was what Hollister loved about Easy. He was starting to feel a lot better about taking command of Juliet Company with Easy there.

"Top, we have troubles around here, and you're going to have to do more than a first sergeant's job to help me get this train on track."

Easy slapped his hands together and grinned. "So where do we start?"

"You can start by finding yourself a company clerk and getting with Captain Browning, the XO. As a team, the three of you might be able to get the admin in this company back in shape."

Hollister started the inspection in the officers' billets. He cut them no slack and instructed them to get their gear in a higher state of readiness, pack a ready bag with gear to be taken into the field on a moment's notice, and to get down to the firing range to fire several hundred rounds through each of their weapons.

He reminded each officer that his personal conduct would be as important as his duty performance. He didn't want to catch any of his officers cutting corners or taking advantage of their rank to avoid unpleasant duty or training. Cross that line, and they were gone.

Once he got to the club, attached to the sleeping quarters, he instructed Browning to have a field phone installed at the bar, connected to allow them to call the orderly room and operations. And the club hours were 2000 to 2400 hours. It would be the only time alcohol would be served there, and the rest of the time the room would be considered a dayroom—no booze. They could read, do paperwork, or write letters there. But no drinking and no poker playing during duty hours.

The real shock came in the team hootches. Hollister found them to be pigsties. The field gear was in sorry shape. He found seven strobe lights with dead batteries and two with broken bulbs. Of the four team leaders he quizzed about URC-10 survival radios, only two knew how to use them and what frequencies they would be on.

The individual weapons were criminal. Rust, crud, and dirt clogged parts, and ammo was corroded and magazines muddy. As far as Hollister was concerned, not one team was in any shape to go to the field with the equipment they had.

He continued through each team hootch and tried to put faces to names as he talked with every member of the company. He felt the resentment of his strict changes in policy, training, and inspection standards. He expected that. Popularity would come at the cost of lives.

The inspection took the entire day. By the time he got through the nightmare in the commo section and the operations section, Hollister was numb. The motor pool was in worse shape than he expected, but he was happy that the motor pool rarely had a negative effect on the combat readiness of a Ranger company. The fact that he had three jeeps that couldn't be accounted for on the property book was only a minor problem Browning could straighten out, while Hollister focused on training and organization.

Organization was a joke—little rhyme or reason how Simonson had assigned new arrivals to jobs. There were medics in the commo section, and radio operators assigned to the motor pool.

Easy stuck his head into Hollister's office. "Sir, Captain Thomas is here to see you."

The announcement set Hollister off. He was irritated that Thomas found it more important to be at a routine dental appointment than at his first meeting with the company officers. He told himself to put his feelings aside and see what the man had to say for himself. "Send him in."

Captain Charles Thomas entered smartly, stopped in front of Hollister's desk, and executed a sharp salute. "Captain Thomas, sir."

"Sit," Hollister said, unsmiling.

Thomas found a chair and then pulled a notebook out of his trousers pocket. He slipped the ballpoint pen from the rubber band holding it to the notebook and looked up at Hollister.

"What's your story?"

"Sir?" Thomas asked, unsure of Hollister's question.

"I show up here to assume command of this company, and you can't seem to find the time to make it to my first meeting?"

Thomas looked at him, surprised. "Sir, it's really hard to get a dental appointment around here—"

Hollister's tone turned tough. "Mister, it's real hard to get a job as the operations officer in one of the two corps Ranger companies. You get my drift?"

Thomas seemed unsure of Hollister's irritation and answered with a noncommittal "Yes, sir."

"I've met every officer in the company now. I've relieved one, and I'm really not happy with the foot you've gotten off on. So tell me what kind of job you do as operations officer around here. But before you do, know I have seen the after-action reports, and they are sorry."

"Well, sir . . . I've only been the ops officer on paper. Major Simonson used me as the part-time XO, and he took care of all the operations, planning, and training. I've never even been up over the area of operations in a chopper. And I've been here for four months."

"Well, I'll get you out in the AO. Count on it."

"That's what I came here for, sir."

"You've been in the field, and you're Ranger qualified. Where'd you get your commission?"

"I went to Rutgers—ROTC, sir."

"So . . . you tell me. You want the job or don't you?"

Thomas's face split into a large smile. "Yes, sir. I can do the job."

Hollister gave him a sour look. "Let me tell you, next to being a team leader, ops officer in this company is the most important job. I've had it. And I know it. I won't take any halfway measures. If you hit the street running and show me something better than I've already seen out of you—I'll keep you in the job. But the minute I find you pulling shit like this dental appointment crap, I'll boot your ass out of here so fast you'll be sorry you ever jerked me around."

It wasn't until well after midnight that Hollister was finally able to think about getting some sleep. He wandered over to the BOQ and walked through the silent hallway flanked by the company officers' rooms.

Browning was sitting at the desk in his room writing as Hollister stopped at his open door. "Good-night," Hollister said.

Browning smiled. "Sir."

"What is it?"

"I'm really glad we got you."

Hollister smiled. "I'll remind you you said that when you are swearing at me and about me. Things are going to get much tougher around here before they get any better."

"I'm sure. That's why I'm glad you have the job."

"Well, okay. By the way, what do you like to be called? Larry?"

"No, sir, since I was a cadet, I've always been Brownie."

"Brownie it is," Hollister said, and he continued to his room.

He slept fitfully during the night and got up at a quarter to four. While he shaved, he could hear First Sergeant Easy bellowing outside in the company street. He knew they were already on their way to becoming a new Juliet Company.

Quickly finishing his shave, Hollister got into his boots, fatigue trousers, a T-shirt, and his black beret. He was glad to see he was the last officer to leave the BOQ.

Outside, there they were—in the dark, but assembled for the first time for him to see—Juliet Company.

Hollister walked briskly to a post in front of the first sergeant.

"Sir, the company is formed," Easy said, executing a sharp salute.

Hollister took charge of the formation and moved them out—for the morning run.

It felt good being out in front of an Airborne company again. Hollister quickly shifted them from a quick time to double time and began the Jody cadence from his position up front, flanked only by Estlin, carrying the guidon.

CHAPTER 10

Juliet Company ran the streets of the Bien Hoa base camp while the sun promised another hot and humid day. Hollister kept raising the force and the tempo of his voice to encourage the troops to do the same. But he could hear coughing and gasping for breath—telling him it had been some time since Juliet Company had done any real running.

His mind wandered to the times his legs were the only things between him and survival as he scrambled to get from a chopper to a tree line under fire, or vice versa. It surprised him that any man in Juliet Company would not take it upon himself to keep his wind and his legs up to be able to sprint under a full combat load when necessary.

He promised to make every run and every PT formation in order to set the example—even though his days scrambling to get to cover or an evacuating helicopter were probably behind him.

They passed the leg companies' billets along their run, and soldiers came out to ridicule the Rangers—it had not changed. But as the light allowed him to see better, Hollister could tell the troops were no longer jeering good-heartedly. There was real friction and some palpable tension between a transportation company—predominantly black—and his almost all-white Ranger company. He knew he would have to make a point of recruiting more black and brown faces if he wanted to cut some of the animosity.

The column ran to the end of the road paralleling the runways and made a wide U-turn back toward Juliet Company's compound. At the top of the turn, Hollister got a glimpse of Easy—at the end of the column, running on his artificial leg. He was limping badly, but keeping up. He was occupying his time badgering three dropouts who were easily twenty years his junior. He reminded them they had both their legs and lower mileage and had no excuse to drop out except they were sorry excuses for Airborne soldiers. Hollister could see Easy's taunts were making them run just to show the old man they could keep up with an over-the-hill NCO with a wooden leg.

The PT formation was followed by the usual army daily dozen calisthenics. The troops were sloppy and out of shape, but they all kept up with Lieutenant Fass, whom Hollister had tasked with leading the exercises.

Hollister had been in the company area for less than two days, and he was already sitting in the front row of the briefing room, receiving a warning order from Master Sergeant Caulter, the operations NCO. Hollister watched as the master parachutist-Ranger announced the few patrol elements he had in his briefing notes. Though Hollister already knew the details, he took meticulous notes, since he would lead the patrol.

Caulter had a good-old-boy, redneck way about him. He stood tall and hardly ever cracked a smile. Hollister had known Caulter— from a distance—when they were both instructors in the Ranger Department. Caulter was a hand-to-hand combat instructor, while Hollister taught patrolling.

He had heard the story around Benning about how Caulter got the ugly red scar running from his earlobe into the neck opening of his T-shirt. It was a mark of firsthand experience in hand-to-hand combat on an earlier tour in Vietnam.

Next to Hollister sat Private First Class Estlin; Lieutenant Fass; Captain Thomas; Specialist 7 Meadows, the senior medic; and Specialist 5 Loomis, the operations radio operator. Those would be his team members—all headquarters personnel. They would go on J Company's first shakedown patrol.

"Y'all'll be leavin' here by ground transport the day after tomorrow at zero six hundred hours. You will be taken to the Hundred Forty-fifth Aviation Battalion over to the other side of Bien Hoa where you'll link up with the lift package that'll insert you into your LZ," Caulter said, pointing to the grease-pencil circle around the landing zone on the map.

"So y'all'll lift off the One Forty-fifth's pad, with gunships, command and control chopper, and lift slicks at 'leven hundred hours the same day.

"Your mission'll be to set up an ambush along a trail located here." Caulter tapped the easel-mounted map at a point north and west of the 25th Division base camp at Cu Chi. "Intelligence has reports of a resupply party frequently traveling that trail to bring batteries and commo equipment to a VC signal unit that's supposed ta be located somewheres in the tunnels in the Cu Chi area."

"Not a prisoner snatch?" Thomas asked.

"No, sir. Field force thinks these guys are just regular replacement gomers who're carryin' extra crap into the country as they pass through the western part of Three Corps. If they have anything of value, you can pick it off them after you hit 'em. They don't want to risk a Ranger looking to tackle a cherry Commie," Caulter said.

"I can go for that," Private First Class Estlin said.

"Your mission is a four-day. You'll be pulled on the morning of the fifth. As it stands, you're the only team to be pulled that day. So, first-light extraction should be possible.

"There's little else in the area of operations at this time other than there're no friendly units operating there, and there ain't no plans to put any in the AO during your mission.

"Indigenous personnel in the area are known to be VC sympathizers, but the rules of engagement prohibit firing on them unless you ID them with weapons and or enemy equipment. So be advised."

There was a universal groan among the patrol members. Rules of engagement *always* seemed to favor the other guys and usually meant trouble for U.S. units. Still, it was their country, and Hollister knew it did little to argue the point.

"I've got some aerial photos, and we've laid on a leader's recon flight for fourteen hundred this afternoon, if it's okay with you, Captain," Caulter said, nodding to Hollister.

"You tell me. I'm patrol leader on this one, not the company commander. Captain Browning is in temporary command of Julliet Rangers effective immediately. When's the patrol order?"

"Straight up, sir—twelve hun'erd hours."

Between the warning order and the patrol order, Hollister had more meetings with the company staff, platoon leaders, and some new faces who wanted to join the Rangers. In a moment of calm between meetings, he walked out of his office into Easy's.

"I hope you have some idea where we are. I'm catching myself in more than one place at a time."

Easy smiled. "Cap'n, need I remind you of the simpler days when you were a mere platoon leader of a fairly sharp group of Airborne soldiers, and we seemed to have some idea what the fuck we were doing over here?"

Hollister returned the smile. "Yeah, Top. Now and then, remind me there were days like that."

At the patrol order, Caulter gave the details of the patrol—times, locations, frequencies, weather, enemy and friendly situations, adjacent units, supporting units—the list went on. Every member of the patrol made precise notes on Caulter's words; the briefing from the intelligence NCO, Sergeant First Class Young, and Captain Dale Tennant—the air mission commander.

Hollister was impressed with the operations section and the pilots attached to J Company. But he reminded himself all those folks were *lifers* and were motivated to do a good job. Still, it was not enough for him. He wanted a company full of Caulters, Easys, and Tennants. He flipped a page in his notebook and made a couple of side notes about things he wanted done while he was out in the bush.

The aerial recon lifted off on time, but Hollister wasn't happy with the weather. A freak storm had blown in off the South China Sea and was tailing the chopper on the way to the insert LZ.

"We're gonna get our young asses wet," Tennant said over the intercom.

Looking back behind the chopper, Hollister could see the large gray loaf of a cloud layer that extended from the treetops to over two thousand feet. "That fucker's faster than you are, Dale," he replied into the mike on his flight helmet.

"I can fly through mud and rocks if necessary," Tennant kidded.

"I hope it won't be necessary," Hollister said. Just then he noticed the door gunner fastening the top button on his Nomex flight suit against the quickly dropping temperature.

"You better suck yourself back into the chopper back there and hold on to something," Tennant said.

But before Hollister could even reply, the rain hit the chopper. It came down so hard that within seconds, he could barely make out the ground from the two thousand feet. He looked up between the two pilot's seats at the altimeter. It read four thousand feet, then zero, then six hundred feet, then a thousand again. "Jesus! How much air do we have below us?"

"Don't pay any attention to that. Gotta remember that it's a barometric gizmo, and we just had a drop in the pressure that'd suck a submarine to the bottom. We're still around fifteen hundred feet—or fifteen thousand," he added, kidding.

Hollister looked up to see if Tennant was laughing. "Can you see anything up there?"

"My side of the Plexiglas, and I'm not too sure about that."

"I hope the hell we don't run into something," Hollister said.

"Yeah, I'm real glad there's only about one mountain between here and Cambodia," Tennant replied, trying to hold the chopper, which was bucking wildly in the turbulence.

"Are we supposed to be flying in weather like this?" Hollister asked.

"No, not like this. We're supposed to stop flying in weather not nearly as bad as this."

Tennant wrestled with the controls, trying to keep the chopper straight and level. He gave away his concern when he slid the small Plexiglas window in his door open so he could look out of it instead of through the torrential downpour splashing against the windscreen.

The water began blowing into the cargo compartment—sideways. Hollister soon found himself soaking as what had been spray turned to sheets of rain hitting him full on. "Shit."

"Hey, things could be a lot worse," Tennant said over the intercom, still struggling with the controls to keep the chopper on course and away from any ground hazards.

"I sure don't see how," Hollister yelled over the intercom, unsure if he could be heard.

"We could be standing on the ground next to this bird waiting for someone to come pick us up."

"I see what you mean. You think this will blow by us?"

"If it doesn't eat us first."

"What do we do 'til then? Can we take much more than this?" Hollister asked.

"This is nothing. Wait 'til you get a load of what's next," Tennant said.

Hollister turned to see what he was talking about and a terrible noise began to bang in his headset. Just as quickly, he realized it was not in his headset. It was the sound of the blades cracking small hailstones into ice pebbles.

He saw the hailstones piling up inside the chopper. They rolled wildly across the corrugated decking inside the compartment, while some bounced off of the nylon seats.

Hollister and Fass moved as near to the center of the chopper as they could. Just then a larger hailstone crashed through the co-pilot's windscreen and landed in his lap.

"Holy shit," the peter pilot yelled over the intercom as he looked down at the golfball-sized stone rolling around on the floor of the cockpit.

"We in real trouble?" Hollister asked.

"Just hold on back there. If I can keep this bronco in control for a little while longer, we ought to break out of this without much more damage," Tennant said.

"Why not put it down?"

"I would if I had any fucking idea where the ground was. Flying on instruments is pretty much wishful thinking in this kind of weather. We're better off flying than trying to land in this tur-bulence on ground we aren't sure of."

"Oh, that's real reassuring."

"You think I'm not doing all I can to get us through this flight in one piece?"

"No, I'm sure you want to hit your rotation date on time." Hollister remembered he hadn't told anyone about their situation. He wondered if they would even know the chopper was in trouble. "S'pose I can reach base from here—in this weather?"

"We already reported our position and situation to my battalion operations. We asked them to call the Rangers landline with the same data."

"Great. Good thinking," Hollister said. The hail stopped as fast as it started, and the winds calmed.

In less than ten more seconds, the sun broke through the large dark cloud disappearing out in front of the chopper—still heading west.

The rest of the flight to the objective area was beautiful. Hollister realized how different the country could look. In just a matter of minutes it went from dark, cold, and dangerous to bright, squeaky-clean, green, and still dangerous.

He pulled out his map to orient on the major rivers in the area.

He recognized his old stomping grounds as he triangulated the chopper's position between the red laterite of Cu Chi, the Sugar Mill, and the Dong Nai River. It hadn't changed since he last flew over the same area some twenty months before. There were a few thousand more bomb craters. But it looked the same to him.

He turned to Fass and yelled to the lieutenant, who didn't have a headset, "You know where we are, Ranger?"

Fass slipped his own map off his lap, folded it for a tight grip against the wind, and stabbed his index finger at a point on it. He then pointed down at the same terrain feature on the ground—a bridge.

"Good call," Hollister said with a smile.

He had plans to put lots of questions to the others on his patrol to make sure he was satisfied with their grasp of the situation. He knew he was unlikely to get a second chance to spend any time with them on the ground again. He wanted to be sure they were up to the job.

"We're about there," Tennant announced over the intercom.

It was a mangrove swamp in the middle of a thickly wooded area with wide dikes through it.

"Where's the trail?" Tennant asked.

Putting his field glasses to his face, Hollister scanned the trees. He caught the reflection of the water between the tree trunks and groaned. It was going to be a very wet ambush.

"It's running northwest to southeast, right near those three bomb craters making a Ballantine symbol in the water."

"I got it," Tennant said. He kicked the chopper into a spiral, up and away from the trail so as not to give away what they were looking at.

Hollister rechecked his map to make sure he had the right trail. "Okay, let's find a place to insert."

He leaned toward Fass. "Pick an LZ." He then watched while Fass looked, checked his map, and looked again. After a few wide orbits over the area, everyone was getting edgy about spending too much time circling.

Fass yelled at Hollister, "It's gonna have to be one of those dike roads."

Hollister smiled. He was right. There wasn't anyplace remotely useful as a landing zone. And while the roads were not the best, they were a lot better than trying to land outside the swamp and having to walk in.

He made a few notes on his map to remind him of the nearest

features that might be trouble. There was a lone stand of trees—separate from the mangrove swamp, but large enough to hide an enemy element capable of putting indirect fire on a Ranger team or shooting at insert choppers.

There was also a canal leading from the wooded terrain to the northwest of the swampy area.

"You got any trouble with landing on that dirt road?" Hollister asked Tennant.

Tennant laid the chopper over in a left turn and looked out his door at the possible landing zone. "It's long enough, a bit narrow, and it'll be easy for your Rangers to get into the tree line. But if we go in there and find out someone's waiting for us, we might be in big trouble because they'll be at a point-blank range. Not much chance someone could fire at a chopper from the trees on either side of the road and miss it."

"Yeah. Well, it's the best we got. I don't want to land way the hell out in the paddies and have to walk in," Hollister said.

"We bring in some good gunship cover, and we'll probably be okay."

"Hope you're right."

It was cool inside his BOQ room back at Bien Hoa. The rain had taken the heat out of the billets, and the winds had blown the moisture away.

Hollister turned the light on and realized, again, there was no mail waiting for him. There was a tug in his chest as he allowed himself a moment to think about Susan and how he was missing her.

He took off his shirt and spread his notes out on the table. He would have to break down the endless details to issue his own patrol order to his team.

He began at the top of a GI writing pad and went through the list of details. With each entry, he made side notes on who would have what responsibilities. He suddenly felt the need for a drink. He knew better, and toughed it out.

He tried to refocus on the order and go into the specific duties of each team member, emergency-action plans, coordinating instructions, and a schedule of rehearsals, weapons tests, and inspections.

He stopped, lit a cigarette, and looked back over what he had done. He realized how long it had been since he had prepared a patrol order. He worried he might be rusty when his intent was to set the example for the others. Dropping his beat-up Zippo onto his pack of cigarettes, next to his notes, he realized he had to just do it—no hesitation.

Once he had finished, he went over it all again—cross-checking against his original patrol order notes he took from Caulter.

He looked at his watch and entered the times in for the brief-back, rehearsals, and the inspection, since the time for the order itself had already been announced.

He dropped his pen onto the lined pad and let his mind wander a minute. What had he forgotten? He was nervous about the patrol. All of them were nervous, but he was the company commander, and there was no room for mistakes or oversights. Not if he wanted to set the example.

Later, Hollister met with the XO, the operations officer, and Captain Tennant. In Tennant's capacity as the platoon leader of the helicopter platoon supporting Juliet Company, he spent the better part of two hours briefing Hollister on what they had and hadn't done since Major Simonson had assumed command.

The others added their summaries. The stories were not surprising, but they still aggravated Hollister—that such a fine company could be driven so far down in combat readiness by its commander. It reminded him how much pressure there was on him to make the fixes and make them fast.

They had little positive to tell about training. More than fifty percent of the aviation company had come from other units drawn down to be sent back to the States as part of the administration's *Vietnamization* of the war. While they had some combat experience, there had been nothing in the way of training in patrolling techniques, communications, rappelling, chopper loading and unloading, map reading, escape and evasion, fire support, combat first aid, weapons training, or immediate-action drills.

They would have to start from scratch.

He gave Thomas the task of putting together a county-fair-type training schedule to allow the troops to cycle through stations of training taught by the most experienced among them. He told Tennant he wanted all the chopper crews to attend the same training.

By dawn the next day, all but the patrol rehearsals and inspections had been completed by Hollister's team. He wanted to spend most of the day on those things, weapons testing, and rest for the team. He might not have been on a patrol in some time, but he was keenly aware of the exhausting demands it placed on ambushers. Sleep would be in short supply in the mangrove swamp.

After breakfast, he had the team run through immediate-action drills—over and over again. It was uncomfortably hot and muggy for all, but each man knew they all had to learn to move like a team if they had to take immediate steps to avoid enemy contact.

Hollister kept them at it for almost an hour and a half, and then swapped positions with Lieutenant Fass. In the event Hollister were to become a casualty, Fass would assume the duties as patrol leader. As in Ranger School, rank was not taken into consideration when assigning responsibilities. He knew if he gave the job to someone senior to Fass, then Fass would be denied the experience he would need as a platoon leader.

DeSantis was just coming out of his hootch when Hollister spotted him. "Hey, just the man I'm looking for."

The lanky platoon sergeant stopped and snapped Hollister an old-fashioned Airborne salute. "Yes, sir. What can I do for you?"

"I want you to be bellyman in the chase ship on my insert."

"Glad to, sir. Say when."

"I don't know enough about too many of the NCOs yet, and I'd like to know I've got someone in the chase ship who I can count on if it goes into the shitter."

DeSantis smiled. "Thanks, sir. I was serious the other day when I told you I'm glad to see you back. We've been in some real trouble around here."

"Well, those days are over. But so are the good times."

"To tell the truth, I'd rather pass on the good times. That's what gets Rangers killed. I got too much time in this company and in this shithole of a country to flush it all because the chain of command has its head stuck up its ass."

CHAPTER 11

The weight of Hollister's rucksack brought back the old unpleasant memories of humping the bush. He had been on so many patrols, but they never got easier. Each patrol taught him something else he had to be concerned about, a new danger facing his teams, a new threat to their lives.

Steadying his load one last time, Hollister jumped up and down to see if his gear rattled.

He looked at himself in the small mirror in his room. Camouflage stick had covered all of the exposed flesh on his face, neck, and hands. And his equipment was void of any shiny metal spots. In earlier years, he would have used shoe polish. The invention of the black marking pen was a Ranger lifesaver.

He picked up his rifle, automatically checking to be sure it was unloaded. He knew it was, but wanted to be true to his habit of checking. It was a small thing, but filled with positive consequences.

He picked up the claymore-mine bag he used to carry several small items in and slung it over his shoulder. Thinking he was ready, he looked around his room for any sign of something he had forgotten. He knew whatever he left behind would stay behind until he returned. There was never a second chopper trip for things forgotten.

Operations had scrounged up two three-quarter-ton trucks to move the team, equipment, and supplies to the airfield. Hollister decided to conduct his patrol inspection next to the vehicles themselves in order to allow some of the gear to rest on the tailgates.

He lined up the five others and began with Estlin, who would act as grenadier on the ambush. In his routine manner, Hollister

started at the top of Estlin's head and worked down. He checked
his camouflage, the gear strapped to the front of him, and his
grenade launcher. He asked Estlin questions about procedures at
the landing zone, movement to concealment, and emergency sig-
nals on the move.

While Hollister inspected his team, acting company commander Browning made last-minute coordination with operations,
fire support, and air force support, and then set up his radio and the
artillery radio on the floor of one of the trucks to make a commo
check.

As Hollister continued with Estlin, he caught sight of Easy
coming out of his hootch wearing his web gear, carrying a rifle, a
map case temporarily clasped in his teeth.

Hollister gave him a questioning look.

Easy stopped near Hollister and finally found a place for his
map case in his pocket. "Morning, sir. Fine day to kill Commies,
ain't it?"

"Where are you going, Top?"

Easy nodded his head toward the west. "Out there—Indian
country. Captain Browning asked me to ride along on the insert."

Hollister looked over toward Browning and got a cross
between a knowing look and a request for an okay for Easy to ride
along.

"You think you're up to this?" he asked Easy.

Easy tapped his plastic leg with the front sight blade of his
CAR-15 and smiled. "If we have to go down out there, I'll take
this off and beat some little zipperhead fucker to death with it."

Hollister tried not to scold his old friend. "I don't have to tell
you what a problem it could be if you ended up on the ground, and
we had to get in to evac you."

Easy's expression changed to one of the most serious Hollister
had seen. "Captain. If it looks to me like I'm holding anyone up or
causing anyone's ass to be out in the breeze—I'll take my chances
and wave you off. I know what the risks are, and I'm in for a dollar
not a dime around here."

Hollister nodded. "Okay. Just make sure you don't go trying to
pull anyone off the LZ again."

"Yeah, I can't afford to lose another leg," Easy said with a grin.

Hollister returned to his inspection.

"You've done your homework," Hollister said.

Estlin smiled, his white teeth gleaming against the camouflage grease on his face. "Yes, sir. I don't mind telling you the thought of going into the AO without the answers to all those questions scares the shit out of me."

"Good. Just hold that thought. A little garden-variety fear will do you good every time." He tapped Estlin on the shoulder and turned him around, then checked his rucksack and the gear attached to it.

"You ain't gonna get me, Captain. I been studyin' up on this since we got the warning order."

"That's what I want to hear. Now tell me what ammo you have with you."

"Got thirty rounds of shotgun and twenty high explosive."

Hollister finished checking the tie-downs on the side pockets of Estlin's ruck and slapped him on the top of the rucksack. "You're okay. Sit down 'til we have to load up."

He moved to the next man, Captain Thomas, and smiled at him. "When was the last time you were out in the bush?"

"Shit, it's been a while."

"What kind of shape do you think you are in?"

"Good enough not to embarrass myself out there, I hope."

"Me, too. I'd sure hate to medevac a captain for heat prostration."

Hollister did the same detailed inspection of Thomas, asking the same kind of questions and checking each piece of his equipment. It became clear to the others there really wasn't going to be any rank out on Hollister's ambush.

Hollister finished the inspection, and then turned to Lieutenant Fass. "Okay, check me out."

Fass handed his rifle to Estlin and began his inspection of Hollister and his equipment.

"Go ahead," Hollister said.

"Go ahead?"

"Run the questions by me."

"Oh, yes, sir," Fass said. He thought a minute and then began to ask Hollister about call signs, frequencies, flight times for medevacs to the ambush location, locations and capabilities of supporting artillery batteries, rules of engagement, and the challenge and password for the day.

Fass finished his inspection of Hollister and tapped him okay.

Hollister turned to the patrol. "I want to make this perfectly clear." He jabbed his thumb over his shoulder toward the Cambodian border. "There might be enough wrong with the way things have been running around here to make it pretty dicey out there. You could get dead because someone back here steps on his dick.

"You don't have to go. You can pass up this patrol. I won't punish you for it. But I'll reassign you to some other unit."

None of the five responded.

"Okay," Hollister said. "I'll take that as an affirmative. Now let's go out and get one."

The roadway to the aviation battalion area was clogged with morning traffic. Hollister watched as the Vietnamese civilians tried to get their wares to the marketplace. He was surprised to see the dramatic increase in numbers of young men—of military age. He had heard there were plenty of Vietnamese soldiers who had deserted as well as those whose families had been able to pay to have their sons exempted from the draft. Hollister had to assume most of the young Vietnamese men he saw fell into both of those categories, and the thought irritated him.

He looked around at the Rangers, soldiers who had been asked to risk their lives for people who wouldn't even risk their own. He tried to put it out of his mind. Out on the ambush, he didn't want to be thinking about how many South Viets were not holding up their end. He knew it would be more than counterproductive.

He tried to find something else to think about and reached into his shirt pocket for his notebook. At least he could focus on some of the details of the mission he might need in the dark—when looking at the notebook would be difficult at best.

As he slipped his hand into his pocket, he wished there were a letter from Susan to take his mind off of the mission, his anxieties, and Vietnam. On earlier tours, he could always count on having a recent letter to reread. It would remind him of who he was, what he wanted to do, and where he wanted to be—all things that got confused in the bush and distorted in the long nights. He missed her.

At the aviation battalion, Hollister made one final check of the chase ship before loading his patrol into the insert chopper. Reaching the chase, he found DeSantis on his hands and knees rechecking the rope routing on the McGuire rig he had tied in.

"Think there's any chance we'll need that?"

DeSantis turned and looked over his shoulder at Hollister. "If we don't, I'll be more than happy to pack it back up later. If we do, I don't want to have to tell you I'm not ready."

They both knew the flat terrain near the ambush site reduced the need for the rig, but it didn't mean they wouldn't run into trouble on the way in or out—something that might cause them to have to use the extraction rigging.

"Good deal. You want me to cross-check it?"

DeSantis scrambled out backward and motioned toward the floor of the chopper. "Please. I'd feel a lot better if I had a second set of eyes and hands go over this rig."

Hollister went over the ropes, snap links, and cabling of the McGuire rig with as much attention as he had paid to packing his own gear, checking out his rifle, and inspecting the members of his patrol. He'd been on enough patrols where McGuire rigs had been used to know they had to be anchored in right. If not, the rig would be more dangerous than the reason for the extraction.

Once he was satisfied with the rigging, Hollister gave DeSantis a nod and headed toward the lift chopper that would carry his team. There was enough unsaid about how he would be relying on DeSantis to be there if the team needed him.

By the time Hollister and the patrol got to the chopper, the pilots had the blades turning at flight idle and were going through the end of their preflight checklist.

Hollister waved to the others. His watch read 1100 hours, exactly. He was pleased they had met their scheduled liftoff time. He didn't want the first mission to start off late—it wouldn't set much of an example for the others in Juliet Company.

He pulled his map out and flipped it open to the objective area for one last look at the prominent terrain features, the relative position of the ambush site to the landing zone, the gun-target line for the only supporting artillery battery, and location of the layup position they had picked.

The preflight seemed to be taking too long. He looked up to the pilots to see if there was any problem. The door gunner tapped Hollister on the shoulder and pointed toward the front of the chopper. "The pilot would like to talk to you."

Hollister nodded and slid off the floor of the chopper and onto the ground. At the pilot's door, Hollister stepped up on the footpad on the skid to be closer to the pilot so they could talk over the chopper noise.

Mister Moody was a CW2 and typical of so many warrant-officer pilots: on his second tour, tired, and not the same hot-dog chopper jock who had arrived for his first tour. He pulled the lip mike away from his face and yelled out the Plexiglas window, "I just got a message from my flight operations folks there's a contamination problem at the refueling point."

"What's it mean to us?"

Before he could answer, the sounds of the turbine changed frequency. The peter pilot had cut the power to shut the chopper down.

"Means we have to check out the fuel on board, and if we have some of the bad fuel, we've got to ground this ship and find another one to take you in."

"Okay. How long do you think this'll all take?"

Moody looked at his watch. "I'd suggest you take your troops to chow. It's gonna be at least that long, even if everything checks out okay."

Hollister gave the pilot a thumbs-up and stepped down off the pad.

After he sent the team to the aviation battalion mess hall, Hollister went back to talk to the pilot. "What's the verdict?"

Chief Moody looked up from his green-plastic logbook, where he was entering some maintenance data. "The crew chief is taking a fuel sample over to maintenance now to have it checked out. I'm pretty sure we're going to have to park this baby and find you another chopper."

Hollister made a face. "So—does a new chopper mean a new crew, Chief?"

"Might. It's still up to operations to decide who drives what."

"Shit! If we get a new crew—we'll get fliers who haven't been on the recon and haven't been to the briefings. If you guys fly us in a new chopper—you won't know much about the new aircraft."

Moody pulled out a pack of cigarettes from his pocket and offered Hollister one. Hollister took one and lit his and the pilot's.

"Tell you what, Captain. I'll head on over to flight ops and see if I can scrounge up a chopper that'll do the job. And I'll push for us to fly it."

Hollister smiled. "That's about as good I can expect, I guess. Thanks."

"Glad to do it. If we don't take your mission, we're liable to end up ferrying little people—chickens, pigs, and screaming kids from somewhere to somewhere they don't want to go. I'd rather fly a new chopper into your LZ."

"You not worried about an insert in a fresh chopper?"

"I'd fly you in wearin' a gasoline suit with lit road flares in each hand before I'd ferry Viets around all day."

Hollister smiled and patted the pilot on the shoulder. "Okay, let me know."

After a meal, the Rangers found a shady spot next to the mess hall, dropped their gear, and tried to make themselves comfortable for the wait.

Soon, the midday sun squeezed out the shade, and they suffered from the direct sunlight and the heat.

"I really hate this shit," Thomas said, wiping the sweat from his face with the medical cravat tied around his neck. He got up, fanned the front of his shirt to try to get some air up in it, and patted his pockets for a lighter to relight his cigar.

"I hate to tell you you'll have to get used to it—but *get used to it*," Hollister said, running his upturned forefinger across his own forehead to keep perspiration from running into his eyes.

"It's like this all the time?"

"When you're humping with a rifle company there's always something to do, and it all goes toward getting another day behind you. But in Ranger ops, everything's a sequence of events, and the next step never happens until you get past the last one.

"The best you can do is look out for this kind of delay and try to figure out a way to slip in a backup plan. Choppers will be choppers. You can't ever get enough blade time out of them. This could be a lot worse."

"How's that?" Thomas asked.

"We were going in in daylight anyhow, and once we get in, we'd be lying up in the sun, sweating there, too. So, if we have to wait, this is good enough," Hollister said, looking up at the sun.

"I sure hope we don't have to put this off 'til another day. I can't get my heart up for this again if we scrub."

"There's plenty of adrenaline where that came from."

Thomas lit his cigar one last time and smiled. "Wish I had a little more ice water in my veins."

"If you did, I wouldn't want you on this team or as my ops officer."

"Okay, Captain. We've got a chopper," a voice said.

Trying to shake the fog from his brain, Hollister sat up and realized he had dozed off. He looked up against the late afternoon sun and squinted at the silhouetted figure. "Moody?"

"Yes, sir. I'm ready to fly if you're ready to ride."

"Old chopper or a new one?"

"New one. The other one had some bad juice in her belly. But the chase ship, the command-and-control ship, and the gunships are okay."

"Problems?"

"It ought to be okay. This is not so tough an insert," Moody said, pulling his Nomex flight gloves out of his pocket.

"All of them are tough until you guys are gone and we are down, in and cold."

"Yes, sir—I guess you're right there. I just mean I'm not as worried about flying a new chopper on this one 'smuch as some others I've been on."

Wiping the sweat from his eyes, Hollister got to his feet and hoisted his rucksack. "Okay, let's do it."

The others didn't need to be told. They were on their feet and making last-minute adjustments of their gear.

"New war paint," Hollister said, reminding the others the sweating had washed away much of the camouflage stick they had carefully applied before loading up the first time.

Hollister looked over to Brownie standing next to the C & C. "We going as is? Any change 'cause of the delay?"

Browning shielded his eyes from the sun with the palm of his hand. "I'd like to put you in first and move the two fake inserts 'til after."

"Okay with me," Hollister said. "You tell the pilots?"

Brownie nodded.

"Mount up," Hollister said.

The hands on his Rolex were straight up and down—six P.M. Hollister leaned against the bulkhead behind Moody's seat and looked out at the sun setting up ahead of the chopper as they headed toward Cambodia.

" 'S gonna be dark by the time we get down and in," Hollister yelled to Thomas, sitting next to him in the left door of the insert chopper.

Thomas made a face, then shrugged as if to say *What are you gonna do?*

Hollister nodded and smiled. "Tough it out."

The five choppers took up a flight formation with the C & C, the insert, and the chase ships in a graceful echelon-left formation behind the two Cobras.

Hollister wasn't happy about their being still twenty minutes from the LZ. If he had had any doubt about it being a night insert, all doubt was gone. He took a deep breath and tried to remind himself there were advantages. His team would be concealed by the darkness and would be less of a target for any LZ watchers.

The ground below the choppers clipped by as Hollister tried to orient himself on the barely recognizable landmarks—the larger river junctions and road intersections. He knew they were close and chambered a round in his rifle. "Lock and load!" he yelled to the others.

The heightened tension in the chopper became more apparent as the insert ship broke out of the formation, along with the chase, while the C & C went forward to confirm the LZ.

Hollister's team made last-minute checks, scooted toward the chopper's open side doors, and started making private deals with their maker.

He knew it was the real thing when he felt the chopper starting to sink to approach altitude. He tried to swallow and realized his throat was dry. He turned up the sole of his jungle boot and looked for a pebble lodged in the cleats. Finding none, he raised the other boot. A small piece of gravel was wedged between two of the rubber ridges near the outside of his sole. He worked it loose, wiped it off on his shirt, and popped it into his mouth.

The pebble immediately caused him to salivate. It was a trick he had learned in Ranger School. The saliva would wet his mouth and throat, and what he swallowed would cause his digestive system to settle down a bit—easing the knots.

The door gunner reached over and tapped Hollister on the back. He held up his hand and gave him a V-sign with his fingers and yelled, "Two minutes."

Hollister gave an exaggerated nod. Thomas and Estlin got the word when Hollister did. Hollister turned to tap the other three. Meadows, Loomis, and Fass spun around from their side of the chopper and moved to the center of the cargo compartment behind Hollister. They would all go out the left side of the chopper—to end up on the same side of their roadway landing zone.

Their faces showed the focus he had seen so many times on men going into combat.

"One minute!" the door gunner yelled.

Hollister leaned forward and looked out ahead for the landing zone. The swampy mangroves appeared to him as a blacker area on the already gray-black ground. He strained to find the roadway and only caught a glimpse of a reflection of one of the gunship's navigation lights off the standing water in the trees. It would be a long, wet night.

The chopper's descent marked the start of a short window where the Rangers would be very vulnerable and unlikely to be able to avoid any accurate enemy fire. As the chopper settled onto the ground, the team could feel the moister air and recognized the sudden loss of visibility as the black curtain of trees came up to a point above the rotor disk.

The right skid tapped the ground.

"Go, go, go!" Hollister yelled as he planted his left hand on the deck and hopped up and out.

The others followed while he looked first up the road and then back toward the tail of the chopper for any signs of enemy fire.

The others jumped off the roadway and slid down the three-foot embankment built up to keep the roadbed above the water table.

Hollister saw the top of Loomis's head disappear into the lush vegetation close to the road. Without hesitating, he followed Loomis as the chopper rolled forward onto the toes of its skids to take off.

Inside the tree line, Hollister fell half his height to the bottom of the embankment and came to rest on top of Loomis, waist deep in mossy water. The collision completely submerged his radioman.

Loomis snapped his head up out of the water, coughing and spitting out the slimy fluid.

Hollister tried to help by grabbing him under the arm, only to lose his own footing in the slippery bog and tumble backward, pulled down by the weight of his rucksack and field gear.

He flailed out with his arms and caught on to a sapling with his left hand, keeping him from completely submerging under the water.

Regaining his footing and clearing the mud and water from his eyes, Hollister grabbed Loomis and turned him around so they could see each other. He leaned over and put his lips to Loomis's ear. "You okay? Can you walk?"

Loomis turned his head, spit out some more debris, and gave Hollister a big nod.

Hollister touched Loomis, Loomis turned and tapped Fass, and the word got up to Estlin, they were ready to move away from the roadway.

They had been moving for less than a minute when Hollister stopped the file and tapped Loomis on the shoulder for the handset to the radio. "Campus Killer Five, this is Six. We are in and cold. Continuing the mission. Over."

Browning answered immediately, "I roger your message. And that you are going to Charlie Mike. We are moving on out of your AO. Will stand by. Out."

CHAPTER 12

The water got deeper not more than a hundred meters into their march from the roadway. Hollister was irritated that they hadn't known how deep the water was and tried to remind himself to make a point to screen old patrol debriefings in the future. He was sure some time in the past couple of years there had been a team in the area who remarked on the water problem. He was sure his team would make several comments on it when they were debriefed.

Their movement slowed to a snail's pace as the thready roots in the mangrove swamp grabbed for their legs while they moved through the chest-deep water.

After thirty more minutes, Hollister passed the word up to Estlin to hold up the file—he wanted to make a map check and consider looking for a change in route to the ambush site.

Loomis opened a poncho, and Fass, Estlin, and Hollister got under it to look at a map with a red-filtered flashlight.

"This is fucked," Estlin said.

"First, we have to find a rally point. I figure we've got less than four hundred meters to the site, and I haven't seen shit for a place to hole up if we need to hide," Hollister said.

Estlin jabbed his thumb up over his shoulder. "There looks like a tight knot of something growing up ahead—a little to the north."

"Okay, we'll check it out. If it looks good, we'll hold up there while I recon the ambush site. If it doesn't work—we'll have to do a little more looking. I *do not* want to go wandering into an ambush position without a place to head for if we get into a bind."

"You want to go check it out now?" Estlin asked.

"I think you and I ought to take a look before we drag the whole team around searching for a rally point."

Hollister turned to Fass. "You keep the team here. If we aren't back in two-zero minutes and you can't reach us on the radio— take over and get the rest of this patrol out to safety."

"Yes, sir," Fass said. "Count on me."

"Just make sure you're ready. Now, we're going forward. You keep things under control around here. Okay?"

"Will do, sir."

Hollister let Estlin lead them forward, even though he wanted to do it himself. He knew if he was going to train anyone in J Company, he had to train them, not do for them.

Estlin hesitated too long at pauses, moved too fast through uneven ground—causing him to lose his footing more than once. And he failed to adopt an organized pattern of searching in front and around him. Hollister would take it up with him when he had the time.

Estlin finally stopped, squatted to reduce the height of that part of him sticking out of the water, and pointed off to his right front.

Hollister looked at the tight stand of trees. It was skirted by a dense apron of bushes ideal for the team to hole up in. He was starting to get cold from standing in the water, and he knew Estlin was starting to tire. He motioned for Estlin to wait while he sloshed forward to take a little closer look at the rally point.

There was no obvious entrance into the dense patch, which was good. Hollister knew if there were, it would most likely be booby-trapped.

He circled the brush and found a couple of small breaks—large enough to pass through without making a racket. It would do. He couldn't waste any more time with it. He had to get the team into position.

Selecting the ambush site was more difficult than finding a suitable rally point. They found the trail they had selected on the aerial recon. It was worthless. While it was not in deep water, the fields of fire from the ambush site to the killing zone were obscured by reeds. Again, Hollister took Estlin and moved toward the path, looking for a better location.

It was difficult to find a site with the elevation to keep the team dry, the fields of fire to cover the killing zone, and the access to get both in and out of the site.

There was also the problem of movement. The more they wandered around in the swamp, the greater their chance of being spotted. Then there was the constant threat of booby traps. And, surviving all that, the team would leave a trail in the fragile marsh.

Hollister considered moving to the alternate ambush location they had picked on the aerial recon. It would mean moving his already tired team five hundred meters to the north through more of the same, only to face the possibility of the same situation.

Suddenly, Estlin tugged on Hollister's sleeve and pointed off toward a spot concealed by a couple of larger trees. "Over here."

Moving gave Hollister a view of the area Estlin was talking about. He took the lead and moved to the darkened area that appeared to be on something like higher, drier ground.

After moving slowly to the site, Hollister stopped and tried to make out the terrain. It was weird in the dark. It had man-made features and appeared to have had some of the vegetation cleared from it. He wasn't going to make any hasty decisions from fifty meters away, so he continued on until he felt his feet climbing a slight incline on the bottom of the swampy ground.

He stopped, squatted, and held his palm over his eyes to shield them from the lighter glow of the sky. It was a dike. An old one, but a dike of some kind built many years before.

Hollister looked back over his shoulder at the section of the trail he would select as the killing zone. It was almost completely visible, save a few branches obscuring a small portion of the trail. He turned back to the dike. The ground rose up out of the swamp, perpendicular to a line drawn to the killing zone. So far, so good, he thought.

He started forward and then stopped himself from climbing the front of the dike. To do so might scar up its forward slope and mark their location. The last thing he wanted was for his team's presence to be announced by disturbing the ground cover. So he sloshed to the left where the brush stood densely in front of the dike and climbed up out of the water.

Standing on the dike, he saw it was dry, long, and flat. The only problem was, it was narrow—only about eight feet wide.

He walked across the top and down the other side of the dike, into the water again. Turning around, he could look over the top of the dike and see the killing zone. Overhead it was concealed by drooping tree branches.

It would do. They would set up on the dike, and if it got to a shooting match, they could easily slip down behind it for cover. It was the best he was going to find.

It took almost an hour to get the patrol to the dike. By the time they were setting up, it was almost ten o'clock. Hollister posted Estlin as the lookout to cover the trail while he positioned each member of the patrol in his respective firing position.

The first order of business after arrival and assignment of positions was to place claymore mines along the side of the path to cover the killing zone with overlapping, earth-hugging blast patterns. Hollister had decided to try to do as much damage as possible with the claymores.

Hollister stopped long enough to report their situation to Campus Killer base—his operations. He also asked for a weather forecast.

Fass, Meadows, Loomis, and Hollister went down to the trail to set up claymores. As the other three started placing mines, Hollister stepped onto the trail to look up and down it for the approach of any VC. He looked back at the ambush site to see if he could make out Estlin and Thomas still covering them.

It was close enough that Hollister could see them when they moved, but not if they stayed still. He would make sure the others saw what he saw and would tell Estlin and Thomas.

The killing zone was adequate. Easy to see, lighter in color than the surrounding ground—which would help identify someone moving on the trail—and long and curved enough for them to see up and down much of the approaches to the killing zone.

He didn't like the steep banks raising the narrow path out of the water. On either side there was a three-foot drop-off. Anyone caught in the ambush and not killed outright could roll off the path into the water and be covered from his team's fire.

Hollister had to decide to go with it as is or place mines on the far side of the path to catch anyone trying to hide there. The problem was the time involved in placing extra claymores there and concealing the detonating wires they would have to stretch across the path. He knew he could probably conceal the wire for the night, but the concealment effort would be plainly evident in the daylight. He decided to risk it and hope any enemy moving down the path would be well within the killing zone before they discovered the wire.

He grabbed one of the claymores from his bag, slipped over the far side of the path, and slid down into the water. He opened the legs on the mine, inserted the blasting cap end of the wire into the detonator well. Making a fast loop around the folding legs to take up any pull if someone tripped on the wire, he sank the four pointed legs of the mine into the bank at the waterline. He tried to line it up so the blast would be parallel to the path, in the low spot where someone would be likely to take cover.

On the path, Hollister stretched the wire across it and left the loose end on the side closest to the dike. He then pulled out his K-bar knife and began to cut a small V slit into the path next to the wire.

Fass and Meadows moved over to help Hollister complete the groove in the trail. In less than a minute, they had dug a little trench, put the wire in it, and covered it with the spoils.

Fass took the lead, and they started back toward the dike, carefully threading their claymore wires behind them as they moved.

They had moved less than twenty meters when someone grabbed Hollister by the shirt at his elbow. He froze, then turned.

Meadows raised his hand for Hollister to see and pointed up the trail.

Hollister listened. *Voices.* He could hear voices. Two, maybe three, but not more. *Shit!* Hollister thought. They weren't in position yet. They couldn't take a chance of executing the ambush without having the claymores wired in. And they were much too close to avoid the backblast if they did detonate them.

"*Do not* fire," he whispered first to Meadows and then to Loomis. Meadows got the word to Fass, and Hollister raised his hand to try to get Estlin's and Thomas's attention at the dike. He then gave the down-and-freeze hand signal, hoping they would understand he wanted no one to fire on whoever was coming down the path.

They flattened out and tried to conceal their location without making any noise. The voices got louder. It soon became clear the voices were Vietnamese men.

Hollister held his breath to strain for more clarity. He wanted to know how many men there were and were they walking casually or running and talking rapidly—as if they were coming to find the team. While he waited, he slipped the binoculars out of his claymore bag.

The voices got louder, and Hollister was more convinced it was just two Vietnamese. He raised his head a few inches above the reeds and slowly brought the glasses to his face.

It took a few seconds to orient the binos and recognize what was in his view. Hollister slowly moved the point of aim of the binos to the mottled light pattern on the path.

The trail images changed from pitch dark to somewhat moonlit to a scattered pattern of shadows. He squinted to try to find movement, signs of life, signs of VC.

Suddenly, there was a light. Moving the binos, he found a pool of light. It was a flashlight! He dropped the binos and tried to locate the light. About a hundred meters from his position there was the unmistakable circle of a flashlight playing on the trail. It was stationary—meaning they had stopped. So had the talking.

He raised the binos again to focus on what the flashlight was illuminating. He recognized the stock of a rifle and the telltale outline of a curved AK-47 magazine. Then he thought they were looking at a box or a rucksack or something about the size of a shopping bag. Looking more closely, he discovered the two men were trying to repair a shoulder strap on a backpack. The strap had come unbuckled. They were simply trying to adjust their gear. They were obviously unconcerned about their security and had no idea Hollister and his men were in the marshy grasses only meters away.

Hollister dropped the glasses and used his finger to wipe away the sweat formed on his brow. He looked around at the others and saw they were frozen and aware of what was going on. He decided not to change his instructions to them. There was no way they could fire on the two enemy soldiers without compromising their position. It would have to be a pass.

He tried to focus on the details: uniforms, weapons, gear, and what they were carrying. Any information was useful.

Raising the binos again, Hollister watched the two men shoulder their loads and begin to walk down the trail—across his front. But no sooner had they taken a few steps when one of them stopped.

This time Hollister was sure they had been discovered. But he was wrong again. One of the soldiers pulled out a pack of cigarettes, put one in his mouth, and lit it. The smell of the cigarette smoke made Hollister want one—and a drink.

Sweat continued to form on Hollister's face, some of it trickling down into his eye, burning, and blurring his vision for a moment. He tilted his head and tried to get the fluid to drain back out of his eye, resisting the urge to reach up and wipe it away.

The two VC reached the leading edge of the killing zone, and Hollister knew they were only eight feet from the claymore wire he had buried in the pathway. If they found it, things could go sour. He said a little prayer—not to let it happen, not then, not while they were split and unprepared for contact.

The VC reached the point where Hollister estimated the wire to be and passed it, without any indication they had noticed it.

He held his breath for a few more seconds, his rifle muzzle pointed at the duo, his thumb on the safety lever, and his index finger resting lightly on the trigger.

One of the VC laughed at something the other said, and their voices started to trail off as they got farther away from the Ranger team in hiding.

The Americans lay still for another ten minutes, until Hollister waved for Fass, Meadows, and Thomas to continue to thread their claymore wires back to the dike. He didn't have to remind them to be careful or to keep the noise down. They all realized how easy it was for someone to come down the path and catch them.

Once they were all in their positions, all facing the trail except Estlin, who was in a tree some ten meters behind the dike, facing to the rear—they were ready for any VC to come down the trail—again.

Around one in the morning, lightning began to snap off to the east. At the same time, the temperature began to drop. It took about thirty minutes for the wind to come up. The clouds boiled in, and it went completely black, save the occasional flash of the lightning.

The trees started whipping, causing even more noise. Hollister knew there was less chance they would be able to catch another VC coming down the path in bad weather, much less execute an effective ambush in the rain sure to follow. He was also worried that if they did spring an ambush, their extraction would be nearly impossible in the downpour—the ceiling was at treetop level.

He decided to cancel the ambush and move the team off the

higher ground on the dike and back down into the water—for safety even if at the cost of more discomfort.

The rain followed the wind and the lightning, as Hollister predicted, and came down furiously until around three A.M. It slacked up but continued to rain at a steady, gentler pace.

By five, all six men were shivering so hard two of them pulled out their floppy hats and bit down on them to keep their teeth from chattering.

Each of them prayed for the sun to come up and the rain to blow over—for some relief from the cold and the boredom of the long, wasted night.

Hollister hugged his chest, his hands tucked under his armpits for the little warmth his own body was giving off. He had not slept. The pressure of honchoing a patrol never let up, and he knew it. He had an endless list of details on his mind. One was his concern that the rain might wash away the dirt covering the claymore wire across the path, making it visible when the sun came up. He would have to send someone down to check it and recover it if need be and hope they didn't get compromised in the daylight.

He had been cold on ambushes so many times before and knew taking his mind off of the discomfort was the only defense against the unrelenting misery. He searched his memory for some moment, some experience he could get lost in. He shifted his weight and the old wound scar on his hip throbbed.

It reminded him of the warm night in Tokyo when he was released from the hospital at Camp Drake and met Susan. They shared a short but wonderful time together. But mostly, they shared each other. He was so excited to see her when she got off the plane. They both tried to talk at the same time—trying to catch up on so much.

He remembered the cozy room in the Japanese hotel and how she looked in the Asian-style bathroom where they shared a hot bath.

She had her hair up and wore a pale blue silk kimono. Her lips were freshly coated with a bright red lipstick.

Most vivid in his mind was when she dropped her kimono. He had waited so long to see her body again. That night, the months of loneliness in Vietnam and the weeks of pain in the hospital were all forgotten in the hot and steamy bath. He remembered holding her, inhaling her essence, and feeling the silkiness of her skin. And he remembered how she cried when she saw the ugly red-blue scar on his body. His stomach tightened at the thought of how it had all fallen apart.

He had asked himself over and over again how he could have had her, then lost her. Crouching there in the water, he had no more answers than he had when she cried back at Benning and told him they were over, they were finished.

The memory only took his mind off the cold for a few moments, but it replaced it with a dull ache he had lived with every second since she told him how unfixable it all was.

He shifted to relieve the pain in his hip. The rain fell on his face and plopped from the trees to the standing swampy water. He fished around in an outside pocket on his rucksack and found a small plastic bag. Without removing it from the pocket, he pulled out two gelatin capsules containing a painkiller Meadows had given him. He placed the capsules in his mouth and forced them down without any water.

He could tell dawn was actually coming by the increase in chopper traffic to the east. Pilots started their days early. They had choppers to preflight and breakfast and briefings and flights to pick up troops and supplies. So the sounds of the skies over III Corps were punctuated by cocks crowing and abuzz with choppers.

Hollister resisted the temptation to go down to check the claymore wires himself. He envied the others who would get to move around and shake some of the stiffness out of their joints. He knew he had to control the team and let them do most of the work. He sent Meadows and Fass to check out the demo, touch up the camouflage, and cover their tracks back to the dike.

While Meadows and Fass were gone, the others began to camouflage their positions and get something to eat.

Hollister found a point behind the dike where he could stay hidden from enemy eyes while watching Meadows and Fass circling around to the path and the claymores.

It was full light, though the sun had not yet broken through the low fog hugging the ground.

After calling in a situation report and making a weapons and ammo check, Hollister opened a pouch of LRP-ration spaghetti and poured almost half a canteen of water into the brown plastic pouch. Resealing the pouch, he slipped it into his shirt and moved

it around to a point over his kidney. His body heat would soften
the dehydrated rations and take some of the chill off the water. But
he had to steel himself for the shock of the cold pouch against his
bare skin.

By the time his rations had softened, the sun was breaking
through the overcast. The winds had stopped, giving promise of
a hot, steamy day in the mangrove swamp. He shook his head at
how quickly the extremes of Vietnam replaced one another and
how all of them were unbearable.

He unrolled the pouch and dug into his spaghetti. His first bite
was tasty if not completely softened. Some of the noodles were
still on the crunchy side. But he wasn't going to wait any longer.
By the fourth spoonful, he started getting thirsty. He raised his
plastic canteen to his lips and tasted the bitter, tepid water—
flavored by the telltale chemical trace of the purification tablets.

He finished most of the spaghetti and rolled up the pouch and
put it in his side pocket for later.

He wanted a cigarette, but knew better—didn't bring them
either. It was an absolute policy—*No smoking in the field.*

The morning was uneventful. The patrol members tried to wave
away flies. They took turns taking off one boot at a time, putting
their foot in a sunny spot to dry out and dewrinkle. Every man was
miserable, so there was no reason to say so. They knew what the
situation was, and there was neither an opportunity nor a reason to
bitch about it.

By midday, the sun had turned the swampy patrol site into a
sweltering pool of rotting vegetation and a hundred different types
of insects and leeches—all determined to improve their own sur-
vivability by feasting on Rangers.

Fass and Thomas chose to fight the heat and the boredom
by eating a second meal. Hollister decided to pass, and faced his
boredom by pulling his small notebook out of the plastic bag protecting it. He jotted down notes about the patrol for his debriefing.

As in all afternoons on ambushes, each man knew he faced
another night without sleep, and they took turns trying to grab as
much of it as they could while the sun was up. The problem was
trying to sleep on cue. Only a couple of them were sleepy enough
to sleep when their opportunity came. Hollister had trouble getting
comfortable and agreed to switch with Estlin, who was the
lookout in the large dense tree shading them for half the day.

From Estlin's tree, Hollister could see considerably farther up the trail toward Cambodia and the farmlands to the south of the mangrove swamp. Out there, Vietnam went on as usual. Lambrettas on the highways, ox carts on the roadways, and choppers. Choppers were everywhere. All were in a hurry to get somewhere or back from somewhere.

The numbers were fewer than at the height of the buildup in Vietnam. Still, there were enough choppers to be a problem for Hollister. He just hoped none of them found something curious on the ground where his team was laying up until nightfall.

About five, the traffic on the nearby roads started to slacken, and the choppers began to head for their parking spots for the night—the pilots destined for the bars in their respective aviation unit clubs.

Hollister had a sinking feeling. The same feeling he always had when he realized he was facing the longest part of an ambush night.

CHAPTER 13

Just after dark, Hollister got up and peered over the dike to decide if it was time to take up firing positions on top of the dike. The visibility was better than the night before because the glow in the sky was throwing an even illumination across the entire swampy area and lit up the path with a pale light.

Hollister dropped his field glasses and listened. He tried to take in the sounds in the night but kept getting distracted by distant choppers and bats flying out of the swamp to feed. He knew the only way he was going to be able to listen was to close his eyes and concentrate.

He had learned as a young lieutenant that the night sounds were very valuable to him in understanding what was happening. He needed to remember the normal sounds—when there was no tension in the air, when there was no threat to the wildlife creating the night harmony. He listened for a long time to the symphony of insects blended into the buzz, occasionally highlighted by the last calls of birds. The swamp had its own sounds, too. Frogs and crickets were an overlay on top of the other sounds. He tried to memorize the night sounds to use the information later—when they might signal the approach of intruders.

The first two hours in the ambush droned on. Hollister felt the warmth of the day's sun leave the ground beneath him, only to be replaced by a cold and damp chill that began its assault on his body. By nine, he was starting to feel the onset of shivering as the muscle sheath covering his kidneys began to spasm in revolt to the chill setting in.

Somewhere north of them, a few short bursts of AK-47 fire

echoed through the wetlands. There was no way to tell who it was. It was just a reminder there were men out there in the dark carrying rifles who could obliterate his six-man team with similar bursts of well-aimed fire. He reached out and checked the position of his extra magazines in his upturned floppy hat.

Loomis called in an hourly commo check to Campus Killer base at Bien Hoa. By ten, Hollister could feel the approach of more bad weather.

Almost as dreaded as the calamity of making contact in an ambush was the onset of maximum fatigue. It took the form of hallucinations and uncontrollable drifting off. That place between sweet sleep and consciousness was a narrow corridor of wild disorientation every combat soldier faced on long night missions in every war.

The first sign for Hollister was when his forehead banged into his rifle. He had dropped off without knowing it, and as fast as he fell asleep, he was abruptly awakened by the pain of the metal sight.

Fass tugged on Hollister's left sleeve and held his hand out in front of his face.

Hollister followed Fass's hand as he pointed out at a spot as far up the pathway as they had ever been able to see in the dark. He tried an old Ranger School trick of not looking directly at the trail. Rather, he let his eyes move in a small circle around the spot. The moment he did, he was able to detect movement.

An enemy patrol? A courier? A farmer? Or could it be an untethered water buffalo? Whatever it was took the longest time to get closer. Hollister and the others held their breath as they readied their weapons, rechecked safeties, and picked up their claymore detonators.

Two figures again. Hollister couldn't tell if they were armed for several more steps, but he was sure they were men. He slowly raised his binoculars. In less than a second Hollister could see enough of them to recognize one was carrying a rifle. He couldn't be sure about the second one. And they were moving more quietly and with far more concern than the pair the night before.

Why? Hollister wondered. What were they expecting? What was different about the path than the night before? Did they have some information there was an American ambush patrol lying in wait?

Paranoia. He knew he had to guard against it. They were

different soldiers and may only have had better training. They might have been spooked earlier by something. He would only find out by watching.

They got closer. Hollister touched his ammo again and made another quick check of the others. They were ready. In no more than eight steps the two VC would enter the killing zone.

Hollister's heart started to race. They had agreed to do the maximum damage with the claymores and not to fire on the enemy unless it was essential.

The signal to execute the ambush was when Hollister fired his first claymore.

The enemy soldiers took another two strides toward the killing zone, and Hollister picked up the detonator for his primary claymore.

Another step, and he slipped the safety clip out of place and prepared to detonate the mine.

The soldiers entered the killing zone.

Then, Hollister hesitated.

Estlin looked over toward Hollister to see if he was ready.

Hollister seemed to squint, and then turned to Fass on his left. He gave him an exaggerated shake of the head—telling him to hold.

He reached over and grabbed Meadows and leaned into his ear, whispering, "Hold it. Don't shoot."

The two enemy soldiers kept walking through the killing zone and approached the point where they would walk out of the blast area of the claymores. Still Hollister didn't detonate his claymore.

The other five Rangers held, waiting for Hollister.

The two soldiers walked out of the killing zone and continued down the trail, passing by the Rangers.

Loomis raised himself up on his hands and looked over at Hollister for some sign.

Hollister raised his hand—as if to say, just wait. He then pointed back toward the trail. He wanted the others to just continue to lie in wait. But he had no way of telling them exactly what was going through his mind.

After they turned their attention back to the killing zone to watch, Hollister looked back down the trail—in the direction the two soldiers went. Where they would end up bothered him. He hated letting them pass and hoped he hadn't made a costly mistake.

Three long minutes passed, and the Rangers held, waiting for whatever Hollister was anticipating. Then they heard voices again, and someone laughing.

Soon the main body of the enemy element came down the path. Five soldiers, two walking abreast, a single soldier, and then two more—hardly concerned for their safety.

Hollister picked up his binoculars and trained them on the five to make sure they were carrying weapons. Three of them had rifles slung across their shoulders, one had a canvas pouch tied to his back with four B-40 rockets in it, and the last man carried the rocket launcher.

He strained to see if the five were followed by even more VC. He saw nothing. And the five moved toward the killing zone. Hollister looked at them, then back up the trail, and then back to them.

With his free hand he picked up the claymore detonator again, quickly pulled the glasses from his face and looked left and right to make sure the others hadn't missed the approach of the VC. They were ready.

He was ready.

The first two VC stepped into the killing zone.

Hollister held.

They continued until the last two crossed the imaginary point on the path.

Hollister let them take two more steps and then forcefully squeezed the handle on his first claymore.

The darkness was broken first by the blast of Hollister's claymore, then by two more, then two more—in rapid succession. Hollister made sure to count each mine. He didn't want to have to ask the others if all the mines were detonated if he could count them.

Hollister had remembered to close his eyes to keep from losing his night vision to the flashes of light, and then quickly opened them to see what damage had been done.

The killing zone was completely obscured by a small cloud of dust and falling leaves, branches, and twigs scattered on the ground.

Not sure if any of the VC had survived the blasts, Hollister counted two beats to himself and then whispered to the others, "Watch your eyes," as he triggered the last claymore covering the dead space on the far side of the path.

More debris hurled into the air.

They waited, each man holding his breath as he strained to see the forms that quickly became visible. Outlines of the lifeless bodies were thrown about on the path.

Each man counted, one, three—five. All five bodies were visible from the dike.

Hollister didn't hesitate. He reached over and tapped Fass, whispering hoarsely, "Go, go! One minute—no more. Understand?"

Fass nodded, got to a crouching stance, and vaulted forward off the dike.

From the right, Estlin took the cue and leaped from the dike, only a step behind Fass.

Hollister turned to the others and urged them to hurry up and pack their gear for a hasty move to their rally point. His efforts were unnecessary. By the time Fass and Estlin were in the swampy bog, the others had scooped up their ammo and were spooling up the claymore wires no longer attached to anything out to their front.

They watched, anxiously, as Fass and Estlin entered the killing zone. The two moved without confusion to their assigned spots on the trail, having split up the small piece of ground to a search sector for each of them.

The two Rangers found a gruesome sight—the dismembered remains of five men who had only moments before walked down a trail with all of the thoughts that normally slip through soldiers' minds—home, family, girlfriends, wives—an end to the war.

Fass and Estlin searched the bodies for anything of intelligence value and collected the weapons. Every man on the team remembered there were still two VC somewhere down the trail who could easily double back. And there was no way of telling if there was still another VC element behind the five dead men.

Thirty seconds had passed. Hollister began to mutter encouragement under his breath. "Okay, come on. Let's get it done. Come on. Move. Move."

Estlin was bent over one of the bodies when Hollister heard the young Ranger gag at the urge to vomit. He hacked to clear his throat and then continued his search. Hollister remembered the sensations of searching his first dead man, and doing it with less composure than Estlin.

At a point where Hollister was about to speak up and hurry them, Estlin spun and reached out to Fass. He slapped him on the shoulder to let him know he was finished. He turned and watched

Fass's back while Fass shouldered what he would carry back to the dike.

Hollister checked his watch, then tapped Loomis, who had his radio handset pressed to his ear while watching the rear.

Loomis gave an exaggerated nod. "Choppers are on the way," he said without turning around.

Back in the killing zone, Fass and Estlin took turns moving back to the dike. One would move a few yards at a time while the other covered his move.

It was nearing two o'clock when the team finally got stretched out in march order to move first to the objective rally point and then on to the pickup zone to meet their chopper. Hollister felt uncomfortable with the swamp, his fatigue, the anticipation of the complex needs of a night extraction, and a nagging sense that things were going too well.

Pulling off an ambush was difficult enough. But pulling one off without having to fire a single weapon and without taking friendly casualties or giving away your position was an incredible success. He tried to convince himself he was just rusty, and he would soon be back into the swing of Ranger operations—ready to deal with the realities.

The move to the rally point was filled with tension for each man, and nothing could make them more alert or more ready.

Hollister held up the patrol and went forward to the point again. He took Estlin and moved forward under the watch of the other four, ready to support them with well-aimed fire in the event of contact.

Hollister and Estlin picked their way through the marshy swamp, avoiding thorny branches reaching out for them.

Estlin reached a break in the brush and stopped. He waved Hollister forward without taking his eyes off the black hole that would be their rally point.

Hollister moved past Estlin and around the wall formed by the thicket. He held up long enough to listen and to allow his eyes to adjust to the darker interior.

Once Hollister was satisfied there was no obvious danger, he waved the others forward while he and Estlin covered their move.

It took another twenty minutes to close on the rally point where they would make the final arrangements for pickup. The team set up a hasty perimeter and readied themselves to defend it.

Hollister, Fass, and Loomis found a place where they could stand less than waist deep in the water and huddled under Loomis's poncho for a map check and to make a radio call to Captain Browning.

The map confirmed Hollister's estimate of their position and the location of their pickup zone. Like the insert, the PZ was another wide spot on the dirt roadway cut through the swamp. The distance was less than three hundred meters, and the ground between them and the roadway was marshy.

"What's the last we heard from base?"

Loomis leaned closer to Hollister and whispered, "They rogered our request for extraction. Captain Browning said he'd call when they get in the C & C."

"Tell 'em we're two-zero minutes away from the Papa Zulu."

Loomis nodded and cupped the mouthpiece on his handset to transmit the message.

Hollister tapped Fass. "This is where things start to go to shit. Everyone's tired, and they feel they're close to the pickup—that combination's real bad."

"What do you want me to do?"

"Talk to the others and make sure they stay alert. I'm not satisfied we weren't seen or followed. I want to be ready if there's shit in the wind."

"Roger that," Fass said.

"Go to it now and send me Estlin."

"Sir?" Loomis said, grabbing Hollister's elbow. "Cap'n B rogered yours. They're lifting off now. He says he'll call twenty-five minutes out."

"Okay, pass the word."

Fass ducked out from under the poncho; Estlin took his place.

"We're only going to have to make it, say three hundred meters, on a compass heading of one hundred degrees. But I want to offset so we can hit the right spot and not spend all morning looking for the LZ. So set your compass for a hundred and twenty, and we'll work our way back left when we find the road."

Estlin set the indicator line on his compass bezel and turned it for Hollister to look at it. Hollister nodded and said, "Get ready. We'll be moving out shortly."

Hollister strained to see the weather between them and the Ranger base. He watched the sky for winds aloft. The skimpy cloud cover seemed to be taking the good weather toward the choppers.

He had a nagging sensation something was not right. He pulled out his binoculars and made a slow sweep of the marshy area around them. As soon as he put the glasses to his face, he saw they had finally become a casualty of the patrol. Water floated in the bottom quarter of each lens barrel. It didn't completely obscure his view, just the bottom part. They would not be much use to him in a day or two unless he got them fixed or replaced. Water in binos in Vietnam was soon followed by mold and other growth that took over the insides.

Hollister checked his watch again. He knew he would be hearing from the C & C any minute. He was anxious to move, and reached over to Estlin. "Move out in five."

Knowing he had been through plenty of water, Hollister wondered what kind of shape his ammo was in. He was sure the magazine in his rifle was waterlogged, but that didn't mean it wouldn't fire. Just to be on the safe side, he fished around in his rucksack, pulled out a new magazine, and replaced the wet one.

He turned the old magazine upside down and whipped it in an arc. The centrifugal force sent a spray of moisture out of the magazine. He decided not to put any trust in the wet ammo and tucked the magazine into a side pocket of his rucksack.

Estlin took up the point, and Hollister moved in behind him—in the slack-man position. Loomis, then Meadows, Fass, and Thomas followed.

Hollister turned to Loomis and whispered, "Stay awake. We're not home yet."

Loomis nodded and passed it back.

The first few steps were into a deeper part of the swamp. Each man held his weapon over his head to keep it out of the water.

Loomis pointed up and back toward Bien Hoa. "C & C, 'n' the slicks are two-five out."

The swamp bottom got a little easier to walk on as the water table dropped, and they found themselves threading through tangled vegetation that limited their visibility to five meters in any direction.

After another ten minutes, Hollister called a halt to listen to the swamp. He knew once chopper noises filled the air, it would be too late to try to listen for anything.

No one moved. They knew what Hollister was doing, and froze.

The only sounds were those of the night and the plopping of water dripping from trees, falling back into the foul-smelling marsh. Hearing nothing else, Hollister signaled for Estlin to move out.

Just before they reached the roadway, Hollister heard the choppers. He slipped back and took the radio handset from Loomis. "Campus Killer Five, this is Six."

He heard chopper noise over the helmet mike before he heard Browning's voice. "Six, this is Five. We're less than five out. The guns should be 'bout breakin' over your heads about now."

Hollister looked up. "Stand by."

In less than a few heartbeats, the first Cobra screamed over the team's position at full crank and then spiraled up and back to the east.

"They're on station and over my head right now."

"We're going to pull up into a circle north of you and wait for your word to pick up," Browning said.

"Shouldn't be too long. Stand by."

Hollister looked up at Estlin. He didn't want the choppers circling any longer than they had to. He waved for Estlin to move.

The team moved out again and moved less than seventy-five meters when Estlin raised his hand to hold them up.

Hollister quickly moved forward alongside the bent-over Estlin.

Up ahead, not more than forty feet, was the roadway, rising ten feet out of the swamp.

The two dropped to their hands and knees to crawl up the slope. At the top, they found a flat, one-lane dirt roadway. They quickly looked to the right for any sign of trouble and then continued moving to the left to the pickup point.

A hundred meters, and Hollister held them up again. He had found it. The wide spot—marked by a large gash on one side of the roadway where the unused part had been eroded over time. He was sure. It was their PZ. He motioned to Estlin, and they slid down the bank, back into the armpit-deep swamp. He looked back toward the remainder of the patrol. He pulled his flashlight from his web gear and partially covered the lens. Pressing the button on the switch, he sent two quick slivers of red light to them.

Fass got the other four to their feet, and they moved out toward Hollister and Estlin. They set up on the west side of the road's slope and waited for the choppers. Hollister posted Thomas and Estlin down in the swamp to watch their backs while the others faced up, down, and across the roadway.

* * *

The radio crackled. "Okay, Six, your ride is inbound. He'll call short final. You ready?" Browning asked over the radio.

Hollister answered quickly, "Roger that. We're at the edge of the PZ. Do you need a mark?"

"Stand by one," Browning said.

Hollister clicked the switch twice to acknowledge Browning.

"Six. This is Five. We could use a small mark on short final."

"Roger," Hollister said. "Holler, and I'll give him a mark."

Hollister felt the muscles tighten across his chest as he looked around at the others. He hated the last few minutes before an extraction. He knew within moments he would be out in the middle of the roadway, exposed to any enemy fire and out of control of the situation.

Hollister looked back up the slope—twice his height. It was steep. And the chopper downwash would make it much more difficult for them to climb up to the roadway and then climb up into the bird with any speed at all.

"Let us have it, Six," Browning said.

The nose of the chopper broke over the trees at the turn in the roadway. Hollister gave the pilot three quick flashes of his flashlight.

"I got it," the pilot said.

Hollister recognized Chief Moody's voice.

The chopper slipped to line up with the roadway and dropped the skids down into the slot between the trees, blades overlapping them.

Hollister yelled over the chopper noise, "Estlin, Thomas—let's go!" He wanted to give them a head start.

The chopper reached a point where the trees were just wider than the rotor disk, and Moody yanked up on the nose, slowing and settling onto the roadway.

The Rangers began their climb up to the chopper even before it was on the ground.

The chopper touched down and slid forward ten feet before stopping.

Hollister helped Loomis, Fass, and Meadows into the chopper, looked back down the slope, and saw Thomas leading Estlin up out of the swamp.

Thomas reached the top first.

Hollister turned to reach out to help Estlin and saw Estlin's eyes widen in surprise as his forward momentum stopped and he was somehow spun around. Hollister was suddenly conscious of a green line crossing between them.

"Fuck! We're taking fire!" Hollister yelled as Estlin twisted from the impact of enemy rifle fire and fell back down the slope.

Hollister had dropped his ruck onto the cargo deck and turned to go after Estlin when Thomas hurled himself out of the chopper, taking a roll as he went down the slope in one somersault—hitting the water just a fraction of a second after Estlin did.

CHAPTER 14

Hollister stepped up on the left skid and yelled into the small chopper window, "I got a man hit. Hold what you got!"

The face in the helmet was Chief Moody's. "Make it fast. They're up in front of us."

Just then, a short burst of tracer fire ripped from the tree line and slashed diagonally across the road, missing Hollister and the chopper by a few feet.

Hollister looked back for Thomas and Estlin. Reaching into the chopper, he grabbed the handset from Loomis. "Five. Six. We have contact. Taking fire! One man hit. Where are the guns?"

"Guns should be rolling in—coming up the road behind you," Browning answered.

A Cobra screamed across the top of the waiting slick and began a minigun firing run. The first rounds spewed from the rotating Gatling gun on the nose of the gunship just as its skids passed overhead. Shell cartridges rained down on Hollister and the pickup ship.

Hollister spotted the first red tracer lines abruptly stopping as each round augered into the roadway. The Cobra gunner wiggled the gun slightly left and right, making the red hose of minigun fire snake into the trees on both sides of the trail.

Reaching the end of his run, the lead gunship jerked up—out of its firing run, into a tight orbit to line up for another pass.

Hollister yelled a correction into the handset. "Add ten meters, lean on the right side of the road!" He spun back around to look for Thomas and Estlin again just in time to catch sight of Thomas powering up the slope, carrying Estlin over his shoulders.

"Hold on," Hollister yelled to Moody in the waiting slick as the second Cobra passed over, making the adjustments from the first gunship's run.

Dropping the handset, Hollister took a large leap from the roadway, landing on his heels halfway down the slope.

He reached out for Thomas to help him carry the wounded point man up the incline, but only got a handful of the slime that covered both of them. So he reached down and grabbed Thomas's pistol belt and pulled up to help him overcome the muscle-burning demands on his legs to climb the slope with Estlin over his shoulder.

Two more slashes of enemy tracers slipped between them and the chopper. The trio reached the side of the bird as the first gunship made another run in front of the pickup chopper.

Thomas dropped Estlin onto the deck of the chopper and crawled in with Hollister pushing and Loomis pulling.

Hollister grabbed for the seat rail to help himself up and in just as another short burst of enemy fire sliced down the narrow space between the side of the chopper and the tree line, hitting the front sight blade of one of the door guns. He counted heads and yelled, "Go! Go! Go!"

Moody jerked some pitch into the blades and rolled the chopper forward just before its skids cleared the ground completely. As he did, Hollister, Loomis and Thomas trained their weapons out the door to fire on the spot the enemy fire was coming from as they passed over it.

But before they got even a few feet off the ground, they heard a frightening thunking sound up front. The chopper jerked first left then right, and a few enemy tracer rounds came over the console between the pilots and slammed into the transmission behind the Rangers.

The chopper lost momentum and altitude. The thought of going down flashed through Hollister's mind, and he instinctively began to look for somewhere to jump.

He tried to figure out where they were. The enemy fire coming through the front of the chopper had distracted him from his reference point on the tree line and he had no idea where the enemy might be. The last thing he wanted was to bail out of a falling chopper into the source of fire bringing down the chopper.

The chopper continued to drift off to the left.

Hollister could see a large tree in their path. He knew if the pilot didn't get some altitude they would hit it.

The chopper yawed to the right, picked up a few feet of altitude—putting it barely fifteen feet off the ground—and struck the upper part of the tree.

The blade strike caused the chopper to jerk wildly. The sounds of the gunships firing behind them gave Hollister some confidence they had passed over the enemy position, and they might be out of range.

The crippled chopper began to shake violently. The passengers and crew were being jerked in a rhythmic pattern—so hard the Rangers grabbed for their weapons to keep from losing their grip on them.

Hollister looked up to the instrument panel. There was no help there. The instruments were jerking so wildly they were useless. Then Hollister remembered Estlin. He held firmly to the seat rail with one hand and reached over and grabbed Meadows, who was trying to stay on his hands and knees while working on Estlin.

"He'll make it back to Bien Hoa. Will we?" Meadows said.

Hollister grabbed the handset from Loomis and tried to keep from slapping himself in the face with the mouthpiece jerking in his hand. "Five. Six."

"Hold on Six," a voice said. "I've got most of my radios shot out. I need this Fox Mike."

Hollister realized it was Moody's voice. "Go ahead, Chief."

Giving the frequency to the pilot, Hollister caught part of Moody's transmission to Captain Dale Tennant, who was flying the C & C chopper. ". . . fucked up my pedals and put my ass into a tree." His voice was choppy. The helicopter was still flying, though not gaining much altitude. "Pretty bad blade strike. Gonna put it down the first spot I can find. You got me?"

"We're on you, Chief. The chase is a hundred behind and a hundred above you. Just give him a place to get in near you," Tennant replied.

"Rog," was Moody's only response.

Hollister saw him roll off RPM with his left hand on the collective. As he did, the violent shuddering seemed to ease up, but the chopper slowed its forward airspeed and began to sink. At the same time the master caution and the RPM limit lights came on on the instrument panel.

The copilot turned and waved his hand to get Hollister's attention and then pointed to his lip mike to let him know Hollister could use the FM radio.

"Five. Six. I've got one Whiskey India Alpha, but it looks like we're putting this ship down and will have to move to the chase. You picking up the crew or what?"

"This is Five. Front seat says he'll take the crew, and DeSantis will pick your element up with the chase. How's your WIA?"

"Don't know. Doc says he'll make the trip."

The chopper flew a long slow right turn over the trees to the margin of the swamp. Hollister looked out again. If they could just fly another thousand meters, the chopper could put down in any one of three rice fields surrounding the marsh.

Hollister looked back at Meadows for a sign. He was still hunched over Estlin, putting a field dressing on Estlin's wound just below his rib cage. He looked up and caught Hollister's questioning eye and gave an exaggerated nod.

"Okay, listen up!" Hollister yelled. "We're putting down, and we'll be picked up by the chase. Meadows, you and Thomas take care of getting Estlin to the chase. Fass, you get his ruck, and Loomis—his rifle, leave the captured weapons."

The chopper lost more altitude and became more erratic. It seemed as if there was a problem with the tail rotor, since the craft kept yawing left and then right and then left again.

The sun broke the horizon as Moody lined the chopper up for a fallow field four hundred meters from the swamp. His control improved and then degraded and then improved again as they got closer to touching down.

Hollister looked out. Easy was in the C & C. The C & C was behind the chase and above it, and the two Cobras were circling the landing zone Moody had picked.

Hollister scanned the nearest tree lines for any sign of enemy activity or fire. Seeing none, he looked out toward the roads. The traffic on the highways was always a good indicator of what the civilians thought the threat was. A well-traveled roadway suddenly void of traffic was a bad sign.

The road nearest the emergency landing zone had little traffic on it—but it had some. That didn't tell Hollister much. They could just be avoiding the area because of all the American choppers and the gunships orbiting. It could also be a good indication they knew the VC were waiting in the nearby tree lines.

As Moody's chopper began to settle, it started to buck and jerk more wildly. Every man in the chopper hoped Moody could hold it together long enough to put the wounded bird on the ground, and they would take it from there.

Just at the moment the chopper reached the weed-covered paddy field, it leveled out and made one of the sweetest landings Hollister had experienced. There was only time to say a silent thank-you as they vaulted from the chopper.

Hollister turned to catch Moody getting out of his seat, the chopper blades still turning.

Moody hit the ground, looked up at the slowing blades, and shook his head. "Amazing machine," he yelled to Hollister, who stepped back far enough to see most of the chin bubble in front of Moody's seat was missing and the right pedal was shot off at floor height. Hollister was equally amazed Moody had survived and had been able to land the chopper.

Moody shrugged and smiled, then pointed off to the rear—to the C & C. "Better get going. There's my ride."

The flight back to Bien Hoa was beautiful in contrast to the moments of near disaster just passed. Hollister had found a dry pack of cigarettes, which he passed around the chopper.

He worked his way over to Estlin's side and lit one for him. "How ya feeling, Ranger?"

"I never saw the bus that hit me."

"You hurting?" Hollister asked, looking for a sign from Meadows.

Meadows shook his head, reassuring Hollister that Estlin was still holding his own.

"I'll hang in there. You gonna give me a couple a days off?"

Hollister smiled at Estlin. "Yeah. But when you get back, I want you to brush up on your landings. That was the worst tumble I ever saw a jumper take."

Estlin laughed and then coughed at the cigarette smoke. "Shit, I'm just glad the fucking water was at the bottom or I really woulda busted my ass."

The last part of the flight to the hospital was bone-chilling for Hollister and the others. They had been so wet for so long, the evaporating, stagnant water dropped their temperatures enough to make them shiver even in the Asian morning warmth.

The C & C landed first. Moody got out and walked to the

hospital entrance. Then the chase replaced the C & C, which took off, leaving Captain Browning on the pad.

Meadows and Loomis lifted Estlin onto a stretcher.

"What's with Chief Moody?" Hollister asked Browning.

"He's wounded."

"Wounded? He didn't let on."

"Looks like he caught some frags."

Inside the clearing station, medics had already stripped Estlin and Moody and put them on tables for treatment. Easy was at the desk, taking care of the paperwork on the wounded Ranger.

Moody was alone, a small lime drape covering his crotch. Estlin was surrounded by a doctor, a nurse, and two medics. Hollister decided to let them work on Estlin without interrupting them. He moved to the far side of Moody's stretcher.

As he did, Hollister could see the multiple puncture wounds up Moody's side and up under his right armpit. The wounds were all small, but some had pieces of metal and scraps of Nomex flight suit material sticking from them.

"How ya doin'?" Moody asked, grinning.

"Why didn't you tell me you'd been hit?"

"Wasn't real sure myself. Then, when I was sure, I didn't see anything anyone could do. So I just sucked it up and waited 'til we got back here."

"How could you have that much crap in you and not know?"

"I'll tell you, when the fucking chin bubble came loose and flew around in front of me, I started pumping adrenaline and hoping I didn't shit in my flight suit. Then when we hit the fucking tree, I figured I was going to put it into the swamp. Then, when the fucker kept flying like it had four flat tires and a busted clutch—I was really freaked. I guess I was a little too busy to worry about it. I just wanted to get the crate on the ground in one piece."

"Well, you did one hell of a job, Chief," Hollister said, taking his hand to thank him and congratulate him.

"Glad to be of help, sir."

Hollister walked around the Quonset hut to make eye contact with Estlin. He gave the Ranger a big smile. "How you doing?"

Estlin looked up at the nurse who was trying to wipe the grime away from his wound with a large gauze swab soaked in surgical soap. "Great, now. Beats layin' up in the ambush site."

Estlin spoke rapidly, the saliva in his mouth drying out, making it difficult for him to speak. Hollister knew the feeling well. Fear, a sense of real vulnerability, and anxiety over what would come next. Still Estlin tried to show Hollister he was calm.

"You going to be okay if we leave you here? They ought to be able to take care of what ails you and get you back to duty soon," Hollister said, trying to diminish the seriousness of the wound to cheer up Estlin.

"Oh, I'll be okay. I have a feeling this is going to get me a week or two of ghost time. I can lay up in clean sheets and eat hot chow."

"Jesus, you guys smell like shit," the doctor said from behind his mask. "What have you been in?"

"A place you'll never understand," Hollister said, surprising himself with his own hostility.

The doctor shot Hollister an angry look.

Hollister looked at the doctor's starched fatigues. "You spend a couple of days lying in a fucking swamp full of shit and see how fresh you smell, Doc."

"You've got a pretty big mouth for a—" He looked for some sign of rank on Hollister's grubby uniform.

Hollister let him search without giving him the satisfaction of identifying himself. "How long you been in the army, Doctor?"

"Twenty months. Why?" the doctor asked, getting angrier.

"Some of us have more time in the chow line."

"What's your name, soldier?" the doctor asked, pointing a surgical instrument at Hollister.

"It's Hollister, two *l*s. You want a piece of my ass, you can find me at the Ranger compound."

"I'll just do that. Your commander is going to hear about your sorry attitude, mister."

"You sure got a way with doctors, Cap'n," Easy said as they walked down the path to the jeep sent to pick them up.

"The fucker pissed me off. He lives in an air-conditioned hootch, wears clean fatigues every day, gets all the class A rations and Stateside booze he wants, and Estlin's smell offends him."

Easy smiled. "You know, if it wasn't for folks like that, we'd have nobody to compare Rangers to. We'd have nobody to talk shit about."

Hollister had to laugh at Easy. "Top, that's the worst defense of a fat rat I've ever heard."

"Well, give me a little time, and I'll come up with something better," Easy said, his broad grin unflagging as he awkwardly backed into the jeep, raising his prosthetic leg over the side.

It was almost two A.M. when Easy stuck his head in the doorway to Hollister's office. "They said they're sending Estlin to the Philippines for a month to heal up. Seems there's no permanent damage."

"Great," Hollister said. "How's Chief Moody?"

"They just finished pickin' all the shit out of him, and they're going to release him tomorrow. He's going to be grounded for at least two weeks."

"You know, I'd heard so much bad shit about what has been going on over here, I was really afraid the Rangers might have gone sour too. But you should have seen this bunch out there. They were good, not great—that'd take some more training. But they never laid down on me."

"So you're feeling better about Juliet Company?"

"Yeah. But we need practice for every swinging dick in this company before we can send them out there."

"I gotcha," Easy said with a wink. "What's next?"

"First, I want some awards recommendation forms for Moody and Thomas and Moody's copilot. They all deserve a piece of colored ribbon. Then, I get some sleep. I couldn't be more tired if you kicked me in the head."

CHAPTER 15

Jrae didn't need to be told there was something wrong. She felt a dark weight.

It was an hour before dawn. The coughing of Montagnards and the distant crowing of an early cock were the only sounds. She sat up, spun on the long axis of her hammock, and reached out for the hard-packed earth with her toes.

In the darkness, all she could make out across the compound was the glow of a cigarette at a point too far from where Krong's hammock normally hung. The hillside behind the structure offered no contrast for Jrae to make out Krong in the blackness cloaking them before dawn.

Jrae decided to use the time before the sun broke the horizon to bathe at the communal water point. Wandering into the men's building that early would be disruptive and might embarrass Krong.

Other women had already gathered to bathe. Washing the dust from the resettlement compound off and cleaning the wood-smoke smell from their hair was a small pleasure.

Jrae wrapped a simple pak cloth around herself and tucked the top in over her left breast. She tightened her stomach muscles to ward off the urge to shiver as water evaporated from her skin.

She found her comb parted in her hair. Krong had made it from the beak of a large bird when she was only five years old. Her mother had used it to comb the lice and small insects out of her hair. When she was older, she used it to help wash out her hair and comb it dry in the midday sun.

She let the morning breeze finish drying her off and gathered

up the few toiletries she had collected in a salvaged one-pound
coffee can she got from Beck's office.

She knew why the other men were approaching her as she walked
from the bath to find Krong. They didn't need to tell her he was
already on his way to the Underworld.

She followed them back to Krong's hammock. He had died in
his sleep, and he looked like an old man still locked in the grip of a
dream. The leathered brown skin and platinum hair all seemed to
have been washed by something that had pulled the richness of his
colors from him and left a pale old man behind. The light green,
cast-off uniform trousers he had been given by the Vietnamese
showed a large dark stain where urine had left his body and puddled
under the hammock.

Two Vietnamese soldiers began yelling over one another as
they disagreed on what needed to be done with the body.

Jrae waited until they tired of arguing and wandered away to
the small headquarters building where the Vietnamese spent most
of their time.

She found a spot in the shade near his hammock to squat and
look at Krong for the last time. He had seemed so large and strong
to her when she was a girl and he was village chief. But his
remains showed the toll the years had taken on him. His fingers
were at once callused and slender. Gone was the sense of power
his hands once projected.

Much of how he looked in death had come on since leaving
Yoon Dlei. She realized she had not really seen how frail he had
become—how old he had grown.

His death marked the loss of the last immediate member of her
family; assuming her brother, Pek, had died in captivity.

Jackie Beck reminded her the Vietnamese were the hosts at the
relocation camp and not the Americans. The fact that they had
refused to take Krong's body back to Yoon Dlei for burial was
their decision. It would be a loss of face for the Vietnamese if he—
an American—insisted. At that moment, she made herself a
promise to find some way of moving Krong's body to the ances-
tral burial grounds—someday.

"What will happen to me now?" Jrae asked.

"Now that what?" Jackie replied.

"Now I not have family here."

"You don't have family here," Jackie corrected.

"Can I stay?"

"Don't you want to?"

"I don't know. You pay me here."

Jackie tapped a strange-looking chart on the wall behind his desk. It was numbered boxes with *X*s in them. "I'm gettin' mighty short here. Be outta here in less than two months."

"You go?" Jrae asked, surprised by his announcement.

"You bet. I'm not planning on spending my life here."

Jrae showed her alarm at the announcement. Jackie Beck had been the only person she had met since leaving her village who had treated her decently.

"Maybe we need to find a new home for you?"

"A home?" Jrae said, confused by the reference.

"No, honey. I mean a new place for you to work—and I guess—live there, too."

Jrae searched his face for some expression of enthusiasm for such a change.

Beck made an *X* on the day's box on his short-timer's calendar and smiled at her. "Don't you worry. I'll talk to the group sergeant major. He'll know of a good place for you."

"Some of the troops thought they'd head out for a little exercise. Would the captain be interested in joining them?"

Hollister woke up, his head on some papers. He had fallen asleep at his desk. Easy was standing in the doorway.

"Shit! What time is it?" Hollister asked as he tried to focus on his wristwatch.

"Zero dark hundred hours," Easy said. "They'll be formin' up in one-five."

"Any coffee around here yet?"

Easy turned to the outer office and pointed at a soldier standing out of Hollister's view, a cup of hot coffee in his hand. "Give it to the CO, son."

The soldier slipped in, put the coffee down, and stepped out as quickly as he had entered.

Hollister stretched, looked at the papers on his desk, and shook his head. "I'm never going to forgive you for forgetting to tell me about all this crap when you were encouraging me to stay in the army, Top."

"I was thinking some chickenshit paperwork wouldn't faze an

authentic Airborne-Ranger, Special Forces, combat-experienced, master parachutist like the captain. So I just didn't mention it."

Raising the coffee to his lips, Hollister blew across the top, then took a sip. He made a face and then checked his watch again. "This shit is strong enough to walk on. And I'm going to be late, and it won't get you off the hook."

The morning run didn't do much to invigorate Hollister. He was conscious of his fatigue and the pain in his hip. He had promised himself to work it out by making all the PT formations. But doing it was more painful than he expected.

He tried to get a sense of the Rangers. They just didn't have the same attitude or esprit de corps his first LRP detachment or the original J Company had. He knew what made them different from the earlier Rangers was attitude. Training would help, and training was essential. But their attitude would come out of feeling special and being special. It was up to him. It would mean he would have to tighten the screws, weed out the losers, and recruit some hard chargers.

The calisthenics were no easier for Hollister's bad leg. Still, he forced himself to do all the exercises and not favor his leg.

At the end of PT, there was very little chatter or grab ass. A sure sign of low morale. Easy announced chow call. Hollister considered breakfast, thought he might pass, and then realized he would have to fight his habit of not eating enough to stay healthy.

Thomas, Browning, Easy, and Hollister huddled in a corner of the mess hall over trays of greasy eggs, toast, sausages, and reconstituted milk.

"Top, get the mess sergeant on this shit," Hollister said, pointing his fork at his food. "This won't cut it."

The first sergeant nodded. "I could use some better chow myself."

"It's not for you, Top," Browning said.

"It never is, Cap'n. It never is. A first sergeant's life is a hard one."

The officers all looked at Easy in mock pity.

"Okay, okay. Don't worry about me. I'll get along fine. I'm used to the sacrifices senior NCOs have to make to do their jobs."

Thomas rolled his eyes.

They all laughed, breaking some of the tension.

"Okay," Hollister said. "Enough grab ass. We've got some serious work to do, and we're already late."

The others calmed down, and the two captains pulled out notebooks.

Hollister looked at Browning. "I want you to call the aviation battalion and see if we can have Mister Moody assigned to us while he's on the mend. He's a terrific slick driver, and I'd like to have him give our troops some of his experience."

"Borrowin' a body from the slick drivers is going to be tough," Browning said.

"He's grounded anyway. If we don't rescue him, he'll be stuck with doing shitty little details around his outfit. So, let's set up a room for him over at the BOQ and make him feel at home."

Hollister took a long sip of his coffee and then pulled out his own notebook. He looked up at Thomas.

Thomas nodded. "Where do we start?"

"I want to see the training schedule you've got worked out now, and we'll see how we can pack it."

"It's pretty tight now."

"It's gonna be one hell of a lot tighter. Training is life insurance. Can't have too much of it."

No one argued with Hollister.

He decided to sign the morning report first because it had to get over to field force, and then proofread the awards recommendations for Moody and the others.

Easy walked in and dropped two letters, two bills, and a copy of the field force daily bulletin on Hollister's desk.

"Thought you might like to see how the headquarters pukes are living." Easy pointed out a paragraph in the daily bulletin announcing the swimming pool would be closed for two days for repairs.

"Too bad," Hollister said sarcastically. "You suppose there'll be something else for them to do?"

"Ah, yes, sir. They're adding on extra weekend passes to Vung Tau for the troops to hit the beaches. That's on the next page."

"Wouldn't want them to lose their tans."

The two of them laughed, and Easy turned to walk out.

"Top, you did a good job out there picking us up yesterday."

"Nothing to it, sir."

"How's that leg?"

Easy smiled. "It's gone. Didn't I tell you?"

"If you are going to be a smart-ass, I'm not going to ask."

"You don't have to worry about me. You got enough to worry about."

"Thanks, Top," was all Hollister could think to say to him. But he meant *Thanks for being there for me for all these years. Thanks for making me understand what soldiering is about. Thanks for caring so much and making it look so easy. Thanks for being the kind of NCO who makes it all work.*

"No sweat, sir."

The morning report signed, the awards recommendations finished, and another cup of coffee later, Easy interrupted.

"Cap'n?"

Hollister looked up and saw Easy standing in the doorway, again.

"There's a doctor here who wants to see the CO. And he's not happy."

Hollister could guess who the doctor was. "Send him in."

The doctor came through the door talking. "My name's Captain Plummer, and I . . ."

"No. Your *name* is Plummer, and your *rank* is captain," Hollister said calmly, enjoying the surprise on Plummer's face.

"What are you doing here?"

"I'm the CO around this lash-up. Hollister's still my name. Now pull up a chair and let's have a talk, Doctor."

"Listen, you son of a—"

Hollister raised his hands to calm him. "Wait a sec." He turned and yelled out the doorway, "Top, can you get the doctor and me some coffee? I'm sure the doctor takes it black."

He turned back to Plummer. "Now let's get off on the right foot. *Good morning, Doctor.*"

"You are the most arrogant, the most self-important, the most, ah, ah . . ."

"I'm all those things. And if I'm not, I'm the wrong guy to command a Ranger Company. You know anything about a Ranger Company, Doctor Plummer?"

"Well, I, ah, think I remember something about them from a briefing I had at Fort Sam Houston."

"The only Rangers you find at Fort Sam were medevacked. I doubt if any of them were in any shape to give you a briefing.

"You ever talk to a Ranger? Got any real idea what they do every fucking night in this shithole? You ever seen a Ranger who is overweight? Sloppy? A druggie? A problem child? I don't think so," Hollister asked and answered his own questions.

A runner from the mess hall brought in the two cups of coffee and placed them between the two captains and left.

"Well, it's not important. What is important is I am particularly pissed off at the crap you gave me yesterday."

"You don't know much about leadership, do you? It runs off of loyalty and looking out for the troops. You fuck with my Rangers, and I'll tear your head off and shit down your neck. That's what they expect of me, and that's what they get. That boy didn't need you bad-mouthing him while he lay there scared shitless of what you were going to tell him about his wounds."

"But you insulted *me*, and I want to let your commanding officer know it."

"Good. I'm sure he'd be thrilled to hear all about it. You do know my boss, don't you? The field force commanding general?"

"He's your boss?"

"Sure is. So you better give his aide a call; get on his calendar. But before you do, why don't you come with me?"

"Where?" Plummer watched, puzzled, while Hollister stood and put his shirt on. He seemed to be quietly impressed with the credentials sewn on Hollister's fatigue shirt. Even at the Medical Field Service School, Plummer learned to recognize master parachutist's wings, the Ranger tab, the jungle warfare patch, and the pathfinder patch sewn on Hollister's shirt. Hollister topped off his ensemble with his Ranger black beret, centering his shiny captain's bars over his left eye.

Plummer put on his stupid-looking, GI-issue baseball hat with the duck-billed brim that made any soldier look less like one.

Hollister took Plummer across the company street to the first team hootch—Team 3-1's. "You working today, Doctor?"

"Working?"

"Yeah, whatever you call it. Do you have to be back at the clearing station right away?"

"No. I'm off 'til noon tomorrow. We work shifts."

"Good."

They entered the hootch, and six Rangers and their platoon sergeant snapped to attention.

The sergeant spoke up without waiting. "Good morning, sirs. Platoon Sergeant DeSantis. Can I be of some assistance?"

"Please, carry on," Hollister said. "This is Doctor Plummer. He patched up Estlin and Chief Moody yesterday, and he wanted to come by here to see what Rangers are all about."

Smiles suddenly appeared on the camouflaged faces of the team and DeSantis.

"Estlin gonna be okay, Doc?" one of the Rangers asked.

Plummer was almost speechless. Every Ranger was in full combat gear with camouflage, weapons, and equipment. It was new to him. He had only seen Rangers stripped of their gear, nearly naked, bleeding, or dying. "Ah, yeah. Yes, he'll be fine. Couple of weeks of mending, and he'll be good as new."

"Tell Doctor Plummer what you all are doing today," Hollister said to DeSantis.

"Sir, this is Sergeant Iverson. He's the team leader of Team 3-1. His team is preparing for a full day of training on immediate-action drills, McGuire rigs, and first aid." He turned to Iverson. "Tell the captain what you've got planned."

"We'll alternate the physical stuff with the sit-on-your-ass stuff so we can get a full day in. But everything we do, we do in full gear—ready for hunting bear. We'll start with immediate-action drills, and when the chopper gets here, we'll practice string rides."

Doctor Plummer looked at the young sergeant, puzzled as much by what he was talking about as what he looked like. "What's in your hair?"

"Kiwi."

"Kiwi?"

"Yes, sir. Shoe polish. All us Iversons are towheads. You can see my hair for two thousand meters in the bush if I don't knock it down with shoe polish. It's not pretty. But I'm still around at the end of a patrol."

The others laughed at the baby-faced sergeant, clumps of shoe polish stuck to the blond stubble on his head.

"String rides?" the doctor asked.

Hollister interrupted. "How'd you like to see just what it is they do and how they get ready?"

"That'd be great, Doc," Iverson said.

The others agreed and tried to encourage an affirmative answer out of the surgeon.

"Ah, okay. I guess I can do that."

Hollister and DeSantis made eye contact, and DeSantis figured out what Hollister was up to. "We'll take good care of you."

"Great," Hollister said. "I'll leave you with these young men, Doc, and check in on you a little later."

Entering the headquarters atmosphere at Long Binh had never been a pleasant experience for Hollister. He always felt as if he was surrounded by people who knew very little about what he did and what his people needed. They seemed to be caught up in their own little world of headquarters politics and headquarters mentality.

"Good morning, Ranger," Lieutenant Colonel Michaelson's voice boomed out. "What brings you out of the snake pit?"

"I got word there was a meeting needing my presence," Hollister kidded. "How ya doing, sir?"

"Better than you, I understand. You took a little fire out there on ambush?"

"Yeah. A little. But we got away without any real serious damage. My WIAs are going to be okay."

"I'm already hearing the whining from the aviation section. If you left it to them, they'd only take the choppers out when the weather was good and the VC were sleeping."

"I'll try to stay away from Colonel Reed."

"I heard that," Reed, the aviation officer, said, entering the staff section.

"Sorry about the scratches we put on your chopper," Hollister said.

"Scratches?" Reed said, mocking Hollister's words. "We damn near had to peel that one off its skids and mount a whole new chopper on top of 'em."

"They just don't make choppers like they used to," Hollister said.

"You keep dinging them up, and you'll be walking to work, young captain," Reed replied with a smile.

"I'll try to remember that, sir."

"Well, we have a meeting in the conference room, folks," Michaelson said as he waved toward the door.

The briefing room was filled with representatives from every staff section and command to hear the first comments of the newly assigned deputy commanding general, William J. Quinn.

After Colonel Terry introduced him, Quinn took the podium.

"Thank you. Gentlemen, it's a pleasure to be here. There are fewer and fewer jobs over here for a buck brigadier, and most of them are shitty."

The general's comment drew a laugh from the room.

He furrowed his brow and took on a more serious tone. "We have got a tough job ahead of us over here, even though the world is acting like we're packing up and pulling out in mass numbers.

"We've turned the corner from our highest troop strength, but the other side is still pouring troops into South Vietnam.

"Our biggest problem? Saigon. While the Americans draw down and the South Vietnamese take to the countryside, there is more and more concern about the safety of the capital. It would be a really tough break if we had another Tet-like invasion with more success than last time. So we have to guard against the complacency that comes with a *going home* attitude, and we have to take the fight to the enemy. Enemy forces have regained their footing in a large number of villages and hamlets, and they're operating freely at night in even more.

"Over the past ten months, our grip on the western provinces has slipped. We have to go where he lives and take back the night from its new owners."

General Quinn smiled, changed his serious tone, and tried to make eye contact with his audience.

"With the changes going on, I think I can get out of this headquarters enough to visit each of you in the field and often. I want you to lean on me for what you need."

CHAPTER 16

"New missions," Michaelson said.

"New?" Hollister asked.

"New to you guys. We haven't spent any time targeting the other side of the fence. Sure, we've sent teams into Cambodia on occasion and for very specific reasons.

"We used to be able to interdict much of the reinforcements and the resupplies as they tried to work their way through the Twenty-fifth Division, the One Ninety-ninth Brigade, and parts of the Big Red One. Things are different with the drawdown. So we're going to try to get them at the end of the trail. And if they slip through, we have time to catch them on the way to Saigon."

"That means cross-border ops?"

"Roger that. The White House is very goosey about this. Every time Nixon's taken limited incursions into Cambodia, he's taken shit from the press and public reaction. But we have to use whatever economy of force we can generate with the loss of U.S. troop strength."

"So we cross the fence."

"But you'll make life easier on all of us if you play this down. Avoid making Juliet Company a household word. If your name comes out of Cronkite's mouth, we've got problems."

"When?" Hollister asked.

"You should be getting the op plan by close of business tomorrow, and your first teams will go in in ten days."

Hollister made a face.

"You still got lots of work to do. Don't you?"

"You bet. I have training and personnel problems I might not get worked out for a month."

"You haven't got a month."

"Ten days, huh?"

"Use them wisely," Michaelson said.

"Launch site?"

"You can stage out of Tay Ninh. There's a lot of shuffling going on up there with U.S. units pulling out and ARVNs moving in. But I'm sure you can find something that will give you shorter flight time to the border. You might be there for a while."

Hollister shrugged.

"I'd get an advance party out there by tonight to get things started," Michaelson said.

"Will do."

"Oh, and you might go a little easy on the profile. Keep it as low as you can. The area will be damn near void of any American units, and the ARVNs and the few remaining advisers will be flexing their muscles," Michaelson said.

"How am I a problem?"

"You haven't worked in an all-adviser neighborhood yet. It's a world filled with Americans jealous of your job and your resources. So be warned and stay low."

"I got it. But I'll still need more blade time to shuttle the troops," Hollister said.

"Count on it. Just try not to break any more choppers."

Hollister looked at Michaelson and caught the smile on his face. He rarely kidded with Hollister, but the chopper comment was one of those moments.

"Cap'n?" Easy said as he got to his feet.

"Yeah. I'm back. What's happened while I was gone?"

"Nothing worth putting in the daily bulletin. So where we goin'?"

"Tay Ninh. Get Captain Thomas over here, and I'll give you both the details. Browning around?"

"I called him over at the motor pool when I heard you drive up. He's gonna be one unhappy XO when he finds out we're moving."

"Well, he better live with it. 'Cause we're going whether he's happy about it or not.

"We got any coffee in here?" Hollister asked, anxiously looking at his watch.

*   *   *

Browning, Thomas, the first sergeant, and Hollister spent the next two hours putting together a plan to move the company and to continue very intensive training while making the move in increments.

Hollister was most concerned about training. Browning was worried about making the move, and Thomas was concerned they might not be able to train and supervise operational needs while the company split between Bien Hoa and Tay Ninh. The war wasn't going to stop just because they were moving.

Hollister reassured Thomas that they'd set up a working company operations section in Tay Ninh before they closed down at Bien Hoa. And he calmed Browning's worries by letting him know there were extra air resources laid on to help them make the move while still remaining operational.

The first sergeant began the tedious job of determining what people and things would have to go to Tay Ninh by road—a convoy. Their cavalry troop reaction force would be the ideal security element for the convoy.

"I'll go with the advance party to get things set up right," Easy said. "Last time I let someone else do this, I lived to regret it."

"What's it mean?" Captain Thomas asked.

Easy grinned. "It means you don't have to be miserable just because you're in Vietnam."

"I'll go along with that," Captain Browning said.

"I will, too—to a degree," Hollister said, giving Easy a warning look.

Easy avoided further scrutiny by getting up and excusing himself. "I got to go put the fear of God in some young Rangers."

In only a matter of seconds he returned laughing. "Cap'n H. You got to see this. Come outside."

Hollister and the other two captains followed Easy out to the steps of the orderly room.

There, hovering over the chopper pad, was a Huey slick holding steady at three hundred feet. Dangling below the chopper on climbing ropes were two Rangers and Doctor Plummer, complete with field gear, weapon, and camouflaged hands, neck, and face.

"That's gonna be one pissed-off doctor when you get him down, Cap'n," Easy said.

"How did this happen?"

"Well, you left him with DeSantis, didn't you?"

"Shit," Hollister said, wondering what the fallout would be.

"Send someone out there to rescue him from DeSantis before we all get sent to Long Binh jail."

Hollister walked into the mess hall to get a cup of coffee and go over his notes from the morning's meeting without all the distractions of his orderly room.

"Coffee, sir?" one of the KPs asked.

Hollister looked up and saw a familiar face—Corporal Greenwood—from Fort Benning. "Greenwood? What the hell are you doing here?"

Greenwood took the hand Hollister extended and pumped it, showing his enthusiasm to be in J Company. "It worked."

"What did?"

"When I got out of your remedial training platoon, your string pulling got me reassigned to the Honor Guard company."

"My old company."

"Yes, sir. And I soldiered my way out of trouble there with the new CO."

"Price? He's a good man."

"I'll say," Greenwood added. "With your help and his I got promoted and got orders to come back over here. I was afraid I'd get sent to one of those fucking leg companies again, but I made it," he said as he puffed out his chest a bit.

"And now you're pulling KP?"

"I'm just in charge of the detail to get the mess hall closed down to move it to Tay Ninh. I only got in last night. The first soldier told me he'll have me assigned to a team by the end of the week."

"You sure you want to be here? In country?"

"Yes, sir. I'd rather be here, as fucked up as it is, than in the World, where it's even more fucked up."

"How about the drugs?"

Greenwood smiled. "Cap'n, I scared the shit out of myself enough; I know I'll never be near that crap again."

"Good. Drop in and see me after you get settled in, and we can talk a little more. I'd like to hear what you have to say about Juliet Company."

The coffee had been simmering most of the afternoon and tasted like it. Still, Hollister needed the stimulation. He filled his cup from the huge pot warming on the field range and found a table in the corner of the mess hall. He pulled a couple of painkillers from his shirt pocket and tossed them to the back of his throat and washed them down with the bitter coffee. But before he could get into his notes, the door to the mess hall opened and Captain Plummer entered.

He was a sight. The starched and headquarters-looking doctor who had arrived at the Ranger compound that morning had been transformed into a combat soldier. Hollister steeled himself for the complaints he expected to hear from Plummer.

"Goddamn, Hollister!"

Hollister raised his hand in apology. "Okay, I know. My guys went a little too far."

"No," Plummer said, pulling up a chair. "This is the most fun I've had since I joined the army."

"What?"

"Hell, you think they teach us any of this stuff in medical training?"

"Hadn't given it much thought."

Plummer took off the floppy hat DeSantis had given him, exposing the white strip of forehead not painted with camouflage stick.

"I have to give it to you. I really didn't understand who your kids were and how hard they train. It must be pretty tough out there for them to go through so much to get ready for it."

"You want to go along on a patrol?"

"Whoa! There's a limit," Plummer said.

"Okay. How about going along sometime on an insert—with me, in the C & C?"

"Now that I'd go for. I'd like to see how this all works."

"When it works—it works well. When it doesn't, we come see you later."

Plummer was silent for a moment. "Yeah. I guess that's what I didn't understand. To me, you were just patients coming into my emergency room. I hadn't ever given any thought to what your guys had just been through before ending up in my world."

"Well, I'm glad you enjoyed a little training with the troops today. I hope you'll come around some more."

"I'd like to do that. I'd like the chance to get to know more about what you guys do."

"Well, you are welcome anytime, Doc."

* * *

Tay Ninh stood only a few minutes' flight time from the nearest point on the Cambodia border and remained a vital hub of communications and traffic for the Communists who had Saigon as their objective. During the course of the war, Americans and South Vietnamese units had staged out of Tay Ninh, conducting operations in the surrounding forested areas, hoping to root out the Viet Minh, VC, and then the North Vietnamese.

Hollister found a different Tay Ninh than he had remembered. Signs of withdrawal were everywhere. Buildings had been taken over by refugees from the countryside. Roadside shops, once filled with black market items, were gone.

More than any city Hollister had been in since his arrival for his third tour in Vietnam, Tay Ninh was the one that screamed of withdrawal and failure.

The compound Browning and Easy had picked had once belonged to a Vietnamese engineer battalion. While it didn't quite measure up to the kind of barracks American engineers usually put together for themselves, it was more than adequate for Juliet Company's needs.

The compound was as big as a football field, surrounded by some wooden, masonry, and chain-link fencing—all of it topped with three rows of razor-edged concertina wire. The structures inside were a mixture of metal sheds and stucco buildings with red tile roofs. In all—fairly comfortable for infantrymen.

The corners of the compound were marked by twenty-foot-high guard towers, offering an unlimited view of the city of Tay Ninh on the east and the reedy plains to the west—toward Cambodia. The central area of the compound featured a single chopper pad marked by a large H made of roofing tiles set into the hardstand.

Easy met Hollister's chopper, and two Rangers helped their captain unload his gear and carry it into the new orderly room. "Chopper pads?"

Holding on to his beret against the chopper's blast, Easy pointed toward a small gate. "Outside-a the wire. Got enough room to park six, and there's a fixed-wing runway about a quarter mile down the road."

"How do we secure it?" Hollister asked.

"The reaction force will have to pull the duty on the bunkers on the far side of the pads."

"Captain Zahn won't be too thrilled about that."

"Not my place to say so, but I think I'd be happy to do that rather than humping through the boonies looking for land mines in a track.

"I'll never understand how those turret-heads do what they do. When they do it, that is," Easy added.

"I'll remind him of that," Hollister said.

Easy waited for Hollister to drop his web gear on the porch of the orderly room and then took him on a tour of the compound.

They reached the most secure looking of all the buildings. "Operations," Easy said.

Inside, they found Captain Thomas, Master Sergeant Caulter, and four other Rangers installing radios and stringing commo wire through a hole on the far wall.

"This gonna work for you?" Hollister asked Thomas.

"I think so." He thumped the stucco wall with the heel of his hand. "I'm a little concerned about its ability to take any fire. Doesn't look like whoever owned this place before ever worried about being shot at."

"You got a plan?"

Thomas pointed the screwdriver he held at Easy. "I asked Top to find me some strong backs so we can sandbag this place."

"I have a feeling we're going to be our own strong backs. Plenty needs to be done to get this place operational, and there is just no manpower pool."

Thomas put down the screwdriver and unbuttoned his shirt. "I had a feeling you'd be telling me that. So don't expect to see me at supper."

The orderly room looked like it had once been a military headquarters. Hollister's office was next to Easy's and had a half counter separating the two. It didn't offer complete privacy for him, but Hollister didn't mind. He was just happy to have a place to work when he was back at the launch site.

He walked to the desk fashioned for him out of the rough wooden planks scavenged from artillery ammunition boxes. On it he found paperwork already starting to pile up.

"Damn, Top! How the hell do I get away from this river of pulp?"

The first sergeant chuckled. "If I knew the answer, I'd be the most popular first soldier in the army. Hell, sir, I could write my own ticket. I'd be having general officers fightin' over making me their command sergeant major."

He raised his artificial foot off the floor and tapped the side of his shin against the wooden desk. "Peg leg and all."

"Well, for now, how about trying to keep this stuff away from my office whenever you can?"

"I'll try, sir. But all I can promise is someone else calling you or writing you to tell you you haven't met some requirements or submitted some stats or some report or other bullshit those headquarters rats think up."

"What are they going to do to us if we don't submit all that crap to them?"

"They'll whine and complain and tell tales on us. In no time, we'll have more headquarters rats snoopin' around here trying to figure out what the problem is with the Ranger Company's admin."

Hollister took his forearm and swept the stack of paperwork aside, replacing it with his map case.

"Screw 'em. I'm going out for a look-see of the AO. You want to get out of here and throw your expert eye on it, Top?"

The first sergeant's face brightened. "You bet I would. I been here two days, and I already hate this place. A little fresh air will do me some good, Cap'n."

Before Hollister had even folded his map, Tennant appeared in the doorway to the orderly room.

"How'd you know I wanted to do some flying?"

"There are good aviators, and there are some special ones like me. Be happy you got a special one. Most maneuver unit commanders don't appreciate the high level of competence and daring a few of us aviators exhibit."

Hollister looked at Easy. "What the hell is going on around here? All you guys been out in the sun getting delusions of grandeur?"

Tennant looked at Hollister and then at Easy. "I don't get it."

Hollister shook his head, grabbed his beret, and waved both of them toward the door. "Let's go find some cooler air."

Tennant had decided to let his peter pilot take care of getting the aviators settled in to their billets and maintenance area, leaving his seat for Hollister. Easy made himself at home in the troop compartment, resting his artificial leg up on the nylon bench seat.

"Jesus," Hollister said, leaning forward, looking down at the terrain to the west of Tay Ninh. "This is some desolate shit!"

"I find it hard to believe those stupid motherfuckers think they can just walk across a wide wet spot and think we can't see them," Tennant said over the intercom.

"Most don't make it. But enough of them do to make it worth our while to go find out how the whole thing starts out across the fence."

"Well, there it is. Right up there," Tennant said, jabbing his gloved finger toward a trail running north-south, just visible over the top of the instrument panel.

"You worried about antiaircraft fire?"

"Aviation G-2 tells us they got 'em, but they're trying not to use them so much unless they have been spotted and are protecting themselves. Seems like they have given their positions away one too many times and brought smoke and destruction down upon their little pointy heads."

Hollister rapped the light metal alloy frame of the chopper door with his knuckles. "Hope you're right. I've never felt too comfortable with the thickness of the skin of these things."

Tennant laughed into his mouthpiece. "If the skin on a chopper was any thicker you'd have a real problem."

"How's that?" Hollister asked, looking over to see if Tennant was kidding or not.

"If a round got in here—you know, through a window or something—it might not be able to get out. It'd rattle around in here for hours, clearing out everything that lived and played inside this flyin' machine."

"Why is it I find this hard to believe?" Hollister asked.

"Don't know. But we had our chance to speak up when they were building choppers, and us pilots wanted thin skin. We'd just as soon the round go out the other side of the chopper as soon as possible."

Seeing Tennant was unable to keep a straight face, Hollister smiled back at his command pilot. "Are you guys this full of shit when they select you for flight school or do you learn this *in* flight school?"

They both laughed for just a minute, until they got closer to the Cambodian border.

Hollister leaned forward and looked at the reed-covered fields stretched out for thousands of meters in front of the chopper. Most of it was abandoned. Rice fields that once produced crop after crop of rice had gone fallow.

And everywhere there were the aquamarine pools of water created by bombs. There were so many of them they overlapped, creating interesting patterns in the grasslands. He wondered if the country could ever return to normalcy if the war ever ended. How could so much damage ever be fixed? Just returning the land to usable condition would take an enormous amount of work and would take generations without heavy earth-moving equipment.

After the war was not his problem.

CHAPTER 17

The rain pelted the palm-frond roofs of the huts sheltering them. A small, hunched-over soldier took off the sheet of plastic he had pressed into service as a raincoat.

"We have much work to do on the trail," Sergeant Dinh said, waving his hand off in the direction of the overflowing streambed.

A frail Montagnard conscript squatted under the thatch, his arms hugging his body for warmth. "It will only wash away again."

Dinh spun around and leaned over, sticking his face close to the man. "Did I ask for your advice? Did I, Rat?"

"My name is not Rat! It is—"

"Quiet. I do not want to know your name. You are a savage of the lowest grade, a pagan who believes the forest is your god. You dress in loincloths and wear your hair like women. You are no different than the rodent who lives off garbage.

"You *will* listen and take my instructions. You will *not* offer your opinion."

Dinh looked around at the others—a mixture of Vietnamese, Cambodians, and Montagnards. All had been assigned to him as laborers. "We have an important mission. If we fail, thousands of our brave countrymen will be slowed or even die while they interrupt their invasion preparations to do our jobs.

"Work hard. If I find you lingering at your duties, I will not hesitate to shoot you," Dinh said.

The laborers glanced at each other to see if anyone would respond, but no one replied.

"Xuan," Dinh said. "You have been with my work parties before. You know I have shot men for less than this *moi*'s insolence. Save his life. Tell him what you have seen."

Xuan, an aging Vietnamese farmer who had been taken from his fields in the Mekong flood plain nine years earlier, nodded to the Montagnard.

"Rat did not mean to insult you, comrade. He is only cold and tired as we all are. When the rain stops, we will consider it our privilege to make the trail passable for our brave comrades from the North."

Rat didn't apologize. Instead, he simply dropped his gaze to the ground in a submissive signal to Dinh. He was sure what Dinh said was right, and he would revel in the chance to shoot him. He thought it better to appear to give in than to argue with Dinh.

The rainwater filled the small streams near the encampment. They swelled and overflowed. The work parties tried to get up off the ground and out of the bone-chilling water until the flooding receded. Rat found himself sitting on top of a crude table built under a thatched roof designed for training transient North Vietnamese soldiers. Next to him was Xuan.

"Why did you defend me in front of Dinh?"

"He is a pig. His temper goes to extremes beyond his control. Once, last spring, he got angry with two women laborers. They stood up to him, and he began to shoot his pistol near them. He made them very afraid. He laughed and kept shooting into the trees near their heads."

"Did he kill them?"

"Not right then. He kept it up until they were hysterical, and then he told them they could leave the work party. He told them not to ever come back."

"They got away?"

"He yelled for them to run. Then he threw a grenade at them. It went off just as it hit the ground behind them—killing them both."

"Why did you speak up for me?"

"I do not care about you. When he threw the grenade at the women, he also wounded two other laborers. I do not want to die just because you might."

Before they could finish the conversation, the sounds of an approaching helicopter scattered them. They were too far from their tunnel complex to run there. Instead, Xuan, Rat, and three others in the training area ran for the bomb shelter only yards away.

The water filled the shelter, but Xuan and Rat had no choice. Rat went first. He slipped through the muddy entrance into the beige water. Chilled from the rain, he sank to the bottom of the water-filled bunker. His head broke the surface, and he found only inches between the surface of the water and the wooden beams holding the sagging earthen roof.

"Slow. Don't fall in," Rat said, hoping Xuan would not splash the muddy water into his face. The debris from the bunker floated in clumps. Twigs, leaves, and dead insects dotted the top of the water. Rat tried to push them away from his mouth, only a fraction of an inch above the surface.

Xuan, too, lost his handhold on the slippery edge of the hole and fell into the water. Rat reached down and found Xuan's sleeve and pulled him to the surface.

Xuan sputtered and tried to wipe the muddy water from his face as he spat out mud.

"Quiet," Rat said.

Xuan stifled his impulse to cough, and they listened for the helicopter blades.

"Americans?" Xuan asked.

"I don't know."

Rat's lip began to shiver from the cold water. "I am getting out of here as soon as they fly away. I cannot stand in this water much longer."

Within minutes of crossing the Cambodia border, the clouds that had boiled up thinned, and the rain let up. Everyone in the chopper was silent for a long time as they looked down at the home of so much of the enemy activity in the III Corps area. Every major operation, every large campaign, and every significant enemy contact had either started below them and moved east or was controlled out of a series headquarters concealed somewhere in the trees.

"You could hide a whole division down there," Tennant said, looking at a large forested area.

"They've hidden lots of divisions in there, Cap'n," Easy said, speaking over the intercom.

"What are we looking for?" Tennant asked.

"Just want to get a feel for it. We haven't spent any time in this area." Hollister said.

"What's first on this operation?"

"First we put some teams in to size up the place, verify the data we have on the maps and in the intel summaries, and then we start running operations in there to screw up their way of doing things, and see what develops."

"Okay, where do you want to go, boss?"

"Let's hang a right and see what we can see," Hollister said.

Tennant eased the cyclic over and the chopper made a gentle turn—deeper into Cambodia.

The ground below them was a maze of cross-threaded trails braiding back and forth across one another, taking advantage of tree cover wherever it existed.

"Tracks every fucking where!" Easy said. "Most of 'em are washed out by the rain. But there's no doubt folks have been through this area—and plenty of 'em."

"Trucks, bicycles, Ho Chi Minh sandals," Tennant said. "Can you imagine walking all the way down here from North Vietnam?"

"Yeah, and no travel pay," Easy said.

"How recently do you think they've used these trails?"

"Can't tell at this altitude," Easy said.

Tennant looked over at Hollister for some sign of response and instructions.

Hollister simply raised his hand and poked his index finger toward the ground.

"Got it. Going down. Next stop, ladies' lingerie," Tennant kidded.

"Don't I wish," one of the door gunners said.

"Don't we all," Tennant said. "Anyway, keep your eyes sharp back there. We want to get back to ladies' lingerie someday."

Hollister grabbed a look at the altimeter again. It passed through fifteen hundred feet and then a thousand.

"What's good for you, Jim?" Tennant asked.

"I'd guess anything below fifteen hundred we might as well be on the treetops."

Tennant accelerated the descent. "My sentiments exactly. Lift your feet up, folks, and hang on. We're going tree trimming."

No one spoke while they passed through more dangerous altitudes on the way down. Finally, Tennant pulled a little power back into the blades and leveled off the chopper only a few feet above the tallest trees.

The view of the ground was almost as good as standing on it. From treetop level, they were able to see fresh tracks. The key was to be able to see enough shadow detail to tell if tracks were fresh or starting to break down from natural weathering. The sharper the shadows, the sharper the edges of the tracks and the fresher they were.

"Shit. Looks like they been holding square dances down here," Easy said. "Look out the left here."

Everyone shifted and craned their necks to see what Easy was pointing at.

"See those vehicle tracks back there?"

"What about 'em?" Hollister asked.

"You got wide tracks and narrow tracks staying pretty much parallel all the way."

"What's that mean?" Tennant asked.

"If they weren't parallel they might be a truck and a jeep. But if a truck was following a jeep the tracks would slop over one another now and then. Since they aren't, you can bet that truck's either towing a trailer—"

"Or wheeled antiaircraft weapons," Hollister finished his sentence.

"Fuck me," came quietly from one of the door gunners.

"Well, we don't have to go looking for 'em with a slick for bait to guess they're in the area. Let's let 'em be and go looking for them when we're loaded for bear," Hollister said.

They flew wide, lazy figure eights over the area for another twenty minutes, and both Hollister and Easy marked areas of interest on their maps.

"I'm going to have to head for the barn pretty soon for some fuel," Tennant said.

Hollister raised his thumb in a gesture of approval. Knowing they were headed back, he took one last look. For as far as he could see, the bundle of trails threaded through the trees and crossed over themselves from the north to Saigon's doorstep. Everywhere, there were tracks of North Vietnamese soldiers, bicycles, and their vehicles.

"Whoa, baby!" someone yelled over the intercom.

At the same moment, Hollister saw what he was talking about. Just ahead of the chopper a lone rifleman opened up on the chopper with a long burst of small-arms fire. The tracers coming directly at the chopper first looked like green balls and then, as their arc maxed out and they fell short, they turned into green lines just before the phosphorous burned out.

The cargo compartment and cockpit area suddenly filled with

green smoke. Hollister couldn't see the windscreen in front of him. If he couldn't see, Tennant couldn't see.

"What we got back there?" Tennant yelled to the door gunners.

Both gunners had opened up on a target below the chopper neither Hollister nor Tennant could see. "Got one in the overhang of the stream we just crossed," the crew chief said between machine-gun bursts.

"Damage?"

The other door gunner stopped firing. "Hit a fucking smoke grenade on the side of my ammo can, and we took some hits in the tail, 's far as I can tell. How's it up there?"

Hollister looked over his shoulder and watched the blurred image of the door gunner let go of his machine gun and lean over. At first he thought the soldier was hit, but when the smoke cleared a bit more, he realized the gunner had just reached under the bench seat, found the smoke grenade, and pitched it out of the chopper.

Tennant leaned forward and finished scanning the instruments for any sign of alarm, and then alternately pressed each pedal, causing the chopper to fishtail a bit. He then rotated the cyclic, causing the chopper to dip, roll, and yaw, and then he raised and lowered the collective to check out the controls.

"Seems like everything still works," he said, coughing from the smoke. He slid the window on his door open. "Let me come around again. I want to know where *that* fucker's hanging out."

"Ya know—unless we start throwing things at them from this slick, there's not much we can do to screw up their day. I'll mark this one and see if we can scare them up some other day—maybe with a team ready to kick some ass."

"Works for me," Tennant said, and he laid the chopper over into a left turn—heading back for the Viet-Cambode border.

CHAPTER 18

Once they settled in at Tay Ninh the training continued around the clock. Hollister inspected every bit of it and gave some of the classes himself. Between classes, he read everything he could find on the enemy situation in southeastern Cambodia and sat in on several planning sessions with Lieutenant Colonel Michaelson and Colonel Terry and General Quinn.

The new Cambodian territory meant added hours of map study for Hollister. And because it was Cambodia, he would have to make do with the maps and aerial photographs of the area. He wouldn't be allowed the freedom to frequently overfly the terrain in a chopper the way he could anywhere else in South Vietnam.

"Cap'n, I got some good news for you—bad for me," Easy said, meeting Hollister as he crossed the compound.

"How can that be?" Hollister asked. "Aren't we on the same side in this war?"

"We are, sir. But you need a new platoon leader for the Third Platoon, and I don't need any more lieutenants in my life."

Hollister brightened. "You got me one?"

"Yes, sir. I aggravated the personnel sergeant major so much he sent us a body—excuse me—an officer to fill our vacancy."

"Where is he?"

"He's waiting in your office."

First Lieutenant Buck Deming was older than Hollister expected. His uniform showed signs of mileage respected in their business. He was a Ranger, senior parachutist, diver, jungle expert, and pathfinder. He looked like just what Hollister needed.

Deming sat drinking a cold soft drink while Hollister went over his file. "How much time have you spent over here?"

"Well, sir, I was a squad leader and platoon sergeant in the Airborne brigade of the First Cav—in sixty-five and sixty-six." His voice was thick with a distinctive dialect Hollister hadn't heard since Sergeant Thibideaux, the MP, ex-LRP, who saved Hollister's butt back at Benning.

Hollister listened to Deming speak and grabbed a look at the place-of-birth box on a form. As he suspected—Deming, too, was from Louisiana. He listed Saint John the Baptist Parish as his home.

"First Cav where you got the Purple Heart and two Silver Stars? I can't remember the last lieutenant I've ever met with a pair. I'm impressed."

"Yes, sir. Thank you, sir. I'm real sure I didn't deserve it, though. It was the Ia Drang Valley," Deming said.

"After that?"

"I went back to the States—the Hundred and First Airborne Division at Fort Campbell. Spent a bit over a year there, and then got selected for OCS. After OCS, I went to Ranger School and stayed on there as an instructor for a while."

"Deming, Deming—oh, yeah," Hollister said. "You were at the mountain camp in Dahlonega, right?"

"Yes, sir. Great assignment. You don't learn much about mountaineering in bayous."

"Then?"

"I got orders back here and spent most of last year as a platoon leader in the Eighty-second Airborne Brigade and then a few months as company commander before the brigade rotated home."

"You extended over here?"

"Yes, sir. I had to do some heavy evasive action to keep from getting sucked into some headquarters job in Cam Ranh Bay. The field force sergeant major used to be my drill sergeant at Fort Polk. He was a great friend to have over here. That's how I ended up here. I hope you have a job for me."

Hollister took a sip from his coffee cup and thought for a moment before speaking.

"How do you feel about being a platoon leader again? I mean after having commanded a rifle company?"

"No problem, sir," Deming said.

"Well, I've got a hole for you," Hollister said.

"I'll take it."

"Good. I expect you to suck up as much as you can from the more experienced members of the company. I don't mind telling you, we place experience over rank when it comes to a toss-up around here. We can't afford the luxury of measuring dates of rank when the shooting starts. You start by going along on patrols headed by folks junior to you. Any problem for you?"

"No, sir. The last thing I want to do is try to pull off looking like I know what I'm doing when I don't. They'll spot it in a New York minute, and I'll never be able to gain their respect then."

"I like officers who remember what it's like to be a PFC. It'll go a long way around here."

"I'll never forget being in a rifle squad in the Cav or a fire team at Fort Riley. It's where I come from. All I want to do is a good job. I figure I do that, and everything else'll pretty much fall into place."

"Good. We're going to get along well. So, welcome to Juliet Company."

At the end of the week Hollister had to report his progress to Colonel Terry and General Quinn. He arrived early and set up his small charts he had put together.

A small briefing room had been set aside. And Hollister paced the room, going over notes he had put on homemade three-by-five cards.

Finally, Quinn, Terry, Michaelson, the operations sergeant major, and Reed, the G-3 aviation officer, entered.

"Good morning, gentlemen," Hollister said. "The purpose of my briefing this morning is to give you an update on the training and readiness status of Juliet Company and direct supporting units."

Some in the room sat back; Michaelson and Reed began taking notes.

Hollister flipped up a chart and held it vertically on the small podium.

"My combat strength looks fairly good on paper—eighty-six percent available for duty is a bit misleading. I'm short of several specialties—radio operators and medics being the worst. Medics, I'm at eighty percent and would like to be at a hundred plus."

Colonel Terry smiled at Hollister, knowing, as would any

colonel, that his motives for wanting more medics than he was authorized was for all the right reasons.

"My equipment status is improving. I want to tell you the G-4 has been terrific at reassigning equipment from units rotating home. I should be at deployable status on equipment, vehicles, and commo gear within six days."

"And your problem areas?" General Quinn asked.

Hollister flipped up another small chart showing subject areas essential for each team member and the percent of completion of training. "You can see our weak areas are those requiring the most training resources. I have to run dummy inserts and extractions with every team to be sure the coordination between teams and choppers is adequate before I put them on the ground. I haven't seen anything yet to convince me the teamwork is anywhere near where I want it."

"How long?" Colonel Terry asked.

"I'd guess about another five days, if I continue to get the same chopper availability."

"Let me tell you five days is about all we can give you. I'm getting heat to quit burning up assets and to start putting your teams on the ground. Maneuver units can't understand why a single Ranger Company needs so much blade time when it's not even putting any notches on its belt."

"I understand," Hollister said. "But on top of that—I have to train my operations people, my ops officer, and my platoon leaders. They're all very short in specialty training."

"How can we help?" Terry asked.

"I could use some help from a pro," Hollister replied.

"A pro?"

"I sure could use Colonel Michaelson to teach a class or two," Hollister said, shooting a hopeful glance at his old friend.

Colonel Terry turned and looked at Michaelson. "What do you say? You want to spend a few days with the troops? Get out of the head shed for a while?"

Michaelson smiled. "I'd love it, sir."

Terry turned to Hollister. "It's a deal. But I expect you to work him hard. His life is too easy for him here."

The briefing continued on for an additional hour as they discussed details of Hollister's problems. The general explained that more and more large chunks of Vietnam would be given to Hollister to screen as U.S. units pulled back to prepare to return to the

States. During the upcoming week of training, the troop strength in Vietnam would drop even deeper below the halfway mark of the one-time high of five hundred thousand plus.

The training continued, and Hollister was able to import some additional instructors. The evac hospital provided doctors to assist in the training. In the beginning, the doctors bristled at the thought of teaching mere medics their trade. But Hollister got Doctor Plummer to explain how the Rangers needed their training. That and the promise of a few sets of camouflage fatigues loosened their objections.

Hollister asked Michaelson to overlook operations while Hollister took Thomas up in a chopper to control dummy inserts and extractions in a relatively safe area of western III Corps. Having Michaelson stand in as the acting commander allowed Hollister to show Thomas the operations officer's job.

Hollister and Thomas boarded a Huey flown by Captain Dale Tennant. The team going in was from the 2d Platoon. Staff Sergeant Chastain had drawn a training mission and was patrol leader of Team 2-3. Lieutenant McIlwain squeezed in as assistant patrol leader.

Thomas only brought along his .45 pistol. Hollister raised his M-16. "Next time, bring a real weapon. You go down with a forty-five and you'll be one very sorry captain."

Hollister then checked out Lieutenant Jack Donaldson, the artillery forward observer. He carried his own PRC-77 radio, maps, binoculars, a thirty-eight on his belt, and a pump shotgun. It was obvious to Hollister that Jack Donaldson had gotten religion somewhere along the line.

The formation of choppers rendezvoused over a major intersection in the Dong Nai River. Hollister had insisted each training mission include a full insert package, loaded with full weapons and fuel.

Chastain's team, 2-3, was given the mission to land in a small PZ that had once been someone's manioc field. On the ground, the team would head north to watch a canal junction with a large river tributary. Their task there was to establish an artillery ambush of the junction. Should an enemy convoy of sampans slip from the canal into the river, Chastain would be expected to identify them as enemy and call effective field artillery and chopper fire on the boats.

Since it was an exercise, one of the slicks would drop two empty fifty-five-gallon oil drums in the canal and let them drift into the river. Then Team 2-3's markmanship and artillery adjustment skills would be tested.

They would spend no more than twenty-four hours on the ground. Hollister regretted it, but he had to cut the training missions short in order to get each team on the ground at least once before the company went fully operational in Cambodia.

Hollister let Thomas sit in the jump seat mounted closer to the open door. It gave Thomas the best view of the other aircraft and what was happening on the ground.

On the approach to the LZ, Hollister quizzed Thomas on frequencies, call signs, and procedures. What if they took ground fire before inserting the team? What if the team was already on the ground? What if a chopper was downed? What if they took a casualty in one of the aircraft? What if they lost commo with the team?

The questions went on for the entire trip until Thomas finally had to focus on preparing the team and the flight for the insert.

Hollister watched Thomas give the okay to the gunships to look for LZ watchers in the trees. They flew ahead, dropping to treetop level. He looked back over his shoulder. The sun was just breaking the horizon and Hollister could see the troops inside Chastain's chopper scooting to the open cargo doors in preparation for the insert.

He looked back at Thomas. He had his map out, orienting it to the terrain below—whipping by at eighty-five knots.

"Raider Three-Six. Looks clear," came the words over the radio headset.

Hollister looked up at Thomas to see if he had understood the gunship lead's message. Thomas didn't hesitate. "Okay, Three-Six. Roger your clearance. We will insert as soon as the slicks arrive—straight in." Thomas then pulled his head back inside the chopper and talked to the back of Dale Tennant's helmet. "Okay with you, Dale?"

Tennant just raised his Nomex-gloved hand and gave Thomas a thumbs-up.

"This is Campus Killer Three. We are clear for the insert. Two-Three, you set?"

Chastain came back over the headsets. "Affirm. Two-Three is ready. Over."

"Roger," Thomas said. "Here we go, folks. Let's take a look," he said over the intercom in the C & C.

Hollister leaned out the left door to look at the landing zone coming up in front of them. From three hundred feet, it was hard to make it out over the rows of trees in his line of sight.

Behind them, the chase and the insert ship peeled off to the left to make a large circle—killing time—while the C & C made a low-level pass over the LZ.

Hollister thought the gunships were a little out of sync— both of them being at a point in their orbits where they were facing away from the LZ. He was tempted to say something over the radio, but stopped himself, leaving the show to Thomas to run. Instead, he just made an entry in his notebook. That done, he reached in his shirt pocket, pulled out a cigarette, and lit it.

Hollister exhaled the acrid smoke as the C & C descended to one hundred feet. They flew the long axis of the LZ, each man looking out—into the trees surrounding the clearing. No one spoke; everyone was alert for the slightest sound or flash of light that might tell them they were being watched or taking fire.

At the end of the LZ, Tennant pulled the chopper up hard and to the left. "Looks clear to me."

"Same here," Thomas said. He turned to look at Hollister.

"It's your call," Hollister said.

"Let 'em go on in, Dale," Thomas said.

Again, things went silent in the headsets. Hollister watched Thomas and then looked back out at the choppers. The C & C loitered at five hundred feet as the two slicks approached the LZ.

Hollister was convinced the insert ship was being too cautious about his approach—exposing the chopper and the team to enemy fire for longer than necessary. He made another note to talk to Tennant about it.

Finally, the slick flared, nose-high, to slow its airspeed. The chase slowed as much as it could and then flew over the top of the insert ship, as it touched down in the landing zone.

Hollister watched the team dash from the right side of the chopper to the tree line. He wasn't happy. They moved in two clumps—each of three men less than an arm's length apart.

He watched the insert ship. It seemed to hold too long on the ground and finally lifted up and struggled for forward motion to get out of the LZ. It had lost its momentum when the pilot let it settle onto the ground while the team unloaded. Before Hollister could make a note, Tennant broke in on the chopper intercom. "I got it. I'll take care of it."

Hollister was getting to like the way Tennant did things. He was in charge and on top of everything his crews were doing.

By the way the Rangers staggered Hollister could tell they were running short of wind. Two of them fell behind and had to be helped by a third. It merited a note in Hollister's notebook. He jotted down: *More PT!*

Finally, the team disappeared into the trees. Now came the wait. Everyone knew the patrol leader was trying to get his team into a hasty defensive perimeter to determine if they had been seen or fired upon.

After a very long pause, Chastain's voice broke the radio silence. "This is Two-Three. Cold. Insert was cold. Charlie Mike. Over."

Thomas repeated Chastain's message for clarity. "I understand cold. And you are continuing the mission. If it is affirm, do not reply. Out."

Thomas looked over at Hollister, who simply nodded his head—*not bad.*

Back at Bien Hoa, Team 4-1, led by the platoon leader, Nathan Hill, was ready to be inserted on a mock ambush position nine miles from Chastain's team. While the choppers went to refuel, Hollister ran into operations to check with Michaelson.

"Your folks seem to be doing things right. But we wouldn't know it back here. They aren't reporting progress. If they want us to jump through our hoops—they'd better let us know what the hell is going on," Michaelson said.

"That it?" Hollister asked.

"Nope. Four-One—bad radios, a bad battery, and the team leader didn't have the alternate freqs."

"Shit," Hollister said. "You think there's any hope?"

Michaelson laughed. "You remember our old detachment in the Airborne brigade?"

Hollister smiled, remembering how screwed up they were when they were so new at it all. "Yes, sir. I get your point. Can you hang around a little longer?"

"'I shouldn't. But I'll see if I can con some more time out of Colonel Terry."

"Great. I need the help."

The second insert went well, but it took too long for Hollister. He made a point out of telling Thomas he had to work on shaving minutes. Sloppiness and extra flying always translated into lost blade time and more risk.

It took almost fifteen minutes for the barrels to float free of the canal and start down the river into the killing zone Team 2-3 had set up.

Hollister, Thomas, and Jack Donaldson circled high above and off to the east of the target area.

Chastain called in a solid fire request.

The first round hit the far bank of the river, beyond the drifting barrels. Chastain knew enough to start too far out and move his way rather than risk hitting his team.

"He's making adjustments—too small," Donaldson yelled across the chopper to Hollister.

Hollister looked down and saw the second round fall closer to the floating barrel, but still dozens of meters short.

Chastain realized his mistake, made a bolder adjustment, and all waited.

The next round hit, and Chastain gave the command to fire for effect to the fire direction center.

The next six rounds hit at the same time—most in the water and one on the far bank.

One round hit the water, detonated, and hurled a barrel up into the air. A cheer went up over the chopper intercom.

Chastain called Thomas and said he wanted to end the fire mission and move to adjusting Cobra gunship fire onto the barrels before they drifted out of sight.

The gunships rolled in; one high, one low.

"We're gonna make a dry pass to make sure we got the right barrels and the right river," the lead pilot said, half kidding, but serious about knowing where he was shooting. By that time in the war, there had been so many accidental injuries and damage done by gunships, checking was overdue.

The lead Cobra rolled out of orbit to just above the water level and popped up its tail—picking up airspeed.

Just about two hundred meters beyond the barrels, the gunship leader punched the power to the Cobra and came almost straight up and out of the river channel to an altitude of more than twelve hundred feet.

"Looks good to me, Two-Three. Whenever you're ready."

"Three, this is Two-Three. We're going to begin the gun runs now."

"Don't wait on us. Go," Thomas said.

"Okay, Two-Three. I have your target eyeballed. We're gonna make a run apiece," the gun leader said.

"Roger," Chastain replied.

Everyone watched again.

Hollister was bothered, knowing every face he could see from the circling C & C was watching the barrels. He grabbed his binoculars and looked down at the Ranger team on the ground. He could see the team members through the limited concealment they had—they were all watching the barrels.

Another note for Hollister's postoperation critique.

The first pass was minigun fire. It started a hundred feet short of the first barrel and popped the surface of the water every few inches and then sliced right through the barrel.

Before the first chopper had turned its tail to the target, the second Cobra began its gun run, pooping out 40mm grenades until one of them hit the first barrel and two hit the second barrel.

Again, a cheer went up over the radio. Hollister looked at Thomas and they both shared a smile. You just couldn't keep Americans from cheering a good shot, a good basket, or a touchdown.

"Enough?" asked the lead gunship pilot as his wingman finished a second successful pass.

"Roger. You sunk both of them," Chastain said. "Thanks. Good shooting."

"We aim to please," the pilot said.

"You got anything else you want done?" Thomas asked.

"Yeah," Hollister said. "Let's go by Team Four-One. They've been far too quiet for me."

The guns, slicks, and the C & C broke out of their orbit and followed Tennant's C & C to the west, toward Team 4-1's position.

"Four-One, this is Three. If your sitrep is negative, give me two squelch breaks."

There was a long pause, and then Sergeant Iverson broke squelch. Once, then again.

Hollister exhaled, realizing he had been holding his breath a bit too long.

CHAPTER 19

"What you have in mind?" Hollister asked Thomas—yelling over the wind in the chopper's cargo compartment.

"We hadn't planned on leaving them on the ground long. They are such a new team together, I want them to have one in and one out under their belt together before I give them anything more complicated to do," Thomas said over the intercom.

"Campus Killer Four-One, this is Three. We are pulling your sister element in about two zero, and then we will be ready for you. Is there any reason you might not be ready for extraction in four-five mikes?"

Lieutenant Hill clicked the squelch once—negative.

Thomas squeezed the transmit button. "Roger, negative, Four-One. I want you to Charlie Mike, and we will be in the area until we—"

Tennant's gloved hand came up to get attention in the backseat. "I got a fucking chip light up here folks."

Tennant pushed forward on the cyclic and pulled up on the collective—next to his seat. The Huey began to gain altitude.

"What do you think?" Thomas asked.

"Can't tell much. Could just be crap in the oil."

"Oh, that's not bad. Is it?"

"Could be this fucker is ready to self-destruct and lose its mastery over gravity."

"That's bad?"

"Only if you are with any other aviator. We specialize in excitement. Lemme turn some dials, press some buttons, and twist some knobs up here."

"That'll fix it?" Thomas asked.

"No. Probably not. But it will look impressive to you guys in the back," Tennant said.

Hollister knew Tennant was doing all he could do to resolve the problem. It could be just a stray flake of metal in the turbine engine. Or it could be a bad chip detector light, or it really could be an important warning that the turbine was about to give out on them.

Thomas seemed to look at Hollister for a sign of hopefulness. Hollister simply shrugged and checked to make sure his seat belt was snugly fastened across his lap.

"What do you do now?" Hollister asked Thomas.

"I, ah . . . better wait until Dale sorts this out before I do anything serious with the teams on the ground."

"You better get on the horn and let Campus Killer Control know you might be making an unscheduled landing out here. Set up a backup crew of slicks and guns to cover you or cover the teams on the ground. You could suddenly find yourself with *three* extractions and a chopper recovery to do before dark."

Thomas shook his head like he knew everything Hollister said was absolutely right and he should have been able to answer right off.

He started to explain when Hollister cut him off. "Hey . . . Get this to Michaelson, *now*! We can talk later."

Hollister watched the white square on the instrument panel flicker on, then off, not giving any indication if it was a real problem. His eyes shifted to the altimeter. He had never been able to reconcile in his mind that the higher you are in a chopper when you get in trouble—the safer you are. Still, he had to trust what he had learned. The altimeter read nineteen hundred feet.

"Somebody up front got the numbers for some good shit-kickin' music?" one of the door gunners asked over the intercom.

"Will that help?" Thomas asked.

"Can't hurt to have Johnny Cash or Buck Owens pulling for you," Dale Tennant said.

The light suddenly went on and stayed on. Hollister saw it, Tennant saw it, and before Thomas could turn to see what Hollister was looking at, the warning tone sounded in the headsets as the master caution light and the RPM limit lights filled the instrument panel with alarm.

Hollister saw the RPM needles split—indicating the rotor RPM was up but they had just lost engine RPM. Hollister caught Tennant's reactions. He slammed the collective lever to the floor—taking all of the lifting pitch out of the rotor blades.

"Hold on back there!" Tennant said, a sudden rise in tone in his voice.

Hollister called back to Tay Ninh. "Control, this is Six. We're putting the Charlie Charlie down. How 'bout taking over the control of the deployed elements until we can get back in the air in the chase?"

"Roger," Michaelson's radio operator replied.

Hollister and Thomas leaned out the left door of the chopper trying to help Tennant select a safe emergency landing zone as the chopper began to fall from its orbit.

"Are we anywhere near the team?" Tennant asked.

"Yeah. They're about five hundred meters north," Hollister said.

Tennant nodded and leaned back to look down through the chin bubble. "I don't think I want to go down anywhere near them. If someone starts shooting at the chopper or from it—they'll be more problem than help."

"Let 'em know," Hollister said to Thomas.

"Four-One, this is Three. You monitor our situation?" Thomas asked.

Lieutenant Hill answered. "Roger. Standing by for instructions. Over."

"Good. Hold what you got," Thomas said.

While they spoke, Hollister watched the altimeter unscrew at a rate he felt was just too fast for a falling chopper to survive at the bottom. His mind filled with random fears. He'd been in a falling chopper before. But then he didn't have time to think about it.

He tried to tell himself Dale Tennant was experienced. He'd get them safely on the ground. *But what about the enemy situation?* They were in bad-guy territory. And just as likely to land safely as run into an enemy element that could kill or capture them all before they stepped free of the chopper.

Hollister placed his rifle across his knees, then picked up his claymore bag and looped the strap around his neck.

The altimeter passed through three hundred feet, the vertical speed indicator maxed out on the descent side of the dial. Hollister grabbed one more look out the open doorway at the trees quickly coming level with the falling chopper. He looked back in time to see Tennant yank the collective up under his left arm and straighten out his leg, using a pedal to compensate for the torque thrown into the rotor blade.

The chopper seemed to shudder to a halt in midair. The sudden downward thrust of the wildly spinning rotor blade created an instant cushion of air only feet before the skids would collide with the ground.

Hollister held his breath as the chopper lost its cushion again, dropping with a sharp jerk to the ground. The aircraft lunged to the right and then rocked back to the left. He hoped it was a sign of uneven terrain and not something more dangerous like collapsing skids. If they collapsed, there was every reason for him to expect the blades to strike the ground and turn the chopper into a wildly bucking machine—bent on self-destruction.

But the chopper stopped rocking. The blades kept spinning as Tennant kept the pitch pulled into them, causing them to quickly slow.

"Out! Out! Out!" someone yelled over the intercom.

Before the second warning, Hollister and Thomas were rolling away from it. Trying to get as much distance between them and the chopper as they could.

Hollister finally dropped to the ground, against a small tree trunk, and looked back at the chopper. Smoke came from the access panel below the rotor head. The crew of the chopper was clear of the aircraft—all except Tennant, who was walking around the chopper looking for damage, a small fire extinguisher in his hand.

Wiping the paddy water from his face, Hollister looked for the other choppers. The chase ship was in a low orbit waiting for some sign.

"I'm going to pull the radios and machine guns and then wave the chase in to pick us up," Tennant yelled to the passengers and crew. "Anybody hurt?"

Hollister shook his head. "Shit! I hope I never have to do that again."

Hollister turned and found Jack Donaldson standing just behind him, bent at the waist, his hands on his thighs—gasping for breath.

"That's as close as I ever want to get to another shitty landing," Donaldson said, straightening up and exhaling to calm himself.

"That working?" Hollister asked—looking at Donaldson's radio.

Donaldson picked up the handset and listened to the rushing noise in the earpiece. "Any station. This is Campus Killer Two-Eight. Over."

He paused for a reply. Getting one, he responded. "Roger, Gunslinger. We are a downed slick. What's your location?"

He listened to the reply and then thanked the distance station. "Roger. You're a bit too far away to help. Not to worry. We have friendlies overhead right now. Thanks for the offer. Out."

Donaldson turned to Hollister. "Works fine. I'm going to drag it over to Captain Tennant so we can talk to the chase ship."

"Good idea," Hollister said.

Donaldson was not more than two yards from the aircraft when a plume of brown water and dirt erupted beneath his feet.

The sound of the explosion reached Hollister a fraction of a second after he saw Donaldson hurled into the air.

He leaped to his feet and ran to Donaldson without thinking. Only after he was running did he hear someone yelling, "Watch it! There may be more of them!"

Hollister knew what the warning was—if it was a mine or a booby trap there might be more. But he was only a few feet from Donaldson, and he hoped there wouldn't be another one close by.

He dropped to his knees and rolled the young lieutenant over. His right leg had been torn away just above the knee and most of the fingers on his right hand were gone. Hollister ripped his jungle fatigue shirt open and quickly looked for any wounds to his torso, then his head and neck.

He rolled Donaldson forward and raised the back of his shirt to examine his back and yelled over his shoulder, "Someone get over here and grab this radio. Get a fucking medevac in here *now*! He needs help—fast!"

It was nearly two A.M. by the time they had recovered the downed chopper and pulled out the teams on the training missions. Hollister sat at his desk toying with the letter to his parents he had started four days earlier. It contained less than two complete sentences and said absolutely nothing of consequence. He pushed it away—promising himself to finish it.

"What's Donaldson's status?" Hollister asked Easy, who had just entered Hollister's office.

"Last update was an hour ago. He was still in surgery. They did tell me he will lose his arm as well as his leg. But they think he has an even chance."

Hollister looked up at Easy. "He's only a boy, Top."

"We're all boys, Captain," Easy said, an uncharacteristically warm smile on his face.

Hollister had to smile at his longtime friend. "I guess you're right. I'm just getting so fucking tired of watching this war eat up the Donaldsons. I didn't even get a chance to get to know him before I'm looking for his replacement. This is really fucked!"

"S'cuse me a minute, Captain." Easy stepped out of Hollister's office.

Hollister looked at the pile of notes on his desk. He had had a call from Colonel Terry while he was out on the ground. He looked at his watch. He decided to call Terry in the morning.

Easy returned with a bottle of bourbon and two coffee cups. "Got some good stuff from an old friend up the road at the ordnance battalion. He was one hell of a radioman in Korea. He's a good contact for several reasons—and this is one of the better." He held up the bottle. "How about a nightcap?"

"Everybody's in? Guards posted on the perimeter?"

"That's affirm."

"A little," Hollister said.

Easy poured a bit more than Hollister asked for. "Bad start, huh?" Hollister said.

Easy shook his head, took a sip of his bourbon, and then shrugged. "It's a fuckin' dangerous business. If we don't train hard, we'll die hard. You know that."

Of course Hollister knew he was right, but it didn't make him feel any better about Donaldson, who would be forever changed by one step on an uncontested landing zone. Hollister's face reddened with a hint of anger. "I want to know what the fuck brought the chopper down."

"Now Cap'n, I'd think twice about connecting the chopper with the booby trap on the LZ. If there's a maintenance problem, Captain Tennant will be quick to find it and fix it. He wants to keep flying more than you want to blame somebody for the boy losing his leg out there in that paddy.

"You didn't ask, but I've decided Cap'n Tennant's one fine

aviator in the time I been watchin' him. You 'n' I been 'round some good ones and some not so good ones. This guy you don't have to worry about."

Hollister killed his bourbon and pushed his cup toward Easy for a refill. "Who do I have to worry about?"

Easy poured more without comment and pushed the cup back. He rolled his eyes skyward and thought for a minute. "It's a long list. But my old soldier's bones tell me you have to watch the chain of command for starters."

"My chain of command?"

"No," Easy said, thumb pointing in the direction of Long Binh. "The links above you."

Hollister was surprised at Easy's reply. "You have problems with Michaelson and Colonel Terry?"

"No," Easy said. "I got nothing but respect for Michaelson, and I think Terry's prob'ly a straight shooter. I'd keep my eye on folks way up higher. They're shaky, and the war's coming unglued. They're liable to do just about anything. Some'll want to find ways to get some more medals. Others'll lay low. They're all fucking crazy about numbers and body counts and keeping discipline figures down—you know. They're running scared, and you can get caught in the squeeze."

"Shit, I can't do very much about changing Westmoreland's or Trickie Dickie's plans now, can I?"

"No, but you can watch your back."

Hollister let Easy's words sink in. "What about around here?"

Easy leaned back, scratched his stomach, and then patted his pockets, looking for a cigar. "Not so bad," he said. He found one, unwrapped it, and began wetting the outer leaves of the dry cigar.

"I think you got good material, but these folks need lots and lots more training. Mostly, I think they need to get religion about what they're doing. They got an attitude like the war is somewhere else. Not enough contact to sharpen them. They run too many dry-hole patrols, and they get cocky and sloppy. Then they get—"

"Dead."

Easy raised his drink. "You're right there, Cap'n."

They looked at each other and said nothing. It wasn't funny—not to them.

*   *   *

Browning had converted one of the buildings into a BOQ for the Juliet Company officers. It was once a supply shed for the former tenant's construction materials. And it still smelled like bags of Portland cement.

Inside, someone had AFN on. Sly and the Family Stone banged out their latest hit. Hollister walked through the arch in the plywood wall that separated the sleeping area from the dayroom-bar they had cobbled up, using the supply counter. He found two platoon leaders, a pilot, the forward air controller, and Captain Thomas listening to one end of a phone conversation Captain Browning was having on the landline near the bar.

"I understand. Yes, yes . . . I'll tell him when he gets here. Roger. Out," Browning said. He hung up the phone, turned, and found Hollister standing in the doorway. "Sir, it's Donaldson."

"Didn't make it?" Hollister asked.

"Some complication with his surgery. He had a fucking heart attack. He died about twenty minutes ago."

All the others were silent.

Hollister tried to fight back the choking sensation rising in his throat. "Shit!" He dropped his head and let it sink in for a moment.

"Pour me a bourbon," he said, moving to the bar.

Lieutenant Fass raised a bottle of Wild Turkey and his eyebrows. Hollister nodded. "It'll do. Just give me a shot."

The others said little, but each moved to the bar and got his own drink.

Hollister waited until they all had something to drink, and he raised his shot glass. "For Jack Donaldson." He downed his bourbon and grimaced at the burn.

The others repeated the toast and followed suit.

"Brownie, I want you to make sure Jack's battery has all the details, and I want to coordinate a letter to go with his battery commander's letter."

"Yes, sir," Captain Browning said. "Anything else?"

"Yeah, get someone on gathering up any of his things that are here and get them over to his battery. And let's have a memorial ceremony—soon."

Hollister had a second drink at the bar and decided to retire to his room. He wanted another drink but didn't want to have it in front of the others. He had been pretty hard on them about drinking when he first arrived. He knew he had to set the example—or at least have another in his room.

His room was dark, smelled of the constant Vietnam mustiness, and felt damp. He twisted on the bulb hanging from the ceiling over the built-in desk and bench near the door.

On the desk, someone had put two letters from his mother, a couple of bills from the States, and a copy of the latest issue of *Stars and Stripes*.

There was nothing from Susan. And he knew it was unlikely he would find anything from her except something that couldn't be avoided.

He threw his hat on the desk, and unbuckled his pistol belt and wrapped it around his .45 and holster. Placing his sidearm on the bench, he stepped over to the ammo crate that served as a headboard, and grabbed the bottle of Dickel nestled between three other bottles of liquor.

He sat and poured himself another stiff drink, and then fished around in his pocket for a cigarette. He found none. Instead, he slipped his finger under the flap of the first letter from his mother.

His mother always spent the first page of her letters saying very little, asking very little, and warming up to the acknowledgment Hollister was in Vietnam. As with all her letters, it was filled with little bits of news from Lansing, Kansas. News about the family and some long discussion about the actual weather and the weather they hoped to get.

Somewhere around the last third of her letters she would try to gently ask her son to be very careful and to try to avoid the perils of war.

Hollister took a long sip of his drink and let his mind wander from his mother's letter to a mental picture of her back on the farm. He couldn't remember a day when they had ever had any friction or tension between them—not until he left for Vietnam the first time.

That day, in the Kansas City airport, he saw her mood change from the mother who had raised him and had always been his best friend to a woman who was angry her son was going off to war. She paced nervously, and there was a strain in her voice he had rarely heard. Still, she didn't want to upset him, so she kept much of her feelings to herself.

It was only through his father's explanations and letters from his cousin Janet that he found out just how much pain was involved in having him in Vietnam—especially for the third time. He missed her breakfasts, and he missed her company.

CHAPTER 20

He was in a deep fog when the CQ shook him.

"Sir? Captain? You gotta wake up," the soldier said, half whispering.

"What? What is it? A contact?" Hollister replied with a start.

"No, sir. We don't have any teams out."

Hollister crawled to a sitting position and tried to clear his head. "What is it?"

"The first sergeant wanted me to come get you. He's over in the orderly room—right now."

"What's it about?"

"Seems there's been some trouble in one of the teams. I don't know the details, only the first shirt sent me to get you."

"Okay. Hustle back over there and tell him I'm on my way."

When Hollister got to his office he found the first sergeant, red-faced and angrily chewing on a stub of a cigar. Also, there was the team leader of 1-4, Sergeant Curry, and Private First Class Parsons. Parsons's face had several large bruises, and the white part of one eye was bright red.

Whatever it was, Parsons had already pushed some buttons for Hollister. He had spotted Parsons his very first day in the company, and he knew the guy wasn't his type of soldier. He had an attitude. That first day Hollister knew there would be a meeting such as the one he was about to have. He didn't know what the first sergeant was about to tell him, but he knew it wasn't good.

"What's the deal, Top?"

"Fuckin' pothead!"

"What? Who's a pothead?"

"Parsons here," Easy said.

Hollister looked at Parsons for a reaction to Easy's charge and saw none. "Sit," he said. "First Sergeant, come into my office."

In his office, Hollister snatched his beret off his head and threw it into the top tray of his in-box. "I just don't get it. I'm completely out of touch with this drug thing. I watched kids destroy their brains back at Benning, and wondered there. But here? Christ, it's hard enough going a round with the bad guys without doing it in a damn coma."

"This is a cancer eating the heart out of every unit in the army," Easy said.

Hollister dropped into his chair and lit a cigarette. "Let me hear it."

"Hear what, Cap'n?"

"Your wise old soldier's recommendation."

Easy took a deep breath and then let it out slowly. "Been in this man's army, man and boy, for over thirty years. I've seen boozers, gamblers, barracks thieves, and race troubles. But I've never seen anything like this."

"That mean you don't have any ideas?"

"Means, years ago I'd tell you to throw this kid in the stockade and forget about him."

"And now?"

"Now? Now's different. You throw him in jail, and his replacement is jus' as liable to be a pothead."

"You think we should keep him?"

The first sergeant looked at the blank wall as if he could see Parsons through it. "You see the mouse under his eye?"

"Yeah. Where'd he get it?"

"His team."

"That's a good sign. They caught him?"

"Yes, sir. And they let him know they weren't going to put up with a druggie."

"How long's he been here?" Hollister asked.

"Got here just about a week before you did. Came from the Airborne brigade when they rotated home," Easy said.

"He been out on any shakedown patrols yet?"

"No, sir. Not yet."

"Well, my guess is if he's even fixable, he'll fix better here than in Long Binh jail," Hollister said.

"Hell, from what I've heard about LBJ, he's more likely to get in the habit of being a screwup there. It's a cesspool."

"Send him in, Top."

"Private First Class Parsons reports, sir."

Hollister returned his salute. "Stand at ease."

Parsons appeared to be unsure if he should look straight ahead, over Hollister's head, or directly at Hollister. He tried all three before he settled on looking at Hollister.

"I'm only going to ask you one question," Hollister said.

"Yes, sir?"

"You want to stay in Juliet Company or not?"

Surprised he was even being given a option, Parsons blurted out, "Stay, sir. If you'll let me."

"It's not up to me," Hollister said. "We're going to leave it up to your team."

"My team?"

"I'm going to let them decide if they want to keep you—if they can trust you."

"You're not going to send me to LBJ?"

"No. But if it happens again . . ."

Hollister didn't have to finish.

"Yes, sir. It won't. I fucked up. It won't happen again," Parsons said.

"Being counted on. Being reliable. Backing up other Rangers is what we're about. Nothing else matters if we can't do that." Hollister leaned forward and raised his voice. "If you don't get it—you don't belong here. The only people you matter to in this world are your teammates. They can't trust a fucking druggie. Would you?" Hollister asked.

Parsons hung his head and almost whispered, "No."

"Go wait out in the orderly room until I find out what your team wants to do with you. And send the first sergeant in."

"I want to see Parsons's team, his platoon sergeant, and the platoon leader in the mess hall after breakfast," Hollister said.

Easy smiled and nodded. "Yes, sir."

"What the hell are you smiling at, Top?"

"Most other company commanders would just dump a guy like that. My guess is you'll be happy you kept him," Easy said.

"Well, I'm glad you approve of my style, First Sergeant," Hollister said—teasing his top soldier. "Oh, and see if Greenwood is still waiting to be assigned to a team and get him into the next hole in Parsons's team. It'll do them both some good."

"You figure Greenwood will be harder on Parsons than his buddies already are?"

"Yep. That kid came close to destroying himself. He's a believer now."

"Well, yer in luck then."

"How's that?" Hollister asked.

"Sergeant Curry's going home next week."

"Talk with DeSantis and see if you two don't think he's team leader material. Will you?"

"And if we think he is?" Easy asked.

"Then see if you can make Lieutenant Fass believe it was his idea to give Greenwood the team."

"Consider it done."

Not finding a butt can on the mess hall table, Hollister crushed out a cigarette, fieldstripped it, and rolled the remaining paper into a ball. He stuffed it in his pocket, spun a folding chair around, and straddled it. He waited for Lieutenant Fass, DeSantis, and the rest of the team to sit. "Smoke 'em if you got 'em."

A couple of the Rangers lit up.

"I guess you all know we're here about Mister Parsons."

The Rangers didn't show any reaction to the statement. They all knew Parsons's pot smoking had come to Hollister's attention.

"I'm not going to dump him unless you folks say so. I know the army is not a democracy, but a Ranger team is a special exception. I'm willing to give him a chance to soldier his way out of trouble if you are. But if any one of you doesn't want to have Parsons watch your back in the bush—just say so. Just one of you, and he'll be reassigned to some leg outfit here in country."

Hollister looked at each man for a response. No one spoke, but each looked around at the others to compare reactions.

"Can you accept this?" Hollister asked Lieutenant Fass.

"Sir, if his team doesn't want to nuke him—I don't either. But if he gets caught again—"

"Count on it. If I even suspect he's using drugs, I'll kick his butt through the front gate. If we can't trust him—we can't use him."

"That's okay with me," Fass said.

The others nodded in agreement.

"Let me make it clear. This is not a wink at drug use. It is a warning. This is an exception only because you all are giving him a chance. If he blows it—he goes."

Hollister pushed the aluminum chow tray away from him and reached into his shirt pocket for a cigarette. "So where do we stand?"

Captain Thomas flipped a page in his GI notebook and scanned his notes. "Near as I can figure, we're about a day over on our schedule. We've made up most of the training we thought we wouldn't get in by stealing instructors and training 'round the clock."

"Can we get the extra training in before we launch the first teams?"

"Let's send out our most experienced teams first and keep the others on the training schedule," Browning said.

"Okay. Do it," Hollister said.

"Captain Hollister," someone yelled from the back of the mess hall kitchen, "phone call for you."

"Hollister," he announced into the mess hall field phone.

"Sir, an American called by radio and wants you to meet him out on the chopper pad in zero five," the radio operator said.

"Who is it?"

"Platinum Warrior, sir. I looked up the call sign, and he's the senior U.S. adviser for the province."

"Okay. Tell him I'll be there."

"Top, I have to go down to the pad to meet a visiting fireman," Hollister said as he entered the orderly room. He stopped in the doorway, surprised to find a trim female dressed in ARVN fatigues, her long black hair falling down her back, nearly reaching her beltline.

"Oh, Captain. I want you to meet your new clerk-typist. Her name is Miss, ah . . ." Easy struggled with the spelling on the card he held in his hand.

"Ray is what the Americans call me. But it is spelled with a *J*," Jrae said as she turned and smiled at Hollister.

Without thinking, Hollister snatched his beret from his head and reached out to take her hand. He was surprised at her arrival, her pretty face, and the smallness of her hand in his. "Well, where did the first soldier find you?"

"It's really amazing what you can do on the jungle drums if you sweeten the tune with a bit of aged bourbon," Easy said.

"That tells me something, but not much, Top," Hollister said, still looking at Jrae.

"Another old Bad Tolz buddy of mine is the Special Forces Group sergeant major. He's closing down some resettlement ops hereabouts, and Miss Ray here is lookin' for a new job."

"I speak English, Vietnamese, Montagnard, and some French," Jrae said.

Hollister released Jrae's hand. "Would you like to sit down while I speak with my first sergeant for a minute?"

Jrae nodded and found a chair near the doorway.

"Close the door, Top," Hollister said.

Easy shut the door to Hollister's office with one sweep of his arm. "I know what you are going to say, sir."

"And just what is that?"

"That we can't have an indigenous female working in the orderly room." He raised one eyebrow and almost asked for confirmation. "Especially one who is so good-looking?"

"You're right. We can't have her here, and she sure is good-looking."

"Sir, we need the help. We got Viets and other locals who none of us can speak to. We have no translators and aren't likely to get any. And I've been told I might get a clerk-typist sometime after hell freezes over."

"So?"

"It means we take her or we go without."

"What about security?"

"Oh, that's the easy part."

"You going to tell me she has a top secret security clearance?" Hollister asked.

"No, sir. But she doesn't have any place to live either. She has agreed to live in the old guard hootch across the compound. That way, we can control her access to foreign nationals, and I'll keep the classified stuff away from her."

Hollister let it sink in for a bit.

"My instinct tells me we're headed for trouble, Top."

"My fatigue factor tells me if I don't get some help around here, we're going to start having some real admin problems."

"What did your old war buddy tell you about her?"

"That she's good people and she's reliable."

"Okay, Top. You keep her out of trouble and make sure she knows she's on probation—indefinitely. And she doesn't leave the compound unless she's accompanied by someone from Juliet Company. If she can't go along with it, we can't use her."

Hollister held his hand up to shade his eyes. The approaching helicopter was a vintage Huey repainted with glossy OD paint instead of the matte finish that had become the SOP.

He impatiently looked at his watch, preferring to be checking on training. He expected nothing much would come of the visit, and he could get back to the team training within a few minutes.

Once the pilot dumped the pitch out of the chopper blades, the dust settled, and Hollister could see an army colonel getting out.

What he wasn't prepared for was Jarrold T. Valentine, his old chief of staff from Fort Benning. The last thing he needed was to be operating out of a launch site with Valentine as the closest thing to the landlord.

"Well, well, well . . . Hollister," Valentine said, positioning his baseball cap on his head.

Hollister saluted and tried to fake a smile. "How are you, Colonel? I didn't know you were in country."

Valentine smiled back and returned the salute. "Yeah, they decided to give me a little more combat time while I'm waiting on my number to come up on the BG's list."

Hollister tried not to show his loathing for the way Valentine described province-level advisory duty as combat time. Equally offensive was the effort Valentine went to to make sure Hollister knew he had been selected for promotion to brigadier general.

Valentine pointed a finger toward the wire surrounding Hollister's compound. "This your headquarters?"

"It's our launch site. We normally base out of Bien Hoa."

"I want to send someone down from my staff to act as a liaison. You know, so we don't have any coordination problems."

The word liaison registered as *spy*. Hollister didn't want any of Valentine's people nosing around his compound.

He scrambled for a reply. "That would be a real imposition on you, Colonel. Since we're visiting in your AO, why don't I have one of my people report to your CP?" He hastened to fill in the void and to not allow Valentine to decline. "I know how understaffed you must be, and I've always got a competent Ranger or two on light duty who can do the job in spades."

Hollister could tell by the look on Valentine's face he had no argument, and without any authority to insist, Valentine accepted.

"Okay. But if I find any lapse in coordination or language problems I'll send *my* man down."

"We'll make sure we don't have to impose," Hollister said, parrying.

The phone line was bad between Tay Ninh and Long Binh, but Hollister had to get some help getting Valentine out of his business.

"I'm more concerned about you ruffling the ARVNs' feathers than Valentine's. Just dodge him where you can, and drag your feet when you can't avoid him," Michaelson said over the echoing phone.

"Things are going to be difficult enough around here without being oversupervised by someone who isn't even in my chain of command."

"I know Valentine from the war college. He was a slippery, ass-kissing, obnoxious SOB. Just goes to show you some real jerks slip through the net and make it to the next rung on the ladder."

"Hell, sir, he wants me to forward copies of all our operational reports to his headquarters."

"Tell him you are not authorized to put anyone on your circulation list because of the sensitive nature of the operations. If he wants copies, he can ask Long Binh to send them. Tell him it's out of your hands.

"If it doesn't work, tell him to go fuck himself. I'll bring Colonel Terry up to speed about Valentine. Let the two old bulls measure peckers."

"That's good enough for me, sir. I'll be as uncooperative as I can be," Hollister said.

"Just be tactful. There's no one more full of himself than a bird colonel on the BG's list," Michaelson said.

It was almost four in the morning when Hollister finally took his jungle boots off and dropped them to the floor in his room. He felt the sticky night air and the sweat in the collar of his fatigue shirt. He considered taking a shower but decided it would be just what he needed to wake him up after the hour of sleep he might get if uninterrupted by some emergency.

He lit a final cigarette and leaned back against the wall, his heels hooked into the side rail on his cot. His mind raced over the endless demands of the day and the one about to break. He watched the tip of his cigarette glow in the dark and then looked out the small window.

On the horizon, the lights of dozens of aircraft crisscrossed the black curtain of night. He watched the blinking navigation lights and then was distracted by a pair of flares wobbling under small parachutes of white nylon.

Somewhere out in the night, an American or ARVN was in trouble. He began to wonder why he was there. Why didn't he just do what Susan asked? He had certainly given the army and Vietnam more than a fair share of his life and his dedication. Another flare caught his eye. There was someone out there who was every bit as worried and every bit as afraid as Hollister had been on so many nights. He would never be able to explain to anyone who hadn't been there how uncomfortable the thought of leaving that unknown warrior out there while he went home felt to him.

He crushed out his cigarette in a C-ration can and stretched out—still in his fatigues. He closed his eyes and thought of Susan.

Sleep came over him in only a few seconds without his knowing it.

The team on the pad waited for launch as the first rays of light promised a hot day across the Cambodian border. They sat on the ground near the insert chopper while the crew made some changes to a relay that had gone bad on them only moments before.

"Sit. Don't get up," Hollister said a split second after one of the Rangers called attention—recognizing their commander.

Hollister reached the side of the chopper and spoke to the back of the command pilot's helmet. "You going to be able to get this thing off the ground anytime soon, Chief?"

"Hell, if we could get some decent maintenance done we wouldn't be in this fix," the pilot said, throwing a switch on the console before turning to see who he was speaking to.

"What's wrong with your maintenance?" Hollister asked.

"Mornin', sir," the pilot said. "Nothing, except we don't have enough people to do the job."

He moved the mike away from his lip. "We're losing our best people, and there just aren't any replacements. A guy gets malaria or the crud and gets evac'd to Japan, and we never see him again."

"How do you take up the slack?"

"We do only critical maintenance, and little, pain-in-the-ass things like this bum relay show up during our flying day."

"Is this serious?"

"No, other than it causing us to lose time we'll never get back before dark."

"How long?"

The aircraft commander looked over to his peter pilot. "What do you say?"

"We're good now. We put enough baling wire and Seventh Army green tape on it to hold it 'til we get back to the barn tonight," he replied.

Hollister slapped the side of the chopper door. "Good deal. Have a good flight."

The pilots ran up the turbine engine on the chopper and continued their preflight checklist.

Hollister walked over to the team. Sergeant Iverson held his hand up to shield his eyes from the brilliant rays of the sun jumping Hollister's shoulder. "Guess we're 'bout ready, sir."

"How you feel? You ready?" Hollister looked around at the others and scanned the equipment and weapons.

"Guess about every team leader'd like to have an extra day or two to prep."

"You really think it would help you do something?"

"No, sir. Guess it'd probably dull the edge," Iverson said.

"Can I do anything?"

"Yes, sir. Wish me luck."

"You can count on it."

"We oughta be lifting off here in a minute or so, sir."

"Yep. We don't want to waste any time getting your folks on the ground. We especially don't want you peaking too early," Hollister said with a smile.

"Don't mind telling you just the word Cambodia puts a little bit of extra pucker in my ass."

"Good. It'll keep you sharp. You get in some shit—we're there."

"All right," one of the seated Rangers said.

"Just do your best, and I'll see everyone else is singing backup."

"Airborne, sir," Iverson said, raising his voice over the full RPM of the chopper blades.

Hollister reached out, shook Iverson's hand, and nodded at the others. "Look out for them."

The radios crackled with cross talk. The pack of cigarettes Hollister had opened just before shaving was almost empty. The first team was on the ground, and he was trying to resist the urge to leave operations, get in the C & C, and go on the last insert. But he knew he just had to let Thomas do some of the inserts without breathing down his neck. He had never really appreciated how frustrating it must have been for his company commander on an earlier tour when Hollister had Thomas's job.

He drained the last sip from the cold coffee in his cup and walked to the door in the operations shack. He squinted against the bright sun and looked at the last team loading up down on the chopper pad.

Hollister watched Easy as he tried to make it look like he was unfazed by the artificial leg that didn't flex at any point from where it attached to his stump to the toe of his jungle boot. Though Hollister couldn't hear what Easy was saying over the sounds of the three idling choppers, it was clear he was busting the chops of a Ranger who had made the mistake of leaving his team hootch without some item of essential equipment.

Easy walked over to operations and simultaneously saluted Hollister standing in the doorway and offered up the morning's mail haul for the two of them. "Somebody back where the peaceniks live found you and me, Cap'n."

Hollister took the two envelopes Easy offered and stepped inside with him.

"Probably bills. No one else I know can write," Hollister said. He recognized the top one as a bill from his insurance company. "Yep. Bills."

Easy didn't respond.

Hollister looked at the return address on the larger of the two envelopes and saw it was from Susan. He opened it and flipped the handwritten cover letter from Susan over only to find the

final court papers for the divorce he had known would arrive—
eventually.

He heard Easy say, "I'm real sorry, Cap'n."

For once there was no trace of bluster, humor, or sarcasm in his
voice.

Hollister looked up at his old friend. "Goddamn this war."

CHAPTER 21

The long hours were beginning to draw off Hollister's energy and his concentration. He paced operations, cautioning himself to let the first night of deployment take its course. He read over the operations log and compared team reports with their locations posted on a map near the radio bench.

He tried several times to write a letter to Susan while he listened to the last of the inserts and the few missed steps during the early evening. He finally gave up on the letter when he couldn't put his feelings down. He realized if he had been able to do it in the first place, Susan might have stayed.

Around midnight, he gave up and went to bed. But sleep eluded him. He gave up on sleep, too, and returned to operations to just check on the teams.

"What's this message from One-One?"

Lieutenant Hill was the duty officer. "They ran across a small trail, and while they were crossing it, they smelled the strong odor of gasoline."

Hollister rechecked the time the report was called in. "This the time it happened or the time they reported it?"

"Both. They called it in just on the other side of the trail," Specialist Loomis, the RTO, said.

"Then it was dark when they crossed the trail," Hollister said. He handed the clipboard holding the radio log back to Hill.

"Meaning?" Hill asked.

"Meaning if what they were smelling came from something or someplace close, they might not have been able to see it. They could have walked right by a refueling point."

Hollister walked back to the map and looked at it.

"There are enough trails in the area that it could well be something like that."

"You want them to double back to the trail, sir?" Hill asked.

Hollister looked at his watch. It was almost three in the morning. "Are they still moving?"

Hill pointed at the map with the eraser end of a pencil. "No, sir. They stopped there about an hour and a half ago."

The map pin showed the team to be almost six hundred meters from the trail.

"Okay. I'll see if we can spot something out there in the morning. If anyone is driving in there to gas up, we ought to be able to see the tracks from the air."

The squelch broke on the tactical radio, and everyone in operations froze, straining to hear the whisper.

"This is One-Four. We have movement. Two-two-five degrees, five to six hundred meters. Over."

Loomis picked up the pork-chop mike and repeated the message. "This is Killer Three Oscar. Roger One-Four, movement two-two-five at five to six hundred mikes. Standing by." Loomis turned to Hollister for guidance.

Hollister poked his thumb at Lieutenant Hill. "Ask the duty officer."

Hill half looked at Hollister and spoke to Loomis. "You let Lieutenant Fass know he has a team with movement. I'll call the Cav hootch to alert them and then call the pilots' shack so they can alert the standby crew."

"Who's the team leader?"

Loomis started to answer, and Hollister held up his hand, waiting for Hill to answer. Hill searched his memory for the name.

"Corporal Greenwood. You have to know these names, Nate. You need to know every soldier in this company. And they need to know you. Got it?"

"Yes, sir," Hill said. "I'll do it."

"Now get on to what you have to do."

Hill picked up the field phone marked Cav and cranked the ringer. He asked for the troop XO and explained the situation.

At the same time, Loomis used the other phone to call Greenwood's platoon leader.

Before everyone was alerted, Greenwood called in more movement, closer to his location.

Fass came through the door still in his trousers, T-shirt, and shower shoes. He stood by and watched.

"Have we heard from the other three teams?" Hollister asked.

Loomis scanned the radio log. "The others all called in routine commo checks within the last hour and a half."

"Anyone still moving?"

"No, sir."

"Get Lieutenant Gannon out of the sack," Hollister said.

Loomis called the officers' hootch to get the new artillery forward observer, assigned after Donaldson's death.

"And tell him to bring his traveling gear. He may get some night flying hours in tonight."

Loomis nodded and added the information to his message.

"Contact! Contact! Contact! This is One-Four. We *have* contact." Greenwood's voice boomed through the small speaker mounted above the operations radios.

Lieutenant Hill reached up and threw the switch setting off a piercing siren mounted outside operations. Everyone in the compound immediately knew there was a team under fire. All those who had been alerted swung into action.

Inside, Hollister grabbed the mike. "This is Six. Okay, Ranger. What have you got?"

Everyone in operations could hear the shooting in the background each time Greenwood keyed his mike. "Grenades. Maybe a half dozen landed in our position all at once. I've got two Whiskey India Alpha, and we're taking close-in small-arms fire."

"Can you use arty?"

"Affirmative. I have a fire mission," Greenwood said, his voice compensating for the noise around him.

"Tell him to send it," Lieutenant Gannon said.

Hollister turned to find the artillery officer standing in the doorway with a pencil and pad in hand, his map tucked under his arm, and his boots unlaced.

"Send it," Hollister said to Greenwood.

While Greenwood recited the identifying target numbers that would allow Gannon to get artillery on its way, Hollister grabbed his web gear and weapon. "I'll be in the C & C. Tell Greenwood we're on the way."

*　　　*　　　*

The cold morning air crept into the C & C chopper. "Jungle fatigues were *not* made for night flying," Hollister said.

"Got my long johns on. I'll be sweating my ass off come noon. But for now, I'm snug and warm," Dale Tennant said, throwing a smile at Hollister.

"You can bet we're going to spend some time out in the AO today," Hollister said. "We've already got two wounded, and I have no idea how bad yet. But the team's gotta come out."

Greenwood's voice came in clearer over the chopper headsets. "Killer Six, this is One-Four. Over."

Hollister stepped on the mike button on the floor near the pedals. "Six, go."

"I've got another Whiskey India Alpha. That's now one walking and two stretchers."

"Shit," Hollister said over the intercom. "This is not good at all." He keyed the mike again to reply to Greenwood. "You still taking fire?"

"Negative. The artillery has 'em hunkered down for now. I think I can hear you coming. Come in out of the northeast. They are still on my Sierra Whiskey."

"Okay. Hold what you've got. How far to a PZ?"

"Two hundred meters. Don't think I can move to it and carry my WIA without hanging my ass out," Greenwood said.

"Okay. Let us get you out of there. Guns should be over you in less than a minute, and you can put 'em wherever you think you need them. Ammo's cheap. Use it."

Even before Greenwood replied, Hollister could see the smoke from the artillery Gannon and Greenwood had fired in.

"Guns are there," Tennant said.

Hollister looked down to confirm they had just flown over the invisible line separating Vietnam from Cambodia. Looking back up from his map, Hollister could see the two prowling Cobras circling Greenwood's position at treetop level.

The lead gunship nosed over and began a firing run; 40mm grenades belched from the stubby chin gun as the gunner zeroed in on the enemy positions.

"Good! Good! Right there!" Greenwood yelled into the handset over the noise of the impacting grenades.

From the orbiting chopper, Hollister could see outgoing red tracers from Greenwood's team. "Come around again, Dale. I want to see if I can spot the incoming fire."

Tennant leaned the chopper over into a hard left turn. After only a few seconds, he reversed the bank and brought the chopper over into a hard right turn, allowing the team's position to be seen out of Hollister's door.

"Good," Hollister said. "Anyone spot any enemy firing positions, yet?"

"Out our right door—due east of you," a gun pilot said. "Let me mark."

"Roger," Dale said.

"How's the clearing just east of the team look to you?" Hollister asked Tennant.

Below them a small clearing not much bigger than a basketball court stood guarded by trees fifty feet high.

"Woo doggie!" Dale said. "We're gonna have to grease one up to slip it in there."

"But can we do it?"

"We got wounded—we can do it."

The gunship pulled out of its high orbit and nosed over into a maximum dive at nearly two hundred miles an hour. Just a few hundred feet above the ground and the team, the pilot pulled up the nose and squirted a short burst of minigun tracer fire.

The snakelike rope of red phosphorous found its mark and the pilot made a hard recovery, causing condensation to form at the tips of his straining rotor disk. "That's it. Five meters south of my impact."

"Roger your mark," Hollister said. "You taking any fire?"

"Negative. After our first run, they stopped shooting at us."

"One-Four, this is Six. You had any more incoming?"

"This is One-Four. Negative. Not in the last one zero. Over."

"Okay. We're going to have a look at a possible PZ to your east about eighty meters. Don't move anybody yet. Wait 'til we check it out. But get ready to move."

"Roger," Greenwood said. "Could you hose down the area between me and the PZ if I'm gonna use it? I'm not sure where they are now. Don't want to find them on the way out while we're carrying wounded Rangers."

"Will do. Hold on." Hollister turned to Tennant. "You feel like testing the water?"

"I'd rather no one do it. But if it has to be done—better us than one of my younger pilots," Tennant said.

"Hold on back there," Hollister turned and said to Gannon and Fass in the back of the C & C. "We're going to look at a possible PZ."

Gannon waved, while Fass nodded and pulled the charging handle on his M-16—chambering a round.

The radios went silent. Everyone in the air and the Rangers on the ground watched as Tennant pulled the C & C into a high hover over the PZ and settled into it, his tail as close to one end as he could get it.

The door gunners gripped the dual handles on their machine guns, waiting to return fire at the first sight of incoming.

The tops of the trees came level with Hollister's eyeline over the instrument panel. He stiffened his back against the armor-plated seat and steeled himself for the worst.

"The team is at our ten o'clock. Don't anyone get squirrelly. They're less than a hundred meters away," Hollister said. "Anybody see anything wrong?"

In turn, five voices came up on the intercom with negatives.

"Can we get a full load out of here?" Hollister asked Tennant.

"I think so. We'll hold the chase close and burn a donut around the clearing with the gunships." Tennant stopped his descent fifteen feet above the PZ and powered straight up and out.

"Good. Let's get 'em out of there," Hollister said to all in the C & C. He then pressed the transmit button and told Greenwood, "Okay, partner. Soon as you can, blow your claymores and get to the PZ eight-zero to your east."

"Will do," Greenwood replied.

Getting Greenwood to the PZ was a difficult part of the extraction. He had to carry two of his wounded while covering his own movement. Hollister instructed the pilots to cover the move and instructed Greenwood to put the emphasis on getting his people out without taking any more casualties. He wasn't concerned about how long it would take.

After almost forty minutes of shuttling the wounded from their contact position to the edge of the pickup zone—they were ready to come out.

Hollister punched the mike button with his boot. "Don't everybody watch the pickup. Keep an eye on the perimeter. Look out! Keep your eyes moving," he cautioned the crews of the choppers circling over the pickup ship.

He counted the long seconds it took for the pickup chopper to come to a stop over the landing zone and settle in. It descended rapidly at first and then gradually slowed as it neared the ground. Hollister could see the skid on his side of the chopper was still off the ground when the other one made contact with something.

The chopper jerked and then settled down on the near skid. Hollister heard his own voice counting the seconds off as the chopper sat there, light on its skids, a little bit of pitch pulled into the blades.

Greenwood was the first one to break out of the tree line. He waved the others on with his rifle while carrying a wounded Ranger across his shoulders. Behind him, another Ranger stumbled over something as he ran, carrying his own gear and two other Rangers' combat loads.

The second Ranger stopped, spun around, and took up a kneeling ready position to cover two more team members who were carrying the second seriously wounded soldier.

Greenwood stopped short of the chopper and also took up security—guarding the backs of the others. As soon as they passed him and dropped the first wounded man on the cargo deck of the chopper, Greenwood motioned for the solo Ranger with the extra gear to get in the chopper. He made the ten-meter sprint to the chopper and threw his load in on top of the others.

Hollister could almost hear himself whispering, "Come on. Move! Move! You're taking too long."

Greenwood took two more long strides and collapsed under the load he was carrying. At first Hollister thought he had been hit by enemy fire. Until he heard the pickup chopper pilot announce: "He just got tripped up. We're still good."

The last Hollister saw was the four boots belonging to Greenwood and the soldier he carried being pulled into the chopper. At the same instant, he heard the aircraft commander announce: "Comin' out. Comin' up. Watch me."

The back ends of the skids came off the ground first and the chopper began to hop on the toes of the skids as it began forward movement. The tail came high and torqued to the left and then overcompensated to the right as the bird picked up momentum and a little altitude.

Quickly, the chopper began to run out of clearing and approached the tree line at the far end. From Hollister's vantage point it appeared as if the chopper would not have enough altitude to clear the trees.

The radio net was silent. Everyone watched the chopper strain to gain enough altitude to avoid running head-on into the trees. The pilot was unswayed by the risky maneuver. He continued on his course, avoiding any maneuver that would cost him altitude.

At the last possible minute, the bulk of the chopper clawed its way to an angle sharp enough to clear the trees. But the skids didn't.

Tree branches grabbed for the skids, and leaves ripped from them scattered into the air. The chopper yawed a few degrees left and right as it powered through the branches to clear air.

Once the chopper cleared the trees, Hollister looked around at the other aircraft and the ground. The area where the team had repulsed the small enemy probe was scarred from the fragmentation of the rockets, the miniguns, and the claymore mines. But he couldn't see any sign of enemy presence.

During the trip back to the Vietnamese side of the border, Hollister tried to find out about the wounded in the pickup chopper. There was a serious belly wound, another soldier had a gunshot wound through his lower leg, and the third casualty was multiple fragmentation wounds, but ambulatory.

The medic with the team recommended the WIAs go directly to the evacuation hospital in Cu Chi. Hollister agreed and radioed operations that he planned to follow the wounded.

CHAPTER 22

Hollister was able to get off of the C & C and over to the pickup chopper before the medics moved the casualties to the triage area. He looked at the lieutenant shutting down the chopper and gave him a wave—letting him know he thought he'd done a good job getting the team out.

The medics and two Rangers pulled out the wounded and laid them out on the two gurneys the medics had brought out to the pad.

Hollister moved to the side of the chopper and found Greenwood. He was very bloody. His face, hands, and most of his uniform were darkened with blood.

"Hey, you okay?" Hollister said, thinking the blood was from the soldier who Greenwood had carried from the contact position to the chopper. But Hollister soon realized he had guessed wrong.

Greenwood was propped up against the bulkhead, bleeding from a slice made by an enemy bullet along his jawline. Two fingers were badly damaged by some trauma—nearly ripped from his hand and bent back at an extreme angle. It was clear to Hollister there were at least a couple of broken bones.

The Ranger's right leg was a mass of small fragmentation wounds, many with bits of trouser fabric embedded in them.

Greenwood's eyes filled with tears, and his lip quivered as he spoke. "Captain. I'm so sorry. I did the best I could. I don't know what went wrong. They just about killed all of us." He dropped his head, his chin resting on his chest, and the tears ran red as they mixed with the blood from his wounds. "I didn't mean to get anybody hurt."

Hollister climbed up into the chopper to help Greenwood out—to the medical attention he badly needed. "Ranger, you did

208

right. You got 'em all out, and you didn't cause this. Now let's get you to some help."

"Airborne, sir," Greenwood said, hardly getting the words out before running out of strength.

Hollister stood out of the treatment area and paced while the medical teams treated the wounded Rangers. He stopped long enough to put a call through to Juliet Company to report the condition of the wounded.

After more than two hours, one of the doctors came looking for Hollister. "I understand you're their CO?" the doctor said.

"That's right. Hollister, Jim Hollister. How they doing?"

The doctor ran down a laundry list of wounds and resulting damage. His prognosis for each Ranger was more reassuring than the last. Hollister relaxed a little, hearing the news.

Tennant came into the hospital and found Hollister sitting in a folding chair, holding his head with the heels of his hands.

"You okay?"

Hollister looked up. "Yeah, frustrated, but okay."

"How are they?"

"The doc tells me they're all going to make it. Two are going home, and Greenwood will probably go to Japan or Hawaii for a while. He might not come back just because of the return policy—not because of wounds. Greenwood's been hit in several places, but he's going to be okay. They're worried he might lose some of the use of a couple of fingers. He's one lucky Ranger."

"Which one's Greenwood?" Tennant asked.

"He's the one who carried one of the wounded over his shoulder."

"With all those wounds? You shitting me? What in hell do you feed these guys?"

"Don't know. But he's one hell of a Ranger. If you only knew where he's been before he got here. I'm putting him in for the Distinguished Service Cross. I just hope the classified location of the contact won't screw him out of it."

It was midafternoon by the time Hollister was able to get back to the launch site in Tay Ninh. The lift package of choppers was still out inserting teams.

He thanked Tennant for his efforts and jumped out of the C & C.

Inside operations, he found Browning bent over the small map on the radio bench. "Any new brush fires?"

Browning stood and spun around. "No, sir. We're clicking now. I hope it stays that way. When you get a minute, I'll bring you up-to-date with our status. Okay?"

"Right. Let me see what has landed on my desk, and I'll be back here in fifteen, and we can recalibrate."

Hollister walked into the much darker orderly room from the brilliant afternoon sun.

"Hello, sir," Jrae said in almost perfect English.

Hollister smiled and stopped in front of Jrae's desk. "And how are you getting along? Is First Sergeant Easy treating you well?"

Jrae giggled for the first time. She had a beautiful smile and some of the tension Hollister had seen in her face when she arrived was gone.

Since leaving her village many months before, she had put on a few pounds. The weight only brought her up to normal for anyone who was not a mountain woman. Someone had taught her how to pin her hair back in a fashion that was more contemporary and less native looking.

She stood to hand Hollister some messages.

"Hey, I like your new uniform. Whose idea was this?"

"Like that?" Easy's booming voice asked from the other side of the room.

"Where'd you get this rig?"

Easy walked over and stood next to Hollister while the two Americans looked at her. She wore the standard issue camouflage fatigues and jungle boots. Over her pocket was a nametape with the letters JRAE embroidered in black, and on her left shoulder she wore the red, black, and white Ranger scroll patch identifying Juliet Company, 75th Infantry.

"This is *not* issue uniform specs," Hollister said. The shirt had been taken in to fit close to her body, showing her nicely proportioned figure and her tiny waist.

" 'Course not," Easy said. "I had them seamstresses in the ville who cut down the ARVNs' uniforms tailor Jrae's."

"Isn't it a little too, ah . . . formfitting?"

"Not for me," Easy said, rolling his eyes. "I think she does a certain something for the uniform. Anyway, we couldn't let her be mistaken for a day laborer. She's now an important member of Juliet Company."

Hollister looked from Easy to Jrae. "Forgive him. He can't help himself."

"What does it mean?" Jrae asked.

"It means he is a great admirer of pretty women. Just take it as a compliment."

She smiled, a little embarrassed. "I will." She turned and stepped back to her desk.

Hollister's and Easy's eyes met. Easy was right. She looked good in her new outfit.

"The way I look at it, we've made some good choices on our first tries over the fence," Captain Thomas said, tapping the team markers grease-penciled in on the map overlay behind him.

Hollister, Browning, the platoon leaders, and two of the platoon sergeants sat in two parallel semicircles in the tiny briefing room.

"Run some of it down for those who haven't been to all the briefings," Hollister said.

Thomas nodded and quickly scanned the notes he had placed on the podium.

"There's a pattern of movement. It seems to end just a few thousand meters north and west of our teams and turns in toward the Viet border. Somewhere nearby, the bad guys must have a release point where they break up into smaller groups to infiltrate across the line.

"We've found some commo wire, and we're tapping it. And we've picked up quite a bit of paperwork from two successful snatches. Both prisoners appear to be local—not new to the area. And if my guess is right, they're part of some kind of service unit that guides arriving North Vietnamese regulars.

"Soon as we get those documents translated, we'll have a better idea about just who the players are," Thomas said.

"I think that we might turn up the brain center of this whole operation and get a chance to screw it up for them. That's basically our short-term objective," Hollister added.

"What are the numbers?" Captain Browning asked.

"We've put eleven teams in, spent a total of fifty-one team days on the ground, had to pull three teams early, made four contacts, and we've stacked up six enemy KIA and two POWs.

"We've gone through two busted choppers, and we're just at a hundred and twenty percent of our allocated blade time," Master Sergeant Caulter read from a clipboard in his lap.

A few heads in the room nodded approvingly at the statistics.

"For some reason, I'm not being advised of the details of your operations, *mister*," Colonel Valentine said, standing on the porch of the orderly room, his face too close to Hollister's.

"I can't understand that. I passed on your wishes to Two Field Force to be added to the distribution list, and I've been running overlays to your headquarters for coordination."

"I've been getting squat through the pipeline, and your overlays don't tell me a thing."

"I can only give your people overlays up to the level of their security clearances. We're working at security levels quite a bit higher than the ARVNs are cleared for," Hollister said, shrugging his shoulders.

"Bullshit! I want to get to the bottom of this. And I want full access to your op plans and after-action reports—starting today. Do we understand each other?"

"Oh, I understand you all right, Colonel. I just can't do that. I don't have the authority to declare you a need-to-know organization."

Valentine's face reddened. "Don't fuck with me, mister. You better find a way to include me or you'll wish the hell you had."

"I'll mention your request to Colonel Terry."

" 'Mention' it? Who the hell do you think you are screwing with? Dump this attitude quickly or you are going to find me on your back. And you *don't* want that. I can promise you that," Valentine said, raising his voice for emphasis.

Hollister was still standing on the porch when Valentine's jeep drove through the wire and out onto the dirt roadway.

"Hope you and the good colonel had a nice chat," Easy said from the doorway.

"Somehow I have a feeling this conversation will come back on me like bad chili."

"Count on it, Cap'n."

"Better call Colonel Michaelson and tell him Valentine is coming his way."

Easy looked at Hollister and smiled. "Ah. The privileges of command."

"Don't be a wiseass, Top."

Hollister sat in the dark in his room and tried to get some perspective on his efforts. Several more patrols went in and out of Cambodia with little or no contact. But movement, sightings, and increased intelligence data were the fruits of the missions. He was pleased with the way the teams were coming around. Training was showing up in preparedness for missions and speed in execution.

Rangers knew each other and seemed to be developing esprit de corps. Morale was up. Appearance was sharper, bravado was getting to be commonplace, and bad-mouthing of everything that was not Ranger or Juliet Company had replaced bitching.

The discipline problems were being handled where they should be—at team and platoon level. Platoon leaders each had a few good patrols under their belts, and their stock was going up in the eyes of the troops.

Hollister lit another cigarette and took a sip of the straight bourbon he nursed. He wondered why, in the face of all the positives, he felt so damn down.

He swallowed a larger sip and faced the reality. He knew what it was. He ached for Susan and had a sinking feeling about Vietnam.

He had lost her. And he was getting sick of the attitude infecting everyone outside of Juliet Company. It was a *why-bother* attitude. The war was closing out soon, and public opinion about the war had picked up downhill momentum, reaching breakneck speed.

Everyone wanted out. No one wanted to recognize the facts—once the Americans left, the South Vietnamese Army would collapse. And the cost of it all would be paid for with the blood of the people. Not the government, not the fat cats—but by the peasants, the farmers and the children. The same people he had thought were worthy of risking his life for and then putting off his personal life for almost seven years.

He shook it off, killed the drink, and decided to get some air.

He walked out to the steps and looked around the compound. Music drifted from a couple of the team hootches, and the smell of rain was in the air.

He turned to go back into his hootch and caught something out of the corner of his eye.

Several yards away stood the remains of what had once been the Vietnamese dependents' living area. On the steps of the poorly constructed building, Jrae sat bundled in a cotton pak cloth. She saw that he recognized her and nodded silently.

"What are you doing up this late?"

She stood. "I cannot sleep, Captain," she said, a hint of a French accent still in her English.

Hollister saw her tuck the corners of the lightweight cloth under her arms, near her waist, to ward off the night chill.

"Are you cold?"

"Oh. No. I am okay," she said, smiling at his concern.

Hollister couldn't miss the contrast between her white teeth and her dark skin and hair. He was pleased that she was getting more comfortable around him. He liked Jrae and was happy she had found her way to Juliet Company.

The troops had taken her on as their mascot. Anyone who might have had other ideas about her was quickly dissuaded by Easy's protective growl. So she became a novelty and a point of pride for Juliet Company and not a cause of friction.

"It's starting to look like we have the area bracketed," Captain Thomas said, pushing his mess hall tray away from the edge of the table.

"We ready to put someone in there?" Hollister asked.

"I think so." Thomas got to his feet and picked up his coffee cup. He thrust it toward Hollister's cup. "You want a refill, sir?"

"No. I think I've had enough to get my heart started."

Beyond Thomas, Hollister spotted Jrae entering the room and getting into the chow line.

"Top, how about scrounging up a couple of GI blankets and sending them to Jrae. She's freezing her butt off at night in that hovel we got her in."

Easy raised an eyebrow. "Would the captain be an expert on Miss Jrae's nighttime activities?"

"Would a one-legged first soldier like to do some push-ups for his company commander?"

"The first soldier respectfully withdraws his question. The captain can consider the blanket situation taken care of."

*   *   *

Michaelson's chopper landed on the far side of the pad at the launch site, and Hollister threw him a large salute. "Mornin', sir."

"Morning, Jim. How are you?"

"I think I'm ready to go, full bore," Hollister said, leading Michaelson to operations.

"We think so, too. We've been watching the results of your early team operations, Jim. I'm glad we were able to talk you into taking the job. I doubt very much if this company would still be on the rolls if you hadn't."

They spent the next two hours in a corner of the briefing room, talking about the possibilities. Hollister's company had turned up several bits of information that suggested iceberg tips. After narrowing it down, they came up with three possible targets to develop.

Michaelson tapped his notes with the plunger on his ballpoint pen. "I'll take these options back to Colonel Terry and see if we can match them with the other intel we've collected. I'd prefer to develop something that has a high likelihood of success rather than a long shot with a bigger payoff."

"I'll buy that. I think it will help build confidence around here," Hollister said.

Michaelson got to his feet and picked his hat up from the field table. "Better get on the road or I'll miss the afternoon briefing back at Long Binh."

The two walked out of the mess hall into the hot midday sun. "So what's the deal with you and Valentine? You know he's not your biggest fan," Michaelson said.

"Isn't his number coming up soon? I'm sure they'll reassign him as soon as he pins on his stars—right?"

"You just better hope he doesn't go over Colonel Terry's head and start whining to General Quinn. There's some kind of brotherhood thing among generals. Even if Valentine isn't a real one yet."

"I'll renew my efforts to dodge him," Hollister said.

Michaelson laughed. "You better."

It took field force less than three days to decide on an operation. Michaelson brought it to Tay Ninh and briefed Hollister on the concept.

After hours of refinement, Hollister, Thomas, and Michaelson finished roughing out the plan to change their operations from heavy intelligence gathering to the destruction of the enemy infrastructure in the Cambodian sanctuary.

CHAPTER 23

The crowd was too large to assemble in the briefing room, so the mess hall was pressed into service. The note on the door and the banner over the map board inside said the same thing: TOP SECRET—NOFORN.

"Let me state at the outset that most, if not all, of what we are about to discuss is classified top secret, no foreign dissemination. Is there anyone in here who is not cleared for this level of information?" Hollister asked the group.

The seated members assembled looked around to see if anyone identified himself—and ultimately excused himself. No one did.

"Good," Hollister said. "Let's get started." He stepped to the podium and scanned his notes. "We can start with the big picture and then go to smaller and smaller ones until we get to the X rays that make up the individual team missions."

He stepped to the map behind him and picked up the pointer made from a rifle cleaning rod. He made a circle on the Cambodian side of a border pocket called the Angel's Wing—a name that sprang from the obvious outline it created. "We've been saturating this area with patrols, sensors, aerial photo flights, and aerial recons for weeks now, and everything points to just what we expected—this is a good hunting ground."

The comment prompted a few in the room to exchange glances and make encouraging noises—nervousness masqueraded as bravado.

"Now, if we were working in Vietnam, we'd back off and let an infantry brigade go in and kick some ass. But we're *not* in country. And mounting large combat operations in Cambodia never fails to become a pimple on the ass of the White House,

Congress, the Defense Department, and on down the line—'til it rattles the windows at Two Field Force."

The comment brought groans of disapproval.

"We don't make the rules, and we aren't in Vietnam to worry about public opinion. But if we're going to do our job and avoid the heat, we have to recognize the problems."

"That mean we aren't going to kick ass?" Lieutenant Hill asked.

"No. It means before we mount any new incursions into Cambodia, we have to justify the shit out of the operation," Hollister said.

"What we've been doing isn't enough?" Sergeant DeSantis asked.

"No. The hunting we've been doing only told us where to hunt for bigger game."

More groans.

"It may be enough for us. And we can often work off of known intelligence and a good dose of Ranger intuition. But we have to have more than a strong smell of bad guys to justify escalating cross-border operations."

"So?" someone in the room asked.

"So we go deeper. Up the ante from armed reconnaissance to prisoner snatches and raids. If we can confirm the presence of larger units—Saigon will have the ammunition it needs to pound the piss out of the area."

"What'll it be, sir?" Fass asked.

"If we can get someone out and get them talking, we can put that together with the intel we've already collected and make our case."

Hollister tapped the map where several red grease-pencil marks were clustered. "We're pretty sure this area is hot with bunkers, tunnels, and hidden way stations that are damn near the equivalent of our replacement battalions. North Viet troops, individual units, and supply convoys slip through this area with the help of service units. They get food, fuel, ammo, and medical attention, and then break up to infiltrate across the border—only to converge later in staging areas north and west of Saigon.

"Most of you weren't here for the Tet invasion in sixty-eight. We kicked some ass and got embarrassed that time. We could not survive another Tet. There aren't enough Americans left, and the South Viets can't do it."

Hollister put the pointer down. "We can save lives if we get them early. Now that we're pretty sure where they're changing buses—we need to punch their ticket."

"Let's go get 'em," someone said.

"We've got some special training to do first. Our inserts will be by chopper and rubber raft. Anyone in here feel comfortable enough to do some rafting tomorrow?"

There was no answer.

"I didn't think so. And we'll need to bone up on our CBR training and equipment. We'll be using gas to flush 'em out."

The room filled with grumbling at the mention of gas. No one in the room had ever had a pleasant experience with gas in training or combat.

After the others were dismissed, Hollister spelled it out for Browning and Thomas. "Brownie, I want you to get them new *working* protective masks and cameras.

"I want enough rubber boats to train ten teams and deploy three heavy teams. Let's not use the same boats to train that we take to the bush. We can count on trashing the boats they train on."

Hollister turned to Thomas. "I want every Ranger in this company to be able to walk, talk, eat, and shit in his protective mask. I know they're hot and a bitch to work with—but they'll save lives and screw up the enemy."

"Why such heavy use of the masks? Can't we just dump some tear gas in the bunkers and tunnels and snatch 'em when they come out with snot running out of their noses?" Thomas asked.

"I don't want to just use gas when the going is easy. I want to be ready to drop tear gas by plane, lob it in by artillery, and leave it behind—everywhere. That, mixed with harassing fire, will account for random losses and won't give away where and what we're up to."

"That means our folks will be operating *in* the gas. Right?" Browning asked.

"That's right. They're going to hate it, but it's the best way to pull this off. So let's build a gas chamber and put everybody—and I mean *everybody* through it."

Browning and Thomas exchanged glances and then nodded to Hollister. *"Everybody?"* Thomas asked.

"Everybody—including pilots and crews. If they go down in a gassed area, it'll be the only thing that'll give them a leg up.

"One other thing," Hollister said. "I want to borrow those

tunnels the Twenty-fifth Division found under the base camp at
Cu Chi and send our folks down there to train in them. In masks."

"In masks?" Browning said. "We're going to have our share of
heat injuries, boss."

"Rather hose 'em down with water and feed 'em salt tablets
than let some eager NVA mole blow their faces off while they're
trying to find 'em in dark tunnels full of gas."

"Okay," Thomas said.

"Oh, one other thing. Plan for each team to take three extra
masks with them."

"You being optimistic about how many we can snatch?"

"No, just a lack of confidence in the masks. If we have some go
sour on the ground, we'll have spares."

By the end of the next day, teams were rotating between training stations that included two days for each team in the Cu Chi
tunnels.

Hollister chose to set the example. He stood first in the line to
enter the gas chamber.

It was nearly eleven when Hollister got to the bottom of his in-
box and found some mail addressed to him. One was from his
mother. His father's health was continuing to decline, and she
made no mention of her frail condition. Hollister worried about
his parents.

He began to draft a reply in his head to encourage them to get
some help without reminding them that the need for help was
directly related to the fact that they were both in their late sixties.
He knew it would take some delicate tap dancing to keep them
from reading between his lines.

Another official-looking envelope had come to him through
the field force message center and had his name and company on
the front. Under the "For Official Use Only" marking printed
on the envelope, the initials PM were hand-lettered in ink. He
knew the envelope was from Perry Mann, his old first sergeant
from Benning—stationed in Saigon.

Hollister opened the envelope and found the casualty list for
the previous week. On the list of 108 Americans killed was one
that had a red check mark next to it. It was Sandy Garland's name.
Sandy had been promoted to captain, assigned to a helicopter battalion in the Mekong Delta, and was listed as KIA as the result of
combat actions.

The news gripped Hollister's chest. He remembered his talented, cheerful, and very bright executive officer from Fort Benning. Then he thought of Sandy's wife and new baby, who had to be approaching her second birthday. He swallowed hard to suppress the pain. Another friend gone. Another widow. Another baby with no daddy. He suddenly wanted a drink.

He decided to write a letter to Jeanie Garland before the time got away from him. In it, he reminded Jeanie of the Sandy Garland he remembered—a good soldier and a good man. He hoped he could help her with the pain of her loss and offered to be available to help her in whatever her needs were. It took him almost two hours to write the letter.

Sealing the envelope, he felt nothing he had said in the letter really conveyed what he felt. Still, he couldn't tell her he was having his own doubts about why they were even in Vietnam.

The other envelope had the return address of Susan's lawyers. He held it for a moment, not wanting to open it. Without needing to open it, Hollister knew anything from her lawyers was bad news. He finally slipped his finger under the flap held down by the folded fastener and ripped it open.

Inside the envelope he found more court papers dissolving their marriage. He leaned back in his chair and let the weight of the document sink in. He wasn't completely sure just what the precise meaning of all the legalese was, but the cover letter announced that the court decree proceedings were complete.

He dropped his head into his hands. It was so easy for him to still see the pretty girl he had met in New York eight years earlier. Though she had changed a little, he always pictured her that way in his mind. He had fallen so much in love with her. He folded the papers and stuffed them back into the envelope and tucked the envelope into his pocket.

Outside, he didn't see Jrae looking out the windows of her quarters at him as he crossed the compound. Had he known she was watching him, he might have straightened his posture a bit more and moved with more authority. Instead, his legs felt like he was walking through water, carrying a heavy load. He was hardly aware of the fact that thunder clouds were forming to the west and promising a storm before the night would end.

He entered the small corner of the officers' quarters they called their club. Browning was nursing a drink, aerial photos and documents spread out on the table in front of him. Seeing Hollister, he raised his drink in invitation.

"No thanks, Brownie. I'll have to take a rain check. I've got things to do and a rack that hasn't seen me in it for too many hours," Hollister said.

"Okay. But that rain check'll be on you," Browning said.

Hollister waved approvingly and slipped off to his room and closed the door behind him. Without stopping to take off his beret or even his pistol belt, Hollister unscrewed the top on the bottle of bourbon on his field table and poured himself a tall, straight shot—not quite a triple. He downed it in one swallow and poured himself another.

The approach and eventual departure of the thunderstorm went unnoticed by Hollister. He drank more of the bourbon and finished the last half of his pack of cigarettes.

Sometime before dawn, he was still awake, sitting in the same chair, looking out his small dirty window toward Cambodia.

He spent the night thinking of Susan and ignored the demands of the day ahead of him. He would start the day drained. He clenched his fists and released them, filled his lungs and said—under his breath: "Suck it up, Ranger." He stood and stripped off his uniform.

The cold shower water was only warmed by a day's worth of sun. During the night, the warmth would dissipate. That time of the morning, the single stream of water slapped him with a sudden shock. He dropped his head forward under the flow and let the icy water hit him on the back of his neck and tried to focus on his day.

The list of things that still had to be done was lengthy. He knew Thomas, Browning, and Easy were on top of everything, but also knew everything needed checking.

He recalled the maxim affixed to every vehicle in Germany when he was a Private First Class. It was one of Gen. Bruce C. Clarke's favorite sayings: The troops do well what the commander checks.

Hollister didn't much believe it when he was eighteen. But on his third tour in Vietnam and an equal number of combat assignments to long range patrol units, Hollister was sure it was a saying worthy of a tattoo.

*   *   *

Inside operations, Browning, Thomas, and Caulter were bent over a map they had tacked to a piece of plywood resting on the backs of a couple of folding chairs.

"Infiltrating them in without being discovered by trail watchers is going to be a trick," Thomas said. "The rubber boats will go a long way to giving them speed and security."

"If they don't drown," Hollister said. "How's the boat training going?"

"I was just down at the river, and they look good," Thomas said. "I guess you know Colonel Valentine isn't happy about it though."

Hollister made a disapproving face. It had been Michaelson's idea to offer rubber boat training to the ARVN soldiers in one of the battalions that Valentine advised. The thinking was if the Americans practiced using boats the word would go out on grapevine that the Americans were practicing for a river operation. Staging boat training for the Vietnamese Army would look more routine.

"I'll head on down to the river and see if Valentine is still there. If he is, I'll try to calm him down," Hollister said.

All four looked at the small marks indicating marshy areas, and the large number of veinlike blue lines indicating small streams and intermittent streams in the area.

"Let's break pattern now with the aircraft. I want to fly up and down an area deeper than our objective and parallel to the border. Shoot, conduct VRs, drop flares at night, overfly in the dark. Mix it up and pick it up. Let's not telegraph our moves, but let's not let the first thing into the area be our boat team insert ships."

"Let 'em get a little tired of us, sir?" Caulter asked.

"Well, let them get used to hearing us thrash around like we're some kind of noisy grunt unit. As a matter of fact, let's let them think that. Send some phony-ass plan over to Colonel Valentine's CP that indicates we will be conducting recon patrols in the area—light ones—and that we'll be backed up by the First Infantry Division. That'll be sure to leak out to the jungle drums."

"Then put some Big Red One markings on the choppers?" Thomas asked.

"You got it. They'll figure we're rooting around for some-place or somebody to drop a few infantry battalions on. They'll be checking with their sources this side of the fence to see if Ameri-cans have moved any battalions to staging areas near the Angel's Wing."

"And until that happens, they won't get froggy," Caulter said.

"Right," Hollister said.

Hollister pulled open his desk drawer and fished around for some aspirin to help his headache. Finding none, he walked over to Easy's desk.

"You need Sergeant Easy, *Dai Uy?*" Jrae asked.

She startled him. He turned to her corner of the orderly room. "I didn't hear you come in."

"Sorry," she said.

"No. That's okay. Anyway, I'm looking for some aspirin."

"Aspirin?" She gave him a puzzled look.

"As-pir-in." He held his hand to his forehead. "You know—for a headache?"

"I will get you something," Jrae said.

Hollister was finishing a letter to his parents when Jrae returned. She put a cup of hot tea on his desk. "This will help your head," she said.

"What is it?" he asked, raising the steaming cup to his lips.

"Just drink," she said.

He drank the bitter tea and soon realized the headache had eased. He got up and walked to the doorway—looking toward Jrae's desk. "So what is this stuff?"

"From tree bark," Jrae said.

He nodded. "Okay—tree bark."

As she walked back to her desk, Hollister realized that the end of the war for the Americans would offer no better situation than she was in. In fact, she might be singled out for punishment or death if the North Vietnamese should conquer the south—which was more likely than not.

He wondered if there was some way he could get her out of the country before the Americans left for good. She wouldn't have to go to America. Almost any other place in South Asia would be better than being a pretty Montagnard woman left behind.

He would put Brownie and Easy on it. They would be able to find someone in Thailand or the Philippines or even Japan who might find a place for her.

Hell, it was the least they could do for her.

CHAPTER 24

He stood on the porch outside the headquarters and looked at the training Thomas and Caulter had set up. The compound resembled some alien planet. Rangers went about their business wearing gas masks in order to get used to the greater demand on their breathing.

Hollister realized he had talked a good game but not played one. His own mask was still in his office. He stepped off the porch and crossed the compound to a large building, once a maintenance shed. The windows had been blacked out for security reasons, and Thomas had set up sand tables inside.

Hollister entered the back door and stood against the wall to watch. Inside, Sergeants Chastain and DeSantis and Lieutenant Deming—each a heavy team leader—gathered their teams around separate sand tables. Every team member in the room was already sporting a few days of beard growth. It was the only place in the army where a soldier could go without a daily shave in garrison. It was common knowledge that the soaps and aftershaves were easily detected by the Viet Cong.

Each sand table had been sculpted into scale replicas of the objectives. The grid lines on the map were represented by strings nailed to the box frames, suspended in squares just inches above the simulated terrain. The trails were drawn in cornstarch from the mess hall. Trees and bushes were made from shredded packing material once used to ship radio equipment. And phase lines, objective markings, and other tactical control measures, normally grease-penciled in on a map, were drawn with pulverized, blue pool-table chalk found in the supply room.

Each man was represented by a Vietnamese piaster coin with

his initials marked on it. And each rubber boat was simulated by a half a bar of GI soap wrapped in brown LRP ration packaging material.

Hollister watched each patrol leader coach his team through their actions, starting from the landing zone. Each man had to explain every move he would make through the objective and back to the pickup zone.

Everyone in the room knew the process was time consuming and often redundant, but it turned up problems and misunderstandings there—rather than on the ground. It was more than worth the time spent.

Hollister pulled Captain Thomas aside. "How's Deming doing?"

"He's really good, boss. This guy has enough bush time and common sense to make me happy. I'd go on one of his patrols."

"Pretty good endorsement," Hollister said.

"I think he's a good choice," Thomas said, referring to Hollister's decision to give Deming's team the most important tasks on the operation.

Hollister hoped by putting Deming's team in near the enemy bunker and tunnel complex that his and a backup team could flush out permanent cadre working there and take them prisoner. The third team would act primarily as security to watch the backs of the other two teams.

Hollister's worry was that either they would come up with a dry hole or the enemy forces would be large enough to overrun the Rangers. With the U.S. reluctance to escalate in Cambodia, he knew he had to make it surgical and effective or risk having to back out with his tail between his legs.

Satisfied the teams had understood their missions and were working out the details, Hollister left the building by the side door.

Outside, he found Sergeant First Class Young, the company intel sergeant, with two other Rangers, setting up a classroom for more training. "What's planned here?" Hollister asked.

"Well, sir, we're gonna teach these youngsters how to use"—the sergeant pulled a small camera from his pocket—"the Pen EE."

Hollister smiled at the advertising pitchman pose Young struck.

Young turned his palm up and placed the camera on it. "Captain, this here camera is *the* Ranger's friend. It's a 35-millimeter, quick-loading, fixed-focus, easy-sighting, hand-operated, fully portable, half-frame, all-weather, black-and-white or color, manual intelligence-gathering device."

"I got all that," Hollister said. "But can our Rangers use it? Or, are we going to get rolls of blank film?"

Young put the camera down on one of the field tables. "Actually, all of our patrol leaders and a few others in the teams have used these cameras in Recondo School in Nha Trang. What I want to do is give them a brushup that'll make them more comfortable with using them and keep us from getting back bad film."

"Looks pretty dark in most places we're sending these teams."

Young reached into a cardboard box on the table and pulled out a handful of film cans. "Got that covered. We were able to get high-speed black-and-white film—400 ASA."

"What's that mean? Will it help, and will it work?"

"It'll work a lot better than the old film we've been used to."

"I hope so. We get in there and find Indians, we'll need all the proof we can get. I hope to avoid spending my nights answering congressional inquiries about why we were wandering around in Cambodia."

"You'll be able to publish this stuff in *Life* magazine."

"I'm counting on you," Hollister said.

"Let's go over this again," Hollister said. "We find nothing—we just walk away and try some other place, some other day?"

"That's about it. We're going on the big picture assembled by the whole intelligence community—your own input being some of the best of it," Michaelson said. He leaned over and put his coffee cup down on the desk in his office at Long Binh.

"Will I still have the aircraft to pull my people out if we don't find the brass ring?"

"What do you mean?"

"I'm going to have thirty-six Rangers on the ground in a fairly small chunk of Cambodia. If this comes up as a dry hole, I want to be able to pull all thirty-six out as fast as if they were under fire. I don't want to have to wait for helicopters."

"I understand. I've already leaned on the colonel, General Quinn, and the aviation guys to dedicate the resources to your operation."

"Okay. It's real important to me."

Michaelson relit his half-smoked cigar and blew the smoke toward the ceiling. "So, how do you feel this one will go?"

"I don't know. Sometimes I can get a feel for it. This time I'm looking at the intel, and it says we'll turn up something. Still, I just don't feel it down deep," Hollister said.

"Just promise me one thing," Michaelson said.

"What's that?"

"You'll keep looking over your shoulder. Valentine is itching to get into a fight before this war's over, and you don't want to be part of it."

"Got it."

Rain blew through the compound and forced the inspections into the larger buildings. Hollister walked through the maintenance shed and found Deming's team.

"How's it going?"

Deming jabbed his thumb skyward. "We were laid out outside our hootch until this storm blew in. I figured we'd be better off taking dry gear in than wet. We don't have time for everything to dry out before we launch tomorrow morning."

"I agree. How's your equipment?" Hollister asked.

"Would you like to take a look, sir?"

Hollister looked around the room. All twelve members of Deming's heavy team had laid out their combat loads for inspection. He singled out Private First Class Keith, a new man, who was one of the radio operators for the team. "You and I haven't had a chance to talk much, Keith."

Keith was kneeling over his rucksack, arranging the contents in front of it.

"How many patrols you have with Juliet Company now?"

The soldier looked up and thought for a moment. "Four, sorta—I mean one of them was only an insert, followed by a pickup about five minutes later. Can't really call that a patrol."

"Anytime you go into bad guy territory and come out, you've been somewhere worth talking about," Hollister said. "What's your call sign?"

"We're Team Georgia this time, sir."

"Lemme see that radio," Hollister said.

Hollister hoisted the PRC-77 and rested it on his hip. He turned the dials to the preset stops and read the number. "What's your primary frequency?"

Keith spit out the numbers from memory.

Hollister spun the dials to the other stops. "Your alternate?"

Keith had the correct numbers that time too.

"How long have you had this radio?"

"A month, sir," Keith said.

"It work?"

"Gets a little staticky in the rain, but most of the time it's pretty good."

"You willing to bet your life on it?"

"I'd rather go with this one I know than a new one, sir."

"Good." Hollister handed the radio back and picked up Keith's two-quart canteen. He unscrewed the plastic top and smelled the water. "Fresh?"

"This morning, sir."

"Water purification tablets?" Hollister asked.

Keith picked up another one-quart canteen and showed Hollister the small brown bottle taped to the canteen.

Hollister swapped canteens and unscrewed the tiny top to the halazone tablets. He turned the bottle upside down, and nothing came out.

"Shit," Keith mumbled.

"If you don't keep these dry, they turn into a rock in the bottom of the bottle. You ever picked up one of the bugs in the local water?"

"No, sir."

"If you had, we'd never need to discuss this." He handed the canteen back to Keith.

"Yes, sir. I'll take care of it."

Hollister looked down at Keith's feet. "Which boot?" he asked.

"Sir?"

"Dog tag," Hollister said.

Keith raised his left foot off the ground. "This one, sir."

Hollister could make out the outline of the single dog tag threaded through the laces of Keith's boot and tucked behind the canvas upper. It was a grim reminder that it was necessary to split the pair up—one dog tag on the neck chain and the other in a boot. In case a Ranger was decapitated and the chain got lost.

Hollister dismissed the solemn subject from his mind. "Okay, Ranger, have a good trip."

"Thank you, sir. Hope I do," Keith said.

Hollister continued to spot-check equipment and ask questions of the Rangers in Deming's patrol. He was impressed with the attention to detail. Deming had put plenty of time into preparing Team Georgia. Hollister finished with another Ranger and turned to Deming. "Let's walk outside. I want to have a word with you."

Hollister pulled a pack of cigarettes out of his pocket and offered Deming one.

"No, sir. I'm trying to quit," Deming said.

Hollister lit one and looked back toward the building. "I don't want to put pressure on you, but I want you to know this is not a normal patrol. Every decision you make will not only affect the eleven other members of your team but the moves and the safety of twenty-four other Rangers and thirteen chopper crews."

Deming looked down at his jungle boot and kicked at a shoot of a weed trying to stretch toward the sun. "I've been thinking about that, sir. It's pretty heavy."

"It doesn't have to be. I mean, you don't have to do it alone. Just don't try to be a hero or an iron butt out there. You have a problem or are unsure about something—let me know. Either me, or Brownie, or Thomas will be a radio squawk away—twenty-four hours a day."

"I appreciate that, sir. You can count on me not to spook or do something crazy out there."

Hollister looked at his watch. "You'll be on the ground in thirty-six hours. What can we help you prepare between now and then?"

"I'd like to spend some more time loading and unloading the choppers. We've never gone in with boats before."

"You got it. I'll set it up."

Deming nodded, and Hollister gave him a supportive slap on the shoulder.

"I don't give a fuck about Colonel Valentine," Hollister said, slamming his fist down on the desktop, upsetting a half-empty soda can.

"Sir, he keeps complaining about our chopper support," Captain Thomas said, reading from cryptic notes in his pocket notebook.

"What the hell does that mean?"

"His story is that his Viets keep seeing chopper after chopper coming and going from our compound, and they can't seem to get their hands on the same kind of chopper support. Two of his regimental commanders here in Tay Ninh are saying it is causing them to lose face.

"He went through channels with his complaint, and it came back down to General Quinn's office. I got the call from the ops sergeant major that Quinn called Valentine directly, and they got in a minor pissing match. So I guess you better stand by for shit to roll downhill, sir."

"What the hell am I supposed to do—not use choppers? Or maybe we should walk into fucking Cambodia?"

Sergeant Caulter came through the orderly room door. "Cap'n . . . chopper's coming with General Quinn on board. Be here in zero three."

"Shit!" Hollister said. He grabbed his black beret and squared it up on his head. "Let's go see what the hell he wants."

Hollister and Captain Thomas stood by the large H sunk into the hard-packed dirt. Quinn's chopper settled onto the pad. Its new paint job and large Field Force emblem on the nose set it off from the working choppers tied down on either side of the runway.

Quinn pushed open the door, slipped free of his seat belts, and jumped out of the chopper. He walked toward Hollister.

"Good afternoon, General," Hollister yelled over the chopper's turbine whine.

"Hollister. Thomas. How are you two?" the general asked, a large smile on his face.

"Good, sir. Is there something we can show you?"

"I came to chat, and then I have to get back to Saigon for a meeting this evening."

The only place they could talk and not have their conversation overheard was in the tiny officers club. Hollister braced himself for what he would find inside. He hoped it looked presentable enough not to be embarrassing.

They stepped through the door into the much darker room and found it completely empty, although smelling of beer and stale cigarettes. Hollister pointed at one of the two plywood tables circled by empty ammo boxes that served as seats; Thomas went to the window and opened the metal shutters to let some air and light in.

"Something to drink, General?" Thomas asked.

General Quinn jabbed his thumb at the wall that blocked his

view of his own chopper. "I've got more flying to do so it better be a soft drink."

Hollister nodded to Thomas, letting him know he'd have the same.

"I have to start by telling you I have had every intention of coming out to see what kind of operation you folks have, but my time has been eaten up by all the shitty little details. I'm the junior BG in the loop—I get all the crap."

Hollister and Thomas smiled at the candid comment; they were not used to a general officer being so informal.

"And with your upcoming operations, this wouldn't be the time to ask you to show me around and brief me on how you folks do what you do.

"I haven't been a general officer so long I don't remember how much work and training gets done when a visiting fireman shows up—none."

"Thank you, sir. Right now we can use every minute we get."

"I don't have to tell you I've been taking some static from the province senior adviser about your folks and your operations."

"I heard, sir, and I'm sorry if we are—"

"I can't think you got this job because something like that would get in your way. You know your own priorities. I also have confidence you can sidestep some of this shit without it blowing up into skunks peeing on one another.

"Now, I'm going to make some noises about all this, and I want you to keep on doing what you're doing. You let me handle Colonel—promotable—Valentine. You got that?" Quinn said.

"Yes, sir." Hollister broke into a smile. He knew there was something about Quinn he liked the first time he saw him.

"I'd like to walk through the compound and say hello to a few of your Rangers while they're warming my chopper back up if you don't mind," General Quinn said.

"No, sir." Hollister stood up. "That'd be no problem at all. As a matter of fact, we're running our teams through some training down at the strip now. Would you like to check it out?"

As Hollister followed General Quinn down the pathway to the airstrip, Rangers passed, recognized the general, and offered snappy salutes.

"They look good, Hollister. I understand you had somewhat of a problem when you took command."

"All they needed was a chance to do a good job."

Before the general could answer, a chopper approached and landed. Several feet off the ground Hollister recognized the passenger as Colonel Valentine.

The chopper settled and Valentine got out. He appeared to be surprised to see General Quinn, but quickly put on a bright smile and saluted the general.

The general turned to Hollister. "Excuse me, Hollister. I'd like to speak with Colonel Valentine."

Without waiting for an answer, the general walked over to meet with Valentine. Hollister couldn't hear the conversation. But it was clear that Quinn was taking the wind out of Valentine's sails.

Valentine continued to nod his head and listen to the general. Occasionally, he would smile and look like whatever the general said was either interesting or enlightened.

The conversation ended with Valentine and Quinn walking back to their respective choppers. Quinn threw Hollister a cramped salute from his cockpit, while Valentine gave Hollister a look that promised more trouble.

On his way back to operations, Hollister heard the unique sounds of an approaching light observation helicopter—known as a loach for its acronym. He held his hand over his brow to cut the glare.

The pilot of the light observation helicopter came in hot, flared abruptly, and put the skids of the small chopper down as easily as if he was pitching pennies into a hat. His total control was evident in the bold moves he made and his decisive flying style.

Hollister didn't recognize the warrant officer at the controls and decided not to waste any more time. He just assumed the chopper was there for some aviation business. After all, he had amassed over a dozen choppers at his launch site, and more of their business was taking place forward than at their base in Bien Hoa.

Inside operations, Sergeant Young had assembled team leaders DeSantis, Chastain, and Deming for a weather update. Hollister came in on the moon-phase information.

Loomis had added backup radios next to and on top of the original ones.

"Nixon could run the White House out of here," Hollister said.

Loomis poked his head up from behind the bench where he was connecting antenna cables. "We aren't gonna get caught with our commo pants down. You need to talk to one of those teams or aircraft, I'll have the tools for you to do it."

Hollister looked at the array of radios and telephones. "Where the hell did all this come from?"

Loomis shot a look at Captain Browning, who had just stepped through the door.

Hollister didn't miss the look. He turned to Browning. "You know anything about all this new commo equipment?"

Browning looked down. "Well, sir, it seems there might be some problems in supply routing. Some of this stuff was scheduled to be given to the Viets—part of Vietnamization—but it ended up here by mistake."

"Where was this *supposed* to go?"

"To province headquarters."

"You mean this stuff was for Valentine's units?"

"Yes, sir."

Hollister shook his head. "Great. This guy is going to be a pain in my butt for the rest of my life. Does he know?"

Browning was unable to hold back a sliver of a smile. "I don't know. I've been meaning to send a message back through channels telling the signal folks some equipment has ended up here by mistake and ask for instructions."

Hollister picked up on the maneuver. "Well, make sure you get the address right before you send it and make sure you identify all of the equipment by nomenclature and serial number. We don't want to screw up the supply system with incomplete messages."

"Yes, sir," Browning said. "I sure hope Colonel Valentine's folks can get along for a few weeks without this stuff. It may take that long to get it and the *complete* information to the right destination."

"It just might."

"Anyone in here tell me where I can find Captain Thomas?"

Hollister turned around and found a chief warrant officer standing in the doorway, his rumpled Nomex flight suit poorly fitting his small frame. The boy couldn't have been a day over twenty. He wore aviator's sunglasses, sported a large handlebar mustache, wore a black leather pistol belt that held up a .38 police special revolver, and had a huge 1st Cavalry Division combat patch on his right shoulder.

"He's not here right now. What can I do for you, Chief?" Hollister said.

The young pilot took off his sunglasses. He quickly recognized Hollister's rank and other insignia and snatched the faded baseball cap from his head. "Sir. My name's Adams. I was told to report to Captain Thomas with a loach ready to do some flying. I'm looking for where to dump my gear and where to park my crew chief. I guess I'm supposed to be here for a week or so."

Hollister stuck his hand out. "Welcome aboard, Chief. Have you eaten?"

The warrant officer's eyes quickly scanned the room, not missing combat markings on the uniforms of the team leaders and officers in the room. "No, sir. I was kinda hoping we'd get lucky. That food back at battalion will ground the average pilot. Thought you folks bein' who you are and doin' what you do would get some priority for better chow."

Browning and Loomis laughed at the notion.

"Well, we have had plenty of complaints about our chow. But folks keep coming back meal after meal. So my guess is the bitching is just bitching. Why don't you round up your crew chief and head on over to the mess hall." Hollister pointed. "Two buildings down. Have Sergeant Kelly give you two something to eat. I'll have someone round up Captain Tennant—the air mission commander—to get you racks and a place to drop your gear."

"Good deal, sir," the pilot said. He turned to exit, and Hollister stopped him.

"Where'd you come from?"

"I was a scout pilot in the Cav, and they started deploying back to the States."

"You got lots of time in a loach?"

"About half and half. Half of it in a loach and half in a Cobra. I started out as a Cobra front seater in a hunter-killer team," Adams said.

"What's your favorite?" Hollister asked.

"It's real hard to say which I like better. I gotta be honest. The Cobra's a real kick in the ass. But I'm about the best loach pilot the Cav ever saw. I can fly that little sucker through the eye of a needle and not ding anything up."

"Well, I'm glad to hear that. We can use all the shit-hot pilots we can get. Now, get on over to that mess hall, and we'll get you an orientation briefing after you're fed and checked in."

*　　　*　　　*

Hollister could see a few lights still on in the team hootches. He remembered how tense those nights before missions had been for him. He could only guess it was the same for the teams going in within a few hours.

Inside one end of an old engineer barracks Team 1–4 had set up housekeeping. They had separated themselves from Team 1–2 with a chin-high wall of empty artillery crating.

Hollister stuck his head in the back door and found one Ranger still awake. "You 'bout ready to go tomorrow, Greenwood?"

"Yes, sir. I'm about as ready as I can be." Greenwood smiled. "Thanks for asking, sir."

"I'm glad you hung in there back at Benning. And I'm happy to have you back again."

"Let's hope I get luckier this time out. I can't spend another month on my back in some lame-assed hospital."

"Yer sure everything's working?"

"Sir, I'm right as rain. Ready to go." He reached up and touched the jagged line on his jaw. "Anyway, the scars are good for picking up women in bars."

The room smelled of cleaning solvents and lubrication for the weapons. Hollister didn't have to be there to know each man spent a considerable amount of time that evening checking and rechecking the action on his weapons.

Private First Class Parsons slept on his back and half-snorted as he rolled over.

"How's he doing?" Hollister asked.

Greenwood simply gave Hollister a nod. Then he added, "Glad I got him. He'll be okay. I'll keep him straight."

"Good. Get some rack time. You've got several long days ahead of you."

CHAPTER 25

Sergeant Dinh spat the rice gruel from his mouth toward the corner of the earthen room. "You cook like you work. Is there nothing your kind can do correctly?"

Rat looked up from his spot on the floor where he tried to finish his own meager bowl of rice. "I'm not a cook. I told you so. Cooking is woman's work."

"You are not a cook," Dinh said. "You are also not a soldier, not a worker, not a brother in the struggle, and not a man. What are you mountain monkeys good for?"

Dinh threw his tin rice cup at Rat. "This is not food. It is pig slop. You did not clean the rice. You did not wash the pot, and you did not cook it correctly."

Rat made eye contact with Dinh, but said nothing. Still his insolent attitude was clear.

"Your people should have been wiped from our highlands centuries ago. Be warned. When we win our just victory over the puppets in Saigon, you will see your kind eliminated. You have no useful function."

Rat refused to allow Dinh to anger him. Every time he did, it always resulted in punishment. He would be given the worst jobs on the repair crew. He would have to dig the holes for all to relieve their bowels. Then he would have to fill the holes and repair the vegetation so it would look as if no one had been there.

To Rat it was undignified for a man to attend to the sanitary needs of another man. He knew Dinh made him do it because there was no dirtier job he could give him. He had never killed a man, but when he thought of Dinh, it didn't seem to him that it would be that difficult.

"Clean up this mess," Dinh yelled. "I want to sleep, and I want not to have to smell your foul, burned rice."

Rat didn't say anything. Instead, he crawled across the floor of the underground room and picked up the bits of rice.

Rat pulled back the crude wooden panel fashioned as a light and smoke baffle at the entrance to the tunnel. All he needed to do was to move beyond that and then separate the bushes that covered the opening, and he would be free of the tunnel.

Outside, in the dark, he stood motionless for a few minutes to absorb the freedom and the fresh smell of the night air. He looked up at the navy-colored sky filled with tens of thousands of crisp stars. The sky and the smell of the breeze after it had passed through the trees reminded him of his childhood. He would go out at night with his father to hunt night creatures. He missed his father, his family, and his way of life. He tried to push the thoughts of how miserable he was from his mind and enjoy the moment.

He looked back toward Vietnam and wondered if there were any of his people left alive. He had been gone so many years. He could only assume the Vietnamese had continued to come to his tiny village to take the grown boys and men. The loss of all the men in the village meant the women were left to work the fields, hunt, cook, and defend themselves. He knew the likelihood of the women being able to do that for any length of time was minimal.

Rat put the grass basket of tunnel waste behind a clump of brush. He would bury it in the morning when he could see to dig. Dinh wouldn't let him keep the garbage in the tunnel during the night. In the morning, Rat would bring out more human waste and cans of urine that had accumulated during the night. After he buried it all, he would join the others in the work party to finish repairing a small bridge.

He looked at the horizon for any sign that the day might be cooler for him. But the trees were too tall for him to venture a guess based on his reading of the wafer-thin line separating the earth from the heavens.

He took one last breath of fresh air and reentered the hole.

Hollister left the maps spread out on the desk in his room and walked to his bunk. He lit a cigarette and then pulled his grease pencil from his shirt pocket. On the wall next to the bunk, he began to draw the schematic of the upcoming operation. It helped him burn a picture in his mind of the important control measures, the major terrain features, and the relative positions of the teams on the ground.

The picture was simple. Two major streams joined just inside Cambodia to form a larger river. In the V created by the junction, the North Vietnamese work parties had created a way station, rest area, and tunnel complex. The tunnel network allowed them to hide from aerial observation, shelter themselves from bombardment, and stage work parties to keep the parallel trails and fords open for the arriving units.

The Rangers would insert three large teams and move to the objective area by rubber boats. Once in position, two teams would set up ambush-snatch sites along the paths paralleling the streams. The third would work its way to a point upwind of the complex and saturate the tunnels with tear gas.

Hollister hoped someone from the complex could be flushed out and captured. Prisoners would provide information and confirmation of the function of the way station. With that information, it would be a simple matter for higher headquarters to justify mounting a more conventional assault on those bunkers, putting them out of business.

Hollister had to remind himself and his Rangers that their purpose was not to destroy the complex or inflict maximum casualties. Rather, it was to capture as many prisoners as they could.

He stepped back from the drawing and looked at it for a long time. He wanted to fix the relationships of the sketch in his mind. He would need to call on his memory in the darkness and in moments of extreme pressure for a decision or an answer from him. He wouldn't always have the luxury of pulling out his map to orient himself.

Convinced he had memorized the diagram, Hollister took a towel from the foot of his bunk and wiped the lines from the plywood wall. He heard himself say, "God—let this one go off well."

Hollister stood in the quiet compound and lit his second cigarette of the day. He surveyed the eastern sky for signs of sunrise. The blackness of the earth was separated from the blue-black sky by a line of teal.

Just then the door to the showers opened, and Jrae stepped out, wrapped in a salvaged nylon poncho liner. She had pulled her wet hair back from her face and tied it in a knot. It was the first time

Hollister had seen how long and thin her cranelike neck was and how prominent her cheekbones were.

"Jrae?"

His voice startled her.

He pulled back the cuff of his jungle fatigue shirt and checked his watch—it wasn't even four A.M. yet.

"Good morning, Captain," she said, shuffling her things and pulling the ragged poncho liner material tightly across her chest.

"Are you all right?"

"Oh yes. I am fine, Captain."

"Isn't this kind of early for you?"

"We only have one shower house here, Captain. If I am to clean myself, I must find a time when the soldiers are not there. This is that time."

"We'll see what we can do about getting you some more privacy."

"That will be very nice, Captain."

"Is everything else okay for you?"

"Everything else?" Jrae repeated, unsure.

"How are you getting along here?" Hollister asked.

"Getting along?" Jrae said, puzzled by the term.

"I mean, are you okay? Is everyone treating you well? Ah . . ." He searched for some easy way to describe it. "Are you happy here?"

She pointed off to the north. "You know, Captain, that I come from the mountains. Many in my family were killed by the VC and the Republicans. I am alone now. I do not think anyone is alive now. Here I am fed, and I have a job, and I do not feel afraid."

"I think it's very important you don't feel afraid. If you have that, you have a chance to work out everything else. Do you understand what I am saying?"

"Yes. I think so," Jrae said. "I must go make ready for work now. I do not want to lose my job."

"Do you like your job?"

"I have so much to learn. I do not understand everything. But Sergeant Easy and the other soldiers treat me better than when I was at the camp. I like my job, Captain."

"Well, we like having you here. And I want you to feel comfortable and want you to know you can come to me if you have any problems."

"Thank you very much, Captain."

Hollister watched her walk away. She moved gracefully, and the fresh smell of her lingered in his nostrils. He realized how long it had been since he had been that close to a woman. He missed the feeling.

Rat woke, shivering from the cold and damp that had seeped into his body while he slept. His nose was clogged with the dirt from the tunnels and soot from the oil lamps. He slowly straightened his legs and searched for the feeling to come back to his toes and fingertips.

It was hard for Rat to tell what time it was with no way to see the sky. He knew if he went back to sleep, it was possible he might sleep too long, and Dinh would wake him and begin screaming at him.

He picked his way to the tunnel shaft that led to the outside. There he had to get back down on his hands and knees to crawl up the angled shaft. As he worked his way through the long, dark, earthen tube, he stopped often to sweep the debris from his neck and hair. In the dark, it was impossible for him to tell if it was only dirt, roots, and pebbles, or the huge poisonous centipedes that were everywhere in the tunnels. He had been stung before. It had made him sick and feverish. The potions his mother brewed from the bark of elder and comfrey roots only relieved the pain for a few minutes. He knew if he was to encounter another centipede, he wouldn't even be able to find that much relief. Even if he knew how to prepare the poultice his mother had made, Dinh would never allow him to stop working long enough to brew it.

Within ten meters of the entrance, Rat could smell the promise of fresh air. Somewhere else in the tunnel complex a vacuum existed that drew the cool, fresh, outside air into the shaft.

Rat moved a few feet and then turned to pull the cans of urine and baskets of waste forward. Then he repeated the process, over and over, until he reached the entrance.

It took Rat two trips from the tunnel entrance to carry all of the garbage to the site he had selected to bury the waste. He knelt down to dig, and felt the pain in his legs. He wasn't sure if it was just soreness from the cold tunnels or if he had just worn out his knees doing all of the digging, carrying, and hauling he had done in the years he had been a slave of the North Vietnamese. He rubbed his legs and tried to find something pleasant to think about while he finished digging the hole. His small hand spade had a split in the wooden handle that pinched the palm of his hand if he didn't take care to avoid trapping his flesh in its grip.

Inside operations was a hive of activity. Patrol leaders were picking up the latest weather data. Pilots made last-minute coordination.

Hollister entered and walked directly to Loomis. He picked up the duty officer's log and read the new entries from the night before. Colonel Valentine had called operations to ask why he didn't yet have a copy of the operations overlay. Hollister reached for a cigarette and lit it.

"Call province and pass the word to Colonel Valentine's office that we sent everything his headquarters needs yesterday."

Captain Thomas looked up from the map he was studying on the far end of the radio bench. "Sir, we didn't send him an overlay."

"I know. 'Everything he needs' doesn't include our fucking overlay."

Thomas made a face.

"I know. It's quibbling. But I'd rather have him take a bite out of my ass for that than have our overlay floating around province headquarters for every fucker under five foot six to see and discuss or even sell."

Hollister looked around the room at the large number of Rangers coming and going. He checked his watch. It was 0428. "We're lifting off in thirty-two minutes, folks. Need I say anything more?"

Everyone in the room acknowledged Hollister's comment and picked up the pace of their activity. The pilots were the first to leave.

Suddenly the sounds of the cocks and the morning birds went silent. Rat felt it before he heard the silence. He put down his hand spade and looked up. Off to the southeast, he heard the approach of helicopters. He watched them for a few moments and decided they were headed somewhere south of him.

When they got nearly due south of the tunnel complex they began circling, dropping flares, and firing at something on the ground.

Dinh stepped out of the tunnel. "What is happening?"

Rat pointed off to the choppers. "They must have discovered something there."

Dinh let out a laugh. "How foolish they are. That area we abandoned in 1968. There is nothing but empty training huts and a trail intersection there. They are so stupid."

Rat didn't speak. For a fleeting moment, he hoped the choppers would come their way and catch Dinh out in the open.

"I am going to eat. Hurry. You have many things to do below," Dinh said before crawling back into the tunnel entrance.

Hollister looked down the length of the runway outside the compound wire. Fourteen choppers stood at flight idle, finishing run-up procedures.

Next to the lift choppers, the teams had stacked their carry-in loads while they underwent final personal inspections only yards away from their assigned birds.

Hollister tried to identify the team members. But in that light, it was hard—made even more difficult by the expert application of camouflage stick. The final confusion was created by the fourteen rotating beacons on the tops of the choppers that painted and repainted the area with red lights.

It was the largest Ranger lift he had ever mounted, and Hollister was more than a little worried about the complexities of the operation ahead.

Across the runway from the slicks, four Cobras and an armed loach stood ready to protect the insert package. Somewhere between Bien Hoa and Tay Ninh, an OV-10 was en route to provide forward air control support. The ground crew and fuel tanker for the sophisticated air force spotter plane were already set up near the maintenance area.

Chief Adams walked up behind and fell into step with Hollister. "Morning, sir. You ready to lift off yet?"

Hollister had decided earlier not to put all of his command and control personnel in one chopper. Thomas and Gannon were going in the C & C, coordinating the inserts. He'd opted to take Adams's loach and oversee the entire insert.

He had spent very little time inside an OH-6A and none of it in the front seat. Chief Adams belted himself into the right seat and began his preflight checklist before Hollister got fully buckled into the left.

Hollister looked around the cramped cockpit of the small

chopper. Compared to the Huey slick, it was half its height, half its length, had half as large a rotor disk, but could cruise through the treetops at 150 miles an hour—just about the same speed as the Huey. It only took a few minutes of watching a skilled loach pilot maneuver one to agree it was the sports car of helicopters.

Hollister watched as Adams ran up the turbine and rotor RPM and then signaled his crew chief outside to leave his post acting as a lookout to warn people about the eight-foot-high rotor blades.

The crew chief got into the chopper and put his machine gun across his lap. He pressed the transmit button on the drop cord running to his helmet. "Clear to the rear, Chief."

Adams pressed the left pedal, pulled up on the collective, and scanned the instruments. Satisfied the chopper was ready, he announced, "Coming up." The tiny chopper almost leaped from the ground. Its whispering rotor blades made the motion seem effortless.

The young pilot took up a left orbit over the airfield to allow Hollister to survey the flight of fifteen as it lifted off for Cambodia.

Hollister slipped the lip mike nearer to his mouth and checked the frequency of the radio on the console. It was the Juliet Company tactical net. "Three. This is Six. How 'bout a sitrep?"

Thomas came back without hesitation. "This is Three. We're about thirty seconds from skids up."

"Roger. I'll take up a slot on the left side of your flight but out of the way. I'll be close if you need me. Good luck."

"Thanks, boss," Thomas said.

The loach had hardly made half an orbit when Hollister saw the gunships lift off. The slicks rolled forward and up. And the pilots took up a flight formation a thousand meters to the rear of the gunships.

"Okay, Chief. Let's get up alongside and try not to get ourselves run over," Hollister said.

The young pilot nodded and rolled the chopper on its nose, sucking the collective up toward his armpit while pushing forward on the cyclic. The loach picked up speed and quickly closed the gap with the larger formation.

Once he leveled off, Adams reached down and punched the button on a tiny reel-to-reel tape recorder Hollister hadn't noticed earlier. Immediately the headsets in all three helmets came alive with Cream singing, *"In a white room with black curtains . . ."*

Adams looked over at Hollister for his reaction and found him smiling at the energetic scout pilot.

To Hollister it was loach music if there ever was any.

The flight to the objective area went off without complication. Hollister watched the flickering morning lights peek from the houses and businesses along the route. After less than five minues, there were no more lights. They crossed over the no-man's-land between populated Vietnam and the Cambodian border.

To the southwest, Hollister could see the flight of six other helicopters, a forward air controller, an AC-47 gunship, and three Cobras.

The AC-47 dropped parachute flares while the Cobras prowled the treetops—firing bursts of miniguns and rockets.

They were shooting at nothing. Hollister and Michaelson knew they wouldn't be able to insert six chopper loads of Rangers without it being noticed by enemy forces on the ground. The solution was to execute a feint just a mile and a half south of the bunker complex as a distraction. While the show was taking place, Hollister's Rangers would slip into two landing zones twelve miles north and west of the bunkers.

Hollister hoped the feint was enough to focus attention on itself and cover the sounds of the three Ranger teams swinging wide to the north at treetop level.

As Hollister's flight crossed the border, the pilots turned off their navigation lights and picked their way through the gentle terrain in the long shadows created by the flares.

Watching the ground rush by only twenty feet below the loach's skids, and flying blacked out, Hollister recognized the chance of collision they faced. The patches of light and dark played tricks on pilots and made it difficult to navigate.

The Ranger flight arced north, crossed the two large streams, hooked back around to the south and then east as they approached their landing zones. Two miles out, the formation split into a flight of one and a flight of two Ranger teams. The first insert on the westernmost stream would put in Deming's and Chastain's teams.

The remainder of the insert package would take DeSantis's to a landing zone near the eastern stream.

Hollister made one last call to Thomas in the C & C with Tennant and Gannon. "Three. This is Six. You okay?"

Thomas immediately responded. "Rog. We think we have it under control. We're three minutes from touchdown for the first element. Over."

"Okay," Hollister said. "I'm going to pull high and out of your way. You need me—you call. Understand?"

"Will do," Thomas said.

Hollister turned to Adams, who had already heard the conversation and needed no instruction. He nodded his head. The tiny helicopter screamed up without strain and put several hundred feet of separation between it and the others within a matter of seconds. The whisper of its rotors was masked by the sounds of the other aircraft and the firing to the south.

The choppers kept circling to the south, firing and dropping flares. Rat thought about how much he hated Dinh. He even considered starting a fire to bring the choppers. As he finished burying the last of the waste containers, he leaned back on his heels to prepare himself to go back underground. He took a deep breath to savor the fresh air. Suddenly he caught some movement on the northern horizon. More choppers, their lights out, flew low over the trees across the border to a point north of the tunnels.

Unlike the other choppers, they were not announcing their presence. They hugged the ground, and then most of them disappeared below his view. Rat considered telling Dinh and then decided not to. He quietly walked back to the tunnel.

At his new altitude, Hollister could see the tops of the slicks' rotor disks approaching the first landing zone, and the prowling gunships.

The landing zone below Hollister was calm and dark. He hoped it would stay that way long enough for Deming and Chastain to get their teams in.

They had selected a large landing zone to allow the four choppers carrying the two heavy teams to land, discharge their loads, and take off without running out of space.

The advantage of a large LZ was maneuverability for the pilots. The disadvantage was it made the run to the nearest tree line longer for the Rangers, and it afforded plenty of uninterrupted visibility for any LZ watchers. What was more, its desirability as a landing zone also made it more likely to be mined or booby-trapped.

Hollister looked up toward Nui Ba Den—the Black Virgin Mountain—to orient himself and then looked out at the approaching choppers closing on the landing zone.

"You are zero one out," Thomas said over the radio to the team leaders.

"Thirty seconds.

"Stand by," Thomas finally said.

The formation consisted of four choppers in trail, with the two chase ships two hundred feet above and four hundred feet behind the insert ships. The Cobras were down in the large tree line, making opposing circles just where the trees became tall grasses.

Touchdown. Hollister let the breath escape from his chest as he strained to see the teams exiting the choppers. From the lead and the third chopper, he saw the large bundles that held the rubber boats bounce out onto the LZ.

Unlike a normal insert, half of each team ran out beyond the choppers' rotor disks and set up a semicircle of security while the other half of each team picked up the heavy boat bundles to carry them off the LZ.

The choppers were up and out of the landing zone long before the first Ranger started for the tree line. Hollister could feel himself silently urging them to *Move! Move! Move!* while he watched them edge toward the trees with all the speed they could muster.

Thomas and the C & C kept on going with DeSantis's insert package to the second landing zone.

The last Ranger left the landing zone, and it grew quiet over the radio net. Everyone was listening for their signal. Every eye in the nine choppers circling above the landing zone was focused on the fringe of the large tree line for any signs of small-arms fire.

Chastain was the first to speak. "Colorado in and cold. I say again—in and cold. Out."

Almost over the top of Chastain's transmission, Deming whispered his report. "Georgia. In and cold. In and cold. Out."

"Move east," Thomas said over the radio. "All aircraft are released to move east—now."

The choppers peeled out of orbit and stretched into a staggered trail formation.

DeSantis's team had its own slicks, a chase, and two gunships. Even before the choppers had inserted Deming and Chastain, Thomas was lining up DeSantis's insert.

"One minute out," Thomas announced over the tactical net.

Hollister caught Adams's eye and pointed back toward the border.

"Yes, sir. We'll be there before you know it." He nosed over the loach and poured it on. The airspeed indicator on the instrument panel broke a hundred knots, and the wind and turbulence inside the chopper picked up.

"You are thirty seconds out," Thomas said.

By that time Hollister and Adams were close enough to see DeSantis's insert choppers—Rangers' legs sticking out of both sides. DeSantis was standing out on the skid of the lead chopper, holding on to the bulkhead with one hand.

"Six. This is Three. They're on short final," Thomas said.

"I'm above and behind you. I copy. Good luck," Hollister said. He turned to look back over his shoulder in the direction of Deming's and Chastain's teams. It was too far away for him to even see the landing zone. But he thought if any shooting started, he might just be able to see the tracers. As he hoped—it was still black.

"Coming out," the lead pilot of the insert chopper announced. Then everything went silent again while they waited for DeSantis to get his team into the trees.

Like the others circling wide north of DeSantis's landing zone, Hollister kept his eyes on the black ribbon of darkness created by the overhang of the tree branches. The shadows in an already dark morning were the only protection available to DeSantis. The stand of trees along the stream bank was only five meters wide and a thousand long. Once inside it, DeSantis had to wait until dusk to unpack and inflate the rubber boats, drag them into the streambed, and start paddling toward his objective.

"We're down. It's cold. I say again—cold," DeSantis announced in a stage whisper.

Hollister felt himself relax into the seat. "Okay, Three. Let's clear the air space around here and let those folks down there get to work."

CHAPTER 26

Rat tried to stretch the dull pain from his lower back. He looked up at the sun still high in the western sky and sighed. The sweat from his brow ran into his eyes and burned. When he tried to wipe it from his face, he only ground in the dirt on his arms.

"What is the matter with you? Do I have to take green bamboo to your back to get some work out of you?" Dinh yelled.

The others on the work party stopped what they were doing and looked at the angry sergeant as he charged up the trail toward Rat.

Dinh thrust his face into Rat's. He pointed to the scars on Rat's legs. "Do you forget so quickly? Do you want more of those to remind you of your lack of motivation and loyalty? Or are you just stupid?"

Rat didn't respond. He knew no matter what he said, Dinh would still beat him. He braced himself and tried to put the pain out of his mind.

Dinh brought the end of the pick handle down on Rat's shoulder, glancing off and down his back. Missing a square, solid blow only seemed to make him angrier. He raised the handle over his head again and swung even harder.

Rat raised his arm to deflect the blow. The pick handle broke through the flesh on his forearm and fractured the bone. He cried out in pain.

"Shut up! You are a woman. You cannot even take discipline like a man. Are there no men among your people?"

Rat bit down hard on his lip to keep from crying out more. The pain shot up his arm, and he grabbed for the wound to stop the bleeding. He could only look at Dinh with all the contempt he could muster. Striking back would only provoke Dinh to more savage beating. He collapsed on the trail in deference to the brutish sergeant.

"Now you have cost me one laborer—a worthless one, but a laborer." Dinh waved his hand toward the trail. "We have to repair the damage to this roadway for our comrades. Now we will not finish before darkness. You will pay dearly for your indolence," he said. "I promise you that."

The work crew stayed well beyond dark and worked to repair the damage done by recent artillery and air strikes. Throughout the extra hours of work, Dinh kept reminding the others in the work crew they were working added hours because of Rat.

He also reminded them it would be dangerous for them to move back to the tunnels after dark. They would risk not seeing the signs to warn them of booby traps and mines at night. That, too, was because of Rat. They would have to move slowly, with extra caution; and that would get them back very late. They would be late to get to their underground hideout and late to eat. They would get very little sleep and be forced to get up earlier the next day to come back and finish their work. They could all thank the mountain man for not doing his share of the work.

The ashtray was made out of an old canteen cup that had lost its handle. Hollister looked into it and realized he had contributed all of its two-inch-deep contents. He picked it up and walked toward the door leading out of operations.

"Lemme get that for you, sir," Sergeant Caulter said, getting up from his chair beside the radios.

"No. I put 'em there. I guess I can find a trash can."

He stepped out into the midmorning sun. It momentarily blinded him after hours inside operations. He found a barrel they used to burn the classified trash and dumped the cigarette butts into it.

He was tired of waiting for something to go wrong. He knew the teams were laying up, waiting for nightfall to start their trips down the streams into the objectives.

"Captain, got some bad news for you."

Hollister looked up to find Easy approaching. "What now?"

"Our friend, Valentine, is on his way over."

"Shit. What's he want?"

"He said he wanted to speak to you. I told him you were in a briefing," Easy said. He kicked out at a small rock to test his leg. "You're just going to hate what I heard."

"Now what?"

"He's been frocked. They pinned on his stars early," Easy said.

"Wait a minute," Hollister said, brightening. "That means he's being reassigned. Province chief is only a colonel's job."

"Well, it doesn't turn out that way. Seems they are reinventing the wheel at MACV, and he's being made into a super adviser. They created a special zone consisting of most of the provinces in Three Corps that aren't underwater. He's the senior adviser, and the other colonels now report to him."

"I s'pose you're going to tell me he's not moving out of Tay Ninh?"

"You're psychic, sir."

General Valentine walked toward operations. New stars were already sewn onto the collars of his fatigue shirt.

"Good morning, General," Hollister said, throwing an obligatory salute.

"Hollister, let's cut the crap. I have been asking your people for overlays and op orders since you got here, and all I get is incomplete and vague paperwork on your operations," Valentine said.

"I'm sending you all I am cleared to send." Hollister stretched the truth.

"Don't argue with me, Hollister. Just get me and my people up to speed on what your goddamn teams are doing over there." Valentine thrust his arm out and pointed toward the Cambodian border.

Hollister didn't say anything.

"Well?"

"Well what?"

"Well, what are you going to do, mister?" Valentine asked, his face reddening and the creases around his mouth becoming more prominent.

"No more than usual. You are getting all your people need to know, and most of our operations are on a need-to-know basis. Anything more than that violates security SOP and may jeopardize the safety of my people."

"What the hell does that mean, Captain?" Valentine raised his voice, emphasizing the word *captain* to remind Hollister of the difference in their ranks. "Are you implying there is a security leak in my organization?"

Hollister locked onto Valentine's gaze. "Giving an overlay to a Viet unit is like running mimeographs for every VC within five hundred miles. I don't want to be the guinea pig to find out just where the leaks are in your organization, General."

"Mister, you have crossed a line. You've not heard the end of this. I'm going to have your tail. You have been a smart-ass since Benning. Don't you know you are not the only officer in this god-damn war? I think it's time we drop you down a peg or two."

Valentine spun on his heel and stepped back to the jeep that brought him from the airstrip. "Take me to my chopper—now!" he yelled at the driver.

Hollister turned around and saw Easy standing in the doorway of the orderly room.

"Thought I'd pretty much weaned you of thumbing your nose at assholes. Guess I was wrong."

"Guess I better call Michaelson and let him know shit is rolling downhill."

"Bad news doesn't get better with age."

"Team Alabama called in movement on the trail east of their position," Sergeant Caulter said.

Hollister snapped out of something between a daydream and outright sleeping. "What was it?" He got up from the uncomfortable folding chair next to the operations radios.

"They weren't close enough to see, but they heard it. They think it was a work party moving from north to south."

"How'd they know?"

"Said they heard what sounded like tools clanking together. Y'know—shovels?"

"He say how many?"

"Several voices—they estimate six to eight," Caulter said, reading the notes in the radio log in operations.

Hollister walked to the situation map. He located DeSantis's position, identified by the code name Alabama.

"Okay. I got it. Let Captain Tennant and the other two teams know, and keep the pilots close to their choppers 'til I say otherwise."

While Caulter put the word out, Hollister sat down and studied the map once again. He needed to see it when he closed his eyes. The fact that he had three large teams on the ground inside a circle not more than five miles in diameter made him much more aware of the demands on his concentration.

Having multiple teams on the ground in a small area meant more consideration had to be given to every decision because it had an impact on more than one team. He no longer had the freedom to support a team in trouble or in contact without regard for the safety of friendlies outside the tiny perimeter of a six-man team. He had to juggle the needs and the vulnerabilities of all the teams. That made everything more complicated and put the responsibility on Hollister to be more surgical.

"I need some coffee. If anything happens you can find me in the mess hall," Hollister said.

"Captain. I must thank you," Jrae said, seeing Hollister sitting in the corner of the mess hall.

He looked up from his notes and saw Jrae standing on the other side of the table, a pot of coffee for the orderly room in her hands.

". . . for the blankets."

"Blankets? Oh, yeah—blankets. I thought we might be able to find something in the supply room for you. I asked Easy to see what we could do."

"You are very kind," Jrae said.

"My pleasure. I can't expect you to work all day if you can't sleep at night."

"In my life I don't know many Americans. But the Americans I know have always been kind to me," Jrae said.

"I hope that continues." He watched her turn and walk out the door. He realized how much he liked her. He had come to admire her dignity and her reserve. He also felt her sadness and her isolation.

Hollister knew if he was going to squeeze in a shower he had to do it before dark. It would be then that the teams on the ground would start moving, and the chance of contact would increase.

He took off his shirt and boots and realized how much the tops of his feet hurt from the long hours of being laced into canvas jungle boots. He took off his trousers and caught sight of his own shadow painted against the wall in the shower enclosure. He had lost even more weight since arriving in Vietnam. He was surprised at how visible the loss was in the outline of his shadow. He felt his ribs, poking out above his equally prominent hip bones.

Hollister pulled the small, tin hand mirror from his shaving kit and looked at his face. He looked awful. The sockets under his eyes had hollowed and darkened. His skin had lost most of the color it had taken on while he was at Benning and Bragg. He saw a level of strain he had never seen. He looked much older.

"Sir," a voice whispered.

Hollister woke up, unsure of where he was. He shook his head to clear the fog and realized he had fallen asleep in a chair in the corner of operations.

"What?"

"You asked me to tell you when all three teams are in the water," Loomis said.

"Any problems?" Hollister asked, rubbing his eyes and searching for a cigarette.

"No sir. DeSantis's was the last team to call in to tell us they're moving."

"What time is it?" Hollister looked at his watch and didn't wait for Loomis to answer. "Twenty-three thirty? What the hell took so long?"

"Lieutenant Deming's team called in that they had found trip wires, and I passed that on to the others—"

"And that slowed everyone down."

"To a crawl."

"Okay. Let's continue the mission."

"That means *wait*, right?"

"Right. And I hate it," Hollister said.

"Join Juliet Company—live a life of excitement and adventure," Loomis said, spoofing the reputation of the Rangers.

Hollister furrowed his brow. "Don't you have something to do?"

"Hollister here, sir," he said into the receiver.

"Jim. I already know what you were calling about. General Valentine already called General Quinn," Michaelson said, his voice breaking over the light static on the line.

"Sir, I don't want to get General Quinn's shorts in a knot, but I'm tired of this guy nosing around in my business. Can't he just be satisfied with his new stars and his new job?"

"Jim, you and I agree. But we aren't running this man's army."

"Am I on General Quinn's shit list?"

"No. But you have to eat a little crow."

"Oh, oh. I feel this coming."

"Not that bad. Might be a little chink out of your ego, but other than that, it's painless."

"What do I have to do?"

"General Quinn was able to strike a compromise. He convinced General Valentine the nature of your operations was far too sensitive to provide full copies of your plans to his headquarters."

"So where's the compromise?"

"Invite Valentine and his American staff over."

"And?"

"And give him a full briefing of the operation and any progress you are making. No paperwork, no maps, no overlays, no classified documents leave the CP with his folks."

"You think that will satisfy him, sir?"

"Don't sweat it. General Quinn wants to sit in on the briefing, too. He wants it to look like the briefing is for him and as a courtesy Valentine is invited."

"That General Quinn's a good man."

"You're right. So, set it up."

"Yes, sir. What's a good time for General Quinn?"

"He said make it convenient for your operational needs."

"I'll take care of it."

"My infallible senior-NCO network tells me Valentine is supposed to be headed to Saigon for the weekend. He even has dinner plans with a classmate at the top of the Rex Hotel tomorrow evening. S'posed to be a pretty classy setup at the Rex—tablecloths and pretty V'namese waitresses," Easy said, a devilish look on his face.

Hollister looked at the handwritten schedule on his desktop. "Damn, Top. Looks like that's the only time we can hold that briefing. I sure hate to take the general away from his steak, martinis, and hot shower in Saigon. But we all have to sacrifice. Don't we?"

"Oh, I'm sure the good general would agree with you. Nothing should interfere with the real war effort."

"Would you be kind enough to extend our invitation to General Valentine for—let's say 1800 hours tomorrow afternoon, First Sergeant?"

"It would be my pleasure, sir." Easy couldn't conceal his

smile. "Damn shame he won't be able to make this briefing and still fly to Saigon."

"Yeah. It's a shame," Hollister said.

During the night the three teams moved closer to their objective areas. Hollister had been concerned from the beginning that using boats was much like posting a sign of their intentions. On normal patrols, the teams would zigzag to their objectives in order not to telegraph their exact direction. With few streams, it wasn't hard for a trail or LZ watcher to guess the direction of a team carrying a boat.

Hollister spent most of the evening in operations, monitoring their progress.

"What's harder?" Sergeant Caulter asked.

Hollister looked at the expression on his face. "You mean, 'What's harder: leading a patrol, being operations officer, or being the CO?' "

"Exactly."

"This is hardest. At least I had more control over things as a patrol leader and operations officer."

The radio broke squelch and DeSantis's RTO reported, "Alabama. Papa Lima Brown. Over."

Caulter picked up the pork-chop mike and keyed it. "This is Three Alpha. Roger Papa Lima Brown. Out."

Hollister stepped over to the situation map and erased the grease-pencil box marking Alabama's old position and drew a new one just below phase line Brown. "That puts them less than two hours from their pullout point."

"How long a hump do they have after that?" Caulter asked, entering the radio message into the log.

"Near as I can guess—about three more hours."

Caulter groaned. "Jesus. What a long-ass night. I'm glad my days of humping rucks are behind me."

Hollister smiled at Caulter. "Don't bet on it. The shit hits the fan around here, I'm putting all my warhorses on the ground."

"Even those horses with advanced cases of arthritis?"

"They never seem to slow you down when you're headed for happy hour."

"That's because happy hour is an anesthetic, sir," Caulter said.

The radio squawked again. "Three. This is Colorado. Papa Lima Greenback. Over."

Caulter answered and copied down the message into the log. Hollister updated the map, and they both sat back down to wait for Team Georgia to report in.

CHAPTER 27

Rat was the first to wake up. The pounding pain in his arm hadn't allowed him much sleep, and the poultice he had put on his wound had dried and needed replacement. He sat up and realized his chest also hurt from breathing the black smoke that filled the tunnel. The oil lamps gave out little light and made the air heavy. He coughed and felt the need to relieve his bladder.

The tin can in the corner was nearly filled with urine from the night, and the ground around it was muddy from those who had not cared to take aim.

Rat tried to avoid the repulsive smell rising from the can as he relieved himself. He felt awkward standing over the tin urinating into it while he held his broken arm above his head to relieve the pressure that brought the pain. He watched the urine splash into the bucket.

He knew within the hour he would have to take the bucket to the surface and empty it. Avoiding the smell was going to be nearly impossible. He hated it all.

Hollister entered operations and found Captain Thomas reading the radio log at the situation map.

"Mornin', boss."

"Morning. How goes it out in the AO?"

"They're in and buttoned up for the day. Georgia is a little worried about concealment. Lieutenant Deming's not happy with what the area has to offer," Thomas said.

"Can we move him to thicker stuff?"

"He opted to stay rather than move during the daylight."

"It's his call. Let's just hope he can hide his ass."

"I've got a lot of confidence in him," Thomas said.

"Me, too. Wouldn't have sent him out there if I didn't."

Rat crawled out into the sunlight and let it warm him for a moment before reaching back into the tunnel for the waste buckets. The morning air was wet and felt sticky against his dirty skin. He dragged his fingernails along the ragged edge of his arm injury. The dirt rolled off in small balls.

He wiped the corner of the wound with the hem of his thread-bare shirt. The pressure caused pus to ooze from the break in the skin. Rat knew his mountain medicine wasn't working, and if he didn't get some real medication, he would be looking at more pain and more infection. And because he was a Montagnard, there was little chance he would be able to get any of the drugs first reserved for the soldiers and then for the laborers.

He stepped over to the small streambed and gathered enough water to remoisten the dried-out poultice. He would try to find more healing plants to make a new poultice later. But until then, he had to make do with what he had.

The bucket of urine needed emptying.

With the injury to his arm, Rat was unable to carry the two cans of human waste in each hand. He walked over to the area where they routinely hid the tools used to repair the roads. Among the hoes and the picks, he found a carry pole they used to spread the load across their shoulders.

The load was a little shaky when it first came off the ground. Rat realized the wound to his arm had drained his energy. He walked slowly. As a boy he had learned he could avoid spilling containers of liquid by not locking his knees out when he walked. He turned up a section of the trail that led to an area he had not yet used to dispose of the waste. On one side of the trail, the small drainage ditch fed into the stream northeast of the underground hideout they slept in. The trail separated the stream from the tree line. He remembered a place they had passed weeks before that was a break in the trees where he could find some soft earth to empty the cans.

After only a few dozen yards, Rat stopped to rest his load. Not wanting to lose his center on the carry pole, he simply bent at the waist until the cans rested on the trail. His arm throbbed, and he felt feverish. He gave up the notion of finding the clearing, estimating it was a hundred more yards beyond the point where he rested.

As he balanced the bar his eyes traveled up the trail, where he spotted a track in the loose surface. The imprint of the toe of a single jungle boot showed the cleated pattern. He could tell it was left by someone running across the trail and into the trees that paralleled it.

He put down the carry pole and looked around for any sign of the boot's owner. He looked in the direction the toe print pointed and saw the vegetation had been disturbed. Americans. No South Vietnamese soldiers wore boots that size or stood that tall. Americans were nearby.

His pulse raced as he realized he could be dropped where he stood by a well-aimed shot. He turned to look back toward the tunnels. Did the Americans know the tunnels were there?

He couldn't risk going back to the tunnels. If they didn't know, they would follow him. He couldn't run away. Where would he go? He was hurt, and he was tired.

Rat stood up straight, pulled down on the hem of his shirt, and stepped off the trail in the direction of the visitors. He tried to hold his hands in view to show he carried no weapons.

Private First Class Keith finished replacing the brick-shaped battery in his radio and stuffed the used one into the side pocket of his rucksack. Out of habit, he raised the handset to his ear and listened for the rushing noise it produced when the squelch was turned off. That only told him there was enough power inside the radio to power the noise. He looked at his watch and saw he was scheduled for a routine sitrep in less than four minutes. He decided to wait.

Keith propped up his radio against his rucksack and then turned around to lean back against his load and wait. He pressed his shoulders against the soft part of his ruck. As he reached up to tilt the visor of his floppy boonie hat down over his eyes, he spotted something through the branches of the trees. For a fraction of a second, he thought he saw a face. He passed it off as his imagination, some weird trick the leaves were playing on his eyes.

He made one more adjustment to get more comfortable and saw the face again. He was sure. There was someone standing outside the perimeter looking in. The man was not more than twenty meters away.

Should he cry out? Should he just shoot? If he sat up and

showed alarm, would it spook the face? He froze and tried not to show the face that he saw him. Instead, he let his fingers search the ground for a pea-sized pebble. He found one and got it into a marble-shooter's grip.

From the corner of his eye he could see Lieutenant Deming's back; he was crouched over the map with Sergeant Iverson. He waited until Deming was still and fired the stone at him.

Deming turned without a start and looked at Keith.

Keith wiggled his fingers—below the eyeline of the visitor—and got Deming's attention. He then closed his hand into a fist and pointed his index finger in the direction of the face.

Deming's field instincts kicked in, and he dropped down slowly as if he were looking for something near the map. Hidden by the nearby bushes, he looked in the direction Keith had pointed.

The face stepped forward slowly and raised his arms above his shoulders in a sign of surrender. The damage to his forearm was clear to the Rangers, even at a distance. He was unarmed, wounded, and passive.

Loomis burst through the door of the officers' hootch and found Hollister's bunk. It was empty. He turned to head back out the door to the mess hall and almost ran over Hollister, who came through the door, his shaving kit and towel in hand.

"Whoa! What's up?"

"Sir, Deming's team just grabbed somebody."

"What? Are they compromised? Any shooting?"

Loomis shook his head. "No, sir. The guy just walked into their perimeter and gave himself up."

"And?" Hollister asked. He threw his gear onto his cot and grabbed the fatigue shirt draped over the back of a nearby chair. Not waiting for Loomis's answer, Hollister headed out the door.

Team medic, PFC Jimmy Ray Smith, finished cleaning the mountain medicine from the wound on the Montagnard's arm and squeezed a large strip of antibiotic ointment from a tube into the break in his flesh.

Rat watched the boy carefully dressing his wound and looked back up to Deming, who was squatting next to the two. Deming whispered to Rat that they were going to immobilize his arm with a wire splint to allow the bones to knit. He held up the strange-looking, ladderlike wire splint he pulled from Smith's aid bag.

Rat nodded, accepting the help.

Deming looked over Rat's head at the sun, then checked his watch. He dropped to both knees and scraped the surface of the ground to create a soft layer of dirt. With his finger he drew the rough diagram of the two converging streams and then poked his finger into the ground at a spot approximating their location.

In simple French he said, "We are here. Can you show me where we must go to find the others?"

Rat took his free hand and scooped up small pebbles near his leg. He dropped four of them in an oblong pattern and replied, "Tunnel entrances."

"All? No more?" Deming asked.

Rat shook his head. No more.

"Good. That's very good."

Rat turned, reacting to Sergeant George holding a camera to his face, snapping and winding, and snapping photos of the mountain man.

Inside operations, Captain Thomas held the ear cups of a headset tight to his ears to listen to an incoming radio transmission.

Hollister and Loomis entered, and Thomas waved for them to stop so he could hear the whispered message.

"Roger. We'll be standing by. Out," Thomas said. He slipped off the headset and picked up his notes. "Here's the deal. Wait 'til you get this one."

Hollister walked over to the map to look at Deming's position while he listened. "Go ahead."

"Deming says a Montagnard forced laborer just showed up. He's been injured, but they have splinted his arm and fired him up with some antibiotics the doc had in his trick bag.

"Seems the guy has been on a work crew for some time and is fed up with the VC busting his balls. The guy told Deming he'd lead them back to the tunnels after dark." Thomas looked up from his note and shot a big grin to Hollister.

"How the hell did Deming get all this from him? When did Deming learn how to speak Montagnard?"

"Sir, the Yard speaks French."

"And Deming's Cajun French worked?"

"Apparently," Thomas said.

Hollister shook his head. "Glad we didn't have someone with German as a second language out there."

"You want to jerk him out of the bush now? He could have lots of good G-2," Thomas asked.

"No. No, not now," Hollister said. He looked at his watch and thought for a moment.

"Listen, we've got that briefing for General Valentine this afternoon. I don't want to bring up the laborer while he is here. Got it?"

Loomis nodded.

Thomas mumbled, "Okay."

Hollister tapped the map. "Make sure nothing around here says we've got someone bagged. I'll call Michaelson to let him know. If the rest of that headquarters finds out, they'll be screaming to get him out and drain his brain. He can do us more good out there for a day. And I don't want to compromise this whole thing to fly out one laborer who just might not have much more to offer."

Hollister looked at the situation map again.

"Get Lieutenant Deming on the horn at the next scheduled sitrep and tell him to find a time convenient to him to call me and tell me what he knows and what changes he needs to make to the plan.

"Make sure he understands I only want the highlights. I don't expect him to include all the details or spend a second longer on the radio than he has to."

Hollister tried to whittle down the pile of paperwork that waited for him on one side of his desk. He worried about the team being discovered by a Montagnard and tried to convince himself it took a special man to find the team. He hoped it was not an indication that their whereabouts was general knowledge in the area.

He read and signed a routine classified-document inventory report due to field force every month. He dropped it into his out-box and reached for his coffee.

Raising the cup to his lip, he found it almost empty and room temperature. "First Sergeant?" He raised his voice to be heard over the divider.

Hollister flipped the cover sheet on the next document. He became more irritated at having to read a change in policy on MPC scrip exchange procedure. It was a waste of his time.

"Shit! This is pure crap," he said to himself.

"Yes, Captain. Sergeant Easy is not here."

He looked up and found Jrae standing a few feet from his desk.

She wore one of her two sets of starched and fitted camouflage fatigue uniforms, her long hair up and tied behind her head. For him, she was a beautiful interruption.

"Can I do something?"

"Oh, Jrae . . ." He picked up his coffee cup. "There any more out there?"

She raised her hand and gestured toward the mess hall. "The first sergeant went to get more coffee," she said, making a face.

"You don't like coffee?"

"No, sir. I think it is bad to taste."

"Tea?" he asked.

"Not American tea. It is not real tea."

"Well, I'm sorry there isn't more of our foods and beverages you like."

Jrae smiled broadly. "Oh, no. I like Coca-Cola."

"Everyone likes Coca-Cola."

She blushed.

He had never seen her blush. He took in her native beauty and recognized the warning in his head to not cross a line he couldn't cross back over. He had seen lots of Americans get into personal relationships with foreign national employees only to end up regretting it.

"Okay, I'll wait 'til he comes back. Thanks, Jrae."

She nodded, turned, and walked away.

He couldn't resist watching her. Her fresh smell filled the tiny corner of his office and tugged at Hollister. He watched her as long as he could, until she turned out of his sight.

Chairs scuffed the floors, and the cross talk stopped when Hollister stepped up to the front of the group assembled in operations.

Thomas, Browning, the platoon leaders, air mission commanders, the FO, Easy, Caulter, and the senior medic sat in the cramped area used to brief teams.

"I just spoke with Deming. The Montagnard they picked up pointed out the tunnel entrances and said there's a work party and a service unit headquarters in the area. They all work out of the same tunnels," Hollister said, tapping the general area of the tunnels on the easel-mounted map.

"What kind of service unit?" Easy asked.

"Seems this guy is not too savvy about things military, but

indicated to Deming they're guiding the North Viet units in transit through the area to crossing points on the border," Hollister said.

"Weapons?" Dale Tennant asked.

"They got enough to raise hell with your choppers, but that's about it—just small arms. He didn't know about any crew-served weapons.

"The plan stays essentially the same. One team slips up to the tunnels and tries to flush them with CS, while the other two watch the trails leading away.

"We still want to snatch someone with some good information. And we don't want to turn this into World War Three," Hollister said.

"How about extractions?" Tennant asked.

"No change—teams with prisoners and no casualties come out first. If we get anyone hurt, that becomes the priority for extraction. We'll know exactly which teams by first light tomorrow. Tonight we see what they flush out."

"And then?" someone asked.

"And then the leg units mount another incursion into Cambodia to exploit the information."

"Bet General Valentine'll be thrilled with that," someone else said.

"Sir. Speakin' of the good general, we have a dog and pony show in a few minutes," First Sergeant Easy said.

Outside, Hollister held his hand up to his eyes and scanned the horizon. Large clouds built far to the south. He stopped long enough to light a cigarette and collect his thoughts. He felt anxious about the upcoming night, but couldn't put his finger on just what bothered him. He'd seen so many similar operations turn out to be completely different than they had appeared only a few hours before.

He also distrusted intelligence from someone who simply walked into a Ranger perimeter. He didn't smell a trap, but he worried about one.

Valentine arrived right on time. He already had a new second lieutenant with him, complete with general's aides insignia on his collar.

Following the duo through the door was Captain Sheldon A. Depplemeier. Hollister recognized him immediately. Depplemeier had been an ass-kissing, lapdog assistant to Valentine back in the States. Hollister never liked him.

"Hollister, you know Shel Depplemeier. Don't you? He's my new provincial recon unit adviser. I thought I'd bring him along," Valentine said.

Hollister didn't want to recognize Depplemeier. Instead he changed the subject. "How could our operation be of interest to your PRUs?"

"Well, son, if your folks turn up something or create an opportunity for us—they'll be the first unit my Vietnamese counterparts commit."

After more formalities and a few introductions, Hollister finally got Valentine seated in the front row of chairs in the old maintenance shed. Sergeant Caulter had created a distraction for the general by dressing one of the sand tables and moving it to the front of the room. He had delicately tilted the table to allow the model to become a three-dimensional briefing aid for Hollister.

Michaelson's chopper arrived only a few minutes after Valentine's. "General," Michaelson said. "General Quinn regrets he won't be able to make the briefing. I'll be standing in for him."

"General," Hollister began. He looked around at the others in the room, put on his more formal face, and recognized them. "Before I begin let me say that this briefing is Top Secret NOFORN. The sensitivity of this information is directly related to the security of the Rangers involved." Hollister paused to let his words sink in.

He continued. "We've inserted three heavy teams on the ground. Here. Here and here." He tapped the corresponding points on the map. "Their mission is to develop intelligence by possibly snatching prisoners from within the permanent contingent that services the units passing through and repairs the damage done to the lines of communication."

It took less than a half an hour for Hollister to go through the motions of briefing the general without really telling him anything specific that might compromise his Rangers.

At the end the general asked, "Just when are you planning on gassing the tunnels?"

Hollister knew he had to avoid an outright lie. He chose to dodge the issue. "We won't be executing that phase of the operation until we feel confident we have identified enough tunnel openings to make our efforts successful."

"But when will that be?" the general pressed.

"At this point, I can tell you we have not yet identified any specific tunnel entrances. We hope to do some or all of that tonight."

The general made a face. He appeared to sense he wasn't getting the straight story, but there was little more he could get out of Hollister.

"I will add, General, if we don't identify enough entrances, we'll scuttle the operation and bring the teams in," Hollister said.

"What kind of attitude is that? I would expect you'd be itching for a good fight," the general said. "You ought to make it your business to find the tunnels, get your people down in them, and find out just what enemy resources are hidden in them."

Hollister caught Michaelson's eye before he spoke. "General, I am never eager to feed my Rangers into a fight. To me, combat is a necessary part of what we do, not the objective."

The general jumped to his feet, his face flushing. "Then I suggest you have your priorities screwed up, *mister*!"

Hollister shrugged. "Maybe you're right."

Valentine looked around for his aide and Depplemeier and found them standing in the back of the room. "We are leaving," he said. Without saying anything to Hollister or Michaelson, Valentine and his staffers hurried out of the briefing room.

The door slammed behind them and the room went silent.

Hollister looked at those remaining. "Gentlemen, this concludes the briefing." He waited for them to clear the room and stood at the map waiting for Michaelson to work his way up to the front of the room.

Michaelson shook his head. "Jim, did you have to do that?"

"Sir, that man has been a bug up my ass since the day I met him. If I ever had a reason to get out of the army, it would be because of the assholes like him salted around."

"Well, that bug up your ass is going to be up mine before dark. You can bet he'll be on the landline to General Quinn within the hour," Michaelson said.

"Sorry to get you in the middle, sir."

Michaelson slapped Hollister on the back. "Don't sweat it, Ranger. I got you into this. I guess I ought to run more interference for you."

"How you going to do that?"

"I think I might have some chopper trouble. Might just have to spend the night here." He poked his thumb toward Cambodia. "The last thing you need while your lads are playing out across the line is clutter from a buck general."

Hollister smiled at his old friend. "Thanks. I do need the help."

CHAPTER 28

Deming leaned toward Doc Smith. "How's he doing, Jimmy Ray?"

Jimmy Ray looked over at Rat resting on a poncho liner under a large tree. "He's responding to the medication; his fever's coming down, and he seems to be more comfortable."

"He going to be able to move to the objective area tonight?"

"I think so. But don't expect much more from him. He really needs some hospital time with that break. I also suspect he's malnourished and probably full of parasites."

Deming nodded. He got to his knees and crawled over to Rat. He smiled at the Montagnard and got his attention. "We will move one hour after dark. Will you be well enough to go?" he asked in his bayou French.

Rat sat up and smiled back at the American who had treated him so well. *"Oui."*

Caulter hung up the phone in operations. "We have some trouble coming. The weather folks at field force tell us a heavy tropical storm is rolling our way. Should blow through here in about two hours and on into Cambodia."

"Shit!" Hollister said. "Just when we need the most control over the winds we get this."

"How about postponing it for twenty-four hours?" Caulter said.

"If we wait any longer, the people in those tunnels are going to wonder what happened to that Montagnard. If they don't find his body somewhere, they'll know he either walked away or was picked up by Americans. Either way they're going to spook."

"What are you going to do?" Michaelson asked.

"First I'll warn the patrol leaders. Then we'll take a relook at the forecast. There still might be a way to pull all this off." He absentmindedly popped the catch on his wristwatch loose and rubbed the skin underneath.

Hollister walked to the door and pushed it open. "Check this out."

On the horizon, the sky was darkening with the approach of night. Below that a thin pillow of yellow-gray clouds separated the sky from the flat terrain of the Mekong Delta.

"Anybody not been through one of these?" Michaelson asked. "If we're lucky, it'll be a freight train that'll blow through in a real hurry."

"And if it happens early, it'll help cover the movement of the teams," Caulter said.

"All depends on timing. Let's get on the horn to the air force weather guys and see what they have. Let's not wait for it to come down from field force."

The sun set within minutes and Hollister received the report that Deming was moving into a position to emplace the gas. DeSantis's and Chastain's teams were moving to positions along the likely trails to snatch anyone escaping the tunnel area.

Again it was time for Hollister to wait. He spent an hour working on contingency plans in his office while Michaelson had a long talk with Colonel Terry over the secure radio net.

When both were finished, they headed to the mess hall.

Michaelson stirred the sugar in the bottom of his cup. "How long have I known you?"

"Not counting Ranger School, it'd be since that day in sixty-five when you grilled the shit out of me about joining the Long Range Patrol detachment in the Airborne brigade."

"You were a lieutenant then, green and eager. Now you have two and a half tours under your belt, you're about to make major, and you've seen more combat than just about any two captains I can name."

"I sure was green then. I look around at some of the lieutenants now, and it scares the shit out of me. How could you have given me such responsibilities?"

"You pamper lieutenants, and you end up with pampered captains and so on."

"That include generals?"

Michaelson took a cigar from his pocket and began the ritual that led up to smoking it. He looked over at Hollister from under his eyebrows, suggesting that Hollister was rubbing it in. "Yes, including generals."

"How'd it go with Colonel Terry?"

"He explained in painful detail the ass chewing Valentine gave him over the phone."

"What did he tell Valentine?"

"That he didn't work for him, and if Valentine had any problems, he could take them up with General Quinn."

"Ouch!" Hollister said. "This is really going to come back to bite me, huh?"

"I figure Valentine has at least ten or more good years of active duty ahead of him. You certainly have that much time left. Chances of you two crossing paths again gets higher every day."

Hollister got up to top off his coffee cup at the makeshift serving line. "You really know how to brighten up a guy's day."

"Hey, you were the one who gave the junior general the finger—figuratively speaking." Michaelson blew a plume of smoke toward the low ceiling.

Hollister was silent for a moment.

"What?" Michaelson asked.

"I can't think about him. I have to focus on those teams, and if protecting them from being compromised gets my root in a wringer—that's why you gave me the job."

Michaelson smiled. "On target, Mister Hollister. Now, what do you say we go find out about the weather?"

It was after eight when Hollister and Michaelson returned to operations. Hollister looked over Loomis's shoulder at the radio log. "What's going on out there?"

"All three teams have been moving since you left. DeSantis is settling into his snatch site. Chastain's team is only about a half hour away from his," Loomis said. He looked back down at the entries in the log. "Lieutenant Deming reported they are still moving and on schedule. He did ask for a weather forecast."

"And?"

"The air force has it nailed," Caulter said. "We can expect heavy rains, winds and gusts up to forty miles an hour out of the southeast in another hour to an hour and a half."

"And out there?" Hollister said, nodding toward Cambodia.

"Half hour after it hits us—it hits them."

"Duration?"

Caulter made a face. "They weren't as positive about their forecast concerning the duration. They said all they could do was narrow it down to being gone on into Cambodia and Thailand by early morning."

"Great. We could have made that good a forecast walking across the compound."

"Sorry, sir," Caulter said.

"Okay. Let's hit them up for an update every hour. Pass this on to the teams?"

"Yes, sir and yes, sir."

Hollister put his hands on his hips and looked around the room. "Okay, folks. Make yourselves comfortable. It's going to be a long, wet night."

Deming stopped the patrol and called Iverson forward.

While Deming waited, he pulled out his compass and rechecked his route. According to his estimate they couldn't be more than a hundred meters from the center of the tunnel complex.

Rat sat down to rest. He had moved well and not caused a delay for the patrol. But Deming knew Rat was hurting. His color was bad, and his brow often showed beads of sweat, even when the team was moving at a comfortable pace.

He crawled over to Rat and asked him to point out the tunnel entrances.

Rat moved to a pool of light on the ground to draw a diagram of the area as Iverson arrived. He began by dragging his finger in the dirt and sketching out the Y created by the river and the two converging tributaries. He punched his finger into a point along the stem and then pointed to the trio.

Deming nodded. It was clear they agreed on their location. He pointed in the direction the team should move.

The trees rustled as the wind came up. Deming looked back toward the southeast and decided they had to move to the upwind side of the tunnels if they hoped to use any of the CS gas against the inhabitants. He felt by being upwind they could control the drift of the CS and would not have to be in the clouds they would create. It would also improve the chance of snatching a disoriented soldier or laborer. Those with any experience at all would try to move into the wind to get away from the CS.

*   *   *

The wind was much stronger at the launch site in Tay Ninh several minutes before the rain began to fall. A shutter on one of the buildings in the compound flapped furiously, slamming into the wall it was hinged to.

"Somebody going to go out there and secure that thing before it drives us all crazy?" Hollister asked.

But before anyone in operations replied, the noise created by the shutter stopped. "Good. Somebody else is tired of listening to it."

The squelch broke. "This is Georgia. Over."

Loomis scooped up the hand mike from the tabletop. "Campus Killer Control. Over."

They could hardly hear Deming's whisper above the wind. "Being slowed up by booby traps. Will Charlie Mike. Over."

Hollister took the mike from Loomis. "This is Six. Roger your transmission. Don't get too eager to beat the weather. Move carefully. Stop if you have to. You understand?"

"Roger. Out."

Hollister looked at Loomis. "Shit. That's all we need."

"We could have expected it near their tunnels," Caulter said, leaning back in a folding chair, balancing it.

"Yeah, but you always hope they get lazy and leave some of the approaches clear."

"Maybe the next war. This one's 'bout over," Caulter said.

The comment stabbed Hollister. It was enough to worry about teams on the ground when there was an all-out war on. Knowing they were part of the drawdown made the feeling that much more distasteful.

Rat pointed to something in the brush a few feet from where they stopped.

Deming leaned over and whispered to Rat, "What? I don't understand."

"Air," Rat said. "They breathe." He motioned for them to follow him.

The small recon party followed Rat. After only a few minutes' movement, Rat reached out in front of Deming and pulled a branch of a bush away. It revealed a wire stretched across their path.

Rat held up his palm to keep Deming from moving forward.

He then reached up and pointed to a new path around the booby-trap wire.

Deming looked back at Sergeant George, a stocky veteran of a previous tour with the Tiger Force in the 101st Airborne Brigade. George held his rifle low enough to fire on Rat if it became necessary. He followed Rat around the trip wire to a spot closer to the clump of bushes Rat had first pointed out.

Rat stopped them and grabbed the edge of a large, leafy plant. Pulling it aside revealed a section of bamboo sticking out of the ground. He motioned for Deming to come closer—to look at the large piece of bamboo.

Deming leaned over and put his hand above the bamboo. Warm air rushed from the opening. He then waved some of it toward his face. It smelled of cook fires and rancid grease. Deming could also detect the distinctive, ammonialike smell of body odor allowed to develop over many, many days.

He looked over to Rat and nodded, then back to the others. He pointed down the breather pipe and then gave the others a thumbs-up to let them know they had struck pay dirt.

Once they got about seventy-five meters away from Iverson's stay-behind element, Deming stopped and turned back to look for Iverson and the other three Rangers who waited near the vent pipe. Because he knew where they were, Deming was able to see the bottom of one of the Rangers' boots. He pulled the handset from Keith's harness and whispered into the mouthpiece, "Three-One, Georgia. I've got a visual on one of your folks. Tighten up your concealment. And good luck. Out."

Deming, Rat, and the other eight members of Team Georgia continued on to another possible tunnel opening. Though the wind covered much of the noise they made, their movement was slowed by the discovery of more booby traps.

Rat suddenly reached out and grabbed Deming by the elbow.

Confused by the gesture, Deming followed Rat's eyeline to the trail.

There, at the limits of his night vision, Deming saw a lone figure walking down the dark trail with a bicycle. He controlled the bicycle by holding on to a pole stuck into the end of the handlebar. He steadied a large load strapped to the seat and crossbar with his other hand.

Deming looked back at the others to see if they too had seen the solo figure. They all waited for a signal from Deming. He held up his clenched fist to reinforce their instinct to freeze.

He looked at the margin of brush separating them from the trail and realized they had few options. It was too far away to spring a prisoner snatch. And if he tried to move an element to the trail to attempt a snatch, they would either take too much time getting there, catch the traveler's eye, or give themselves away by the noise they would make.

If he decided to fire on the bicyclist from their position, they would alert everyone in the area to their presence.

He turned back to the patrol and gave them a hand signal to stay down and hold what they had. They would just let the man pass and see where he went.

The cyclist moved slowly down the trail toward Deming's patrol, unconcerned about his safety. He devoted much of his attention to keeping his load balanced and staying in the center of the path. The wind blew the bushes along the trail in gusts, and spits of rain promised more.

Deming raised his binoculars to his eyes and watched the figure pass immediately to his front. The clouds had moved across the moon, and the shadow detail was muddied. But he could make out a man in his thirties or forties and the large soft bags on his bicycle. The shape of the bags suggested rice or flour or salt, but not weapons or equipment.

Slung across the man's back was an old bolt-action rifle. Deming couldn't see more than that.

They watched as the man stopped, leaned his bike up against a tree, and knelt down. He pulled aside some loose brush and lifted a trapdoor made from an oil-barrel lid, which led to the tunnels.

Michaelson got to his feet and stretched, rubbing his back. "Damn, I'm just getting too old for this shit."

Hollister looked up from the report he was drafting. "Wait 'til that news gets back to infantry branch. I'm sure they can find a nice, out-of-the-way job for you in the basement of the Pentagon."

"I've done my time in the puzzle palace. I'm not ever going back there," Michaelson said.

"Not good, huh?"

Michaelson lowered his voice. "You ever wonder where they breed the Valentines?"

Hollister dropped his face into his hand. "Please don't blow my confidence in the system," he kidded. "I was kinda hoping Valentine was more of a fluke than a cultivated crop."

"I'm going over to the piss tube and then to the mess hall for some more coffee. Anyone want some more of that evil black substance?"

Caulter declined, and Loomis and Hollister raised their cups affirmatively.

"I'd go with you, but it's about time for the sitreps to be called in. I'd like to be here," Hollister said.

"Come find me if something jumps the track," Michaelson said as he grabbed the large, metal mess hall pitcher and left.

Hollister watched Michaelson go through the door. The bad weather blew into the room, and Hollister caught a glimpse of the black night. Rain was coming down at a sharp angle, and the wind continued to blow. Michaelson just put his head down and charged out into it.

For a moment, Hollister wondered where he would be when he had as many years' service as Michaelson did. He admired Michaelson and trusted him. He had been a tough boss when Hollister was a lieutenant and a good friend ever since.

What he liked most about Michaelson was his priorities. He never let his own needs or wants get in the way of taking care of the troops or accomplishing the mission—and in that order. Hollister hoped he could someday be more like Michaelson.

After several minutes, the rain began to fall and swirl in the strong winds. Deming looked around at the others. To a man, they were still and ignored the rain running down their necks into the collars of their fatigue shirts. He was pleased with the way they had been performing and hoped they would not soon tire and get sloppy. Skill and discipline were the only things that balanced the risks they were taking.

Private First Class Keith reached over and tapped Deming on the leg and directed his attention back to the tunnel entrance.

There, the pajama-clad bicyclist emerged from the tunnel with two others. They went to the bicycle and unstrapped the three bags and took them back to the entrance. The bicycle man said good-bye to the others and stood by while they disappeared back into the tunnel. He then covered the entrance behind them and got on his bike. In only seconds, he pedaled back up the pathway and out of sight.

After several minutes, Deming moved to the far side of their perimeter—as far from the tunnel as he could get without moving the patrol. Satisfied he was far enough away not to be heard, Deming got on the radio to call the other teams to look out for the bicyclist moving in their direction.

He instructed them to snatch him if they could without compromising the major effort to grab someone from the tunnels. Otherwise, let him pass.

The report of the sighting and locating another access to the tunnel was good news back at operations. Hollister looked at the message he had heard over the speakers after Loomis finished writing it in the log. "Call over to the pilots' hootch and tell them what we know. Call Lieutenant Gannon and tell him to relook at his fire support plan and slip on his jungle boots. Call the forward air controller and tell him we may need him up within the hour. Tell him that I can't wait. If I need air force birds over the objective—I'll need them on a short rope, and I'll need a FAC there first. Oh, and give them all the latest weather forecast for here and the objective area.

"Things are about to happen," Hollister said.

Deming had pulled the patrol back from the tunnel entrance and briefed the small element, headed by Sergeant George, that would stand by to drop CS into the second tunnel opening. Satisfied George understood, Deming moved on.

Rat led the remaining members of the patrol toward another tunnel entrance. The fact that Deming had his twelve-man patrol broken up into three elements bothered him. If they made contact or were compromised, the distance between elements would cause endless complications. Deming had drilled and drilled the team members and the subelement leaders on immediate actions if they were hit while split up, and hoped he had done enough.

It began to rain harder.

"Jesus! I hope the hell we don't make contact now," Michaelson said. He came back through the door, soaking wet, his free hand protecting the open top of the coffee pitcher from the rain.

"How bad?" Hollister asked.

"Bad enough that I don't think we could lift these choppers off right now."

Hollister walked over to the shuttered window and pulled the plywood away. He looked across the compound to the airstrip.

"Hell, I can't even see the choppers. Are we sure we still have them here?"

Caulter laughed, got to his feet, and filled his coffee cup. He raised it a bit to Michaelson. "Thank you, Colonel. I'll get the next jug."

Michaelson looked at the graying sergeant. "What do you think?" he asked, nodding toward Cambodia.

"Well, sir, I think they got a real good chance of grabbing another VC groundhog if their luck holds out. They been running good, getting breaks, and moving smart. But that could all go to hell real fast, and they're in a bad place with bad weather."

Deming watched as Rat tried to explain the location of the third tunnel entrance by pointing at bushes and the safe approach to it.

The entrance was very different from the other opening and the vent pipe. Instead of being a hole in the ground camouflaged with vegetation, it was tucked into a rock outcropping next to a bank of the main stem of the river.

Deming raised his field glasses to his eyes and strained to see the details. A simple cluster of rocks concealed an entrance just inches above the swelling river. He soon realized they might have been able to paddle right up to the entrance had they not already destroyed and buried the boats.

Without the boats it would mean that all or some part of the remaining members of Team Georgia would have to work their way upstream, get into the water, cross the stream, and then float down to the entrance.

At the entrance, they would place the CS, arm the timing device, and then reverse the process to get back on the near side of the bank—to move back north to link up with the others.

Deming wiped the rain from his forehead and eyes again to clear his vision. He would follow the same routine, placing a team at the third opening to the tunnels.

He decided to take himself and Keith forward with Rat and let the other two cover their movement from the near bank. He had trusted Rat to show him the final tunnel opening. If all went well there, they would be able to emplace the CS grenades inside the tunnel opening and get away—upwind.

Deming waited for the three remaining Rangers to move to

him. Once there, he leaned over and whispered over the rain and
the rushing water, "According to our man there, this hole is only a
backup escape. It hasn't been opened in several weeks and isn't
booby-trapped. That's good. They just might panic and use the
damn thing."

The others nodded to let him know they heard him and
understood.

"Okay," Deming said. He raised his wristwatch to his face and
looked at the radium hands. "I've got four zero minutes to get over
there and back. If it hits the fan—leave me and Keith. Go to the
rally point. We'll find you there."

Jimmy Ray gave Deming a thumbs-up and helped Deming slip
his light pack off his back.

CHAPTER 29

The growth along the bank of the small river slowed their movement to a crawl. Vines tangled around their feet, and the thickets tugged at their already wet uniforms.

Deming had to guard against fatigue setting in. They were getting very tired, and it showed up in a stumble now and then or a distraction. Deming noticed it when Keith forgot what he was doing. Rat stopped for a moment, causing Keith to do the same. But when Rat began to move forward again, Keith just stood there, confused and disoriented.

Deming turned and walked back to Keith. "Okay?"

"Yes, sir," he whispered. The contact seemed to bring him back into focus.

Deming patted him on the shoulder—reassuring him—and then returned to the point position to lead them to the tunnel entrance.

The door to operations burst open with a kick of a jungle boot. Hollister looked up to find First Sergeant Easy, wearing his combat gear, his face camouflaged, leaving only the blue of his eyes and the pink from his mouth exposed.

"Where are you going, Top?"

"Cross the fence. I'm riding belly on that young lieutenant's chase ship. I may be old, but I'm still the meanest som'bitch in this man's Ranger company."

"I don't know that's true. But I do know you're the best goddamn belly man that ever flew an extraction. Let's just hope no one really needs you tonight."

The squelch broke on a radio speaker. "Base. This is Georgia. We are to execute phase four in zero five minutes. Over," Deming said.

Hollister picked up the mike and answered, "This is Six. Roger your last. Good luck and be careful."

Hollister didn't miss the background noise of the winds blowing at Deming's end. He also knew the rain was coming down as hard there as it had at the launch site in Tay Ninh.

"Something wrong?" Easy asked.

"Not any more than the usual. I just wonder how long you and I can keep our fingers crossed in this business."

"Long as we need to, to get 'em home," Easy said.

Rat reached out and grabbed Deming's shirtsleeve. He motioned for Deming to stop, and pointed at a place on the bank nearly twenty meters upstream from the rock outcropping on the other bank.

Deming took a breath, shrugged to adjust his load, and raised his rifle up to high port. He took one last look up and down the river and then stepped into the water.

It was cold and fast flowing. Deming had to widen his stance on the bottom and shift his weight upstream to keep from being toppled over. As he got to deeper water, the claymore bag carrying the CS and the timing devices began to float. It worked its way around Deming and found the downstream side.

Rat stepped into the water. Unlike Deming, he moved gracefully and with little difficulty. He had walked through streams his whole life on a daily basis. For him it was as easy as walking on dry ground.

Suddenly, a noise came from the trees on the far bank nearly two hundred yards upstream. Deming and Rat froze. It happened again. They quickly recognized a cough—as if someone was trying to spit something from his throat.

Rat waved his hand from side to side to let Deming know it was one of the Vietnamese from the tunnels. The fact that the man was hacking and coughing without fear of being heard was reassuring to Deming. No one who suspected an American patrol was in the area would act so recklessly.

They waited until the coughing stopped and then continued across the stream.

"Damn, she's a really pretty girl. Ain't she?" Sergeant Caulter said, spreading out the photographs on the table.

Hollister got up from the field desk, stretched, and walked over to the two NCOs. "What you got?"

Sergeant Young proudly pointed at the small photos on the table. "I had to test out the darkroom. So I stopped Jrae out in the company area and grabbed a few snaps of her. She looks pretty good, don't she, Captain?"

Hollister spun one of the photos around. It was a shot of Jrae from the waist up. Her long black hair flowed undisturbed down her shoulder and the full length of her back. Her figure was flattered by the tight-fitting fatigue shirt, and her bright teeth were exaggerated against so much black and gray in the photo. "Got to admit. She's a real heartbreaker."

"She never saw her own photo before. She told me no one had ever photographed her," Sergeant Young said.

"Did she like it?" Caulter asked.

"You ever see a Viet who wasn't crazy about their own photograph?"

"She's not a Vietnamese. She's a Yard," Caulter said.

"Well, maybe it's because she's such a pretty girl. She liked it all right. Promised her a better print as soon as I get some bigger paper in from field force," Young said.

"Well, as long as you don't start your own photo studio, I guess it's okay," Hollister said.

Young held up another very flattering photo. "You want one for your scrapbook, sir?"

Hollister laughed. "No. I don't think so. If I had a picture like that of her, I might let my mind wander."

They all laughed.

The cover to the tunnel entrance was almost overgrown with weeds and matted deadfall. Deming pulled out his folding Buck knife. He slowly opened the blade to avoid making a loud snap as it locked into place.

He knew if the cover was booby-trapped and he tripped it, it could kill him and compromise every man on the ground. He looked up at Rat, who shrugged again—not knowing for sure if it was booby-trapped. There was no other way. He had to probe it the hard way.

Deming looked at his watch. He only had twenty minutes to find a way to set the CS and get back to the other side of the river and head back to their rally point.

He decided not to try to lift the cover. That would reduce the need for him to completely clear the circumference of the woven-twig cover that concealed the opening. He needed to find a small section of the cover that was clear of booby traps, dig enough dirt and rock away from it, and slip the CS grenades into the opening. He could then set the timer, cover the small opening with mud to keep the gas in the hole, and rejoin the others.

He gingerly slipped the four-inch blade of the knife under the edge of the cover and felt for anything that might be part of a trip wire or a mine.

Nothing.

He slowly withdrew the knife and did the same to the next section of the cover. He would have to do it several more times—without tripping a detonator before he was finished. The job was harder than usual because of the rain and the runoff of muddy water seeking the river's edge where he stood.

Hollister ran across the compound to his hootch and tried to dodge the larger puddles. The sprint only took him nine long strides. Still, he was soaked by the time he hit the porch of the officers' hootch.

Inside, he found his web gear and pulled it off the hook on the wall above his bunk. He pulled his M-16 off a nearby nail, holding it by the front sight blade, and then checked his holster for his .45. He kicked his footlocker out from under his bunk.

Just inside the lid he found several pairs of dry wool socks. He grabbed two pairs and stuffed them into his cargo pocket. He grabbed a couple of packs of cigarettes out of the locker's top tray and headed back out.

Deming took a deep breath and poked Keith. "Commo?" he whispered, wanting to know if Private First Class Keith had confidence in his ability to speak with the Rangers near the other tunnel entrance and the vent tube as well as the other two patrols.

Keith looked up from under the drooping rim of his floppy hat and gave Deming an exaggerated nod.

"Okay. Give them the five-minute warning. Get an up from each of them."

Keith cupped his hand around the mouthpiece of the handset and called Chastain first.

Deming looked up at the sky. The rain was coming down so hard he couldn't keep his eyelids open long enough to even see what the cloud cover looked like. He wiped the rain from his face and then pulled back the cuff of his jungle fatigue shirt to check his watch.

Hollister returned to operations. Michaelson had found a way to get comfortable enough in two folding chairs. He had pulled his cap down over his eyes to grab a nap.

Easy slept in a seated position on the floor, his back against the commo bench. Loomis had set up a canvas cot under the commo bench, where he slept while Caulter spelled him on radio watch.

"What's happening out there on the ground?"

Caulter twisted to make eye contact with Hollister. "The young lieutenant's about to pull the string on all the CS. Everyone's in position, and he's gonna drop a pile of it down the vent tube first and then pop the other two entrances about five minutes later."

"The other two teams?"

"Alabama and Colorado are both at one hundred percent alert and ready to snatch."

Hollister looked around the room. "Choppers, arty, and the FAC?"

Caulter held up the log. "All notified," he said, tapping the entries on the page.

"Okay. Let's take a deep breath and rub a rabbit's foot or something." Hollister dropped his field gear on the end of the commo bench and started his methodical inspection of every item.

"Thought Cap'n Thomas was going out to pull 'em if they need to get yanked," Caulter said.

"Three heavy teams? Too many people out there to think Thomas can handle 'em all alone. He'll need two more arms and a blow torch out there if it goes to shit."

"Well, sir, you better take your hip waders out on a night like this."

"Morning."

"Huh?"

"On a morning like this," Hollister corrected, nodding toward the wall clock.

Deming looked around one more time. The rain still sheeted, rolling across their position in waves of hard rain, then soft steady rain. The winds had subsided a bit, and that encouraged him.

Less wind would keep the CS confined. The more gas the

enemy had to fight, the better the chance of disorienting them and snatching a prisoner.

Deming grabbed the straps to his own protective mask and tugged at them anxiously. He looked at his watch and then over at Keith, who sat with the handset pressed to his ear.

Keith suddenly straightened. "Roger," he whispered into the mouthpiece.

He dropped the handset to his lap and leaned close to Deming. "Sir. They've popped at the breather tube."

Deming looked at his watch again. Any second either one or both of the other two tunnel openings would fill with gas. He raised his mask, held it up for the others to see, and then put it on his face.

The rubber dragged against his gritty skin and the elastic straps pulled at his short-cropped Airborne haircut. Once he got it in place, he checked its seal against his face. He tucked his floppy hat into his pocket and looked around at the others.

Keith was helping Rat put on the unfamiliar mask. The two awkwardly slipped the mask onto his face, and Keith tugged the straps tight around the chignon on the back of the mountain man's head.

Operations had filled with the key players for what was about to happen. Captain Tennant had made one final check of his chopper crews before coming in. Next to him in the briefing area was gunship boss Joe Raymond. He sat with his elbows resting on his knees, a map in his hands. He looked up at the weather chart on the easel and then back to his map.

"What?" Tennant asked.

"I want to find a way to stay upwind as long as I can," Raymond said.

"Don't want to fly through the CS?"

"Don't want to wear this fucking mask," Raymond said, kicking at the canvas mask carrier on the floor near his boot.

Caulter walked around the room with a fresh pitcher of coffee. He poured some for Captain Thomas. "Well, sir, you look bright-eyed."

"I knew there wouldn't be shit happening during the night. I slept like a baby in all this rain."

"Well, I hope you brought your poncho," Hollister said. "I have a feeling you're gonna get wet before the day's over."

Lieutenant Gannon laughed, not taking the handset from his ear.

"You got good commo with your firing batteries?" Hollister asked.

Gannon gave him a nod.

Deming pulled the mask up from his face and sampled the air. He smelled the sweet, roselike scent of the CS gas. Though he couldn't see any gas escaping from the riverbank entrance, he knew it had filled the tunnel. He leaned toward the others and, in a stage whisper, said, "Stand by. If they're coming out, it'll be any second now."

He turned to Keith. "Get a commo check from Alabama and Colorado."

Keith nodded and keyed his mike in a coded pattern worked out with DeSantis's radio operator. In a fraction of a second, he got a keyed reply. He did the same and got the same reply from Chastain's radio.

Keith held up his hand and made a large O with his thumb and forefinger.

"Chastain's got movement," Loomis said over his shoulder.

Hollister walked over to the map and looked at the map symbol for Chastain's Team Colorado. "Coming up the trail?"

"Yes, sir. He said moving toward him from the Sierra."

Hollister looked around the room. "Okay, folks. The fish are swimming toward the net. Better take your places."

The pilots left; Easy followed. Gannon gathered up his maps and balanced them on top of his web gear—sitting in a pile on a chair. "I'm ready anytime."

Keith mumbled to Deming through the rubber mask, "Chastain's got movement."

Deming had barely heard Keith's message when he noticed a small puff of CS gas drifting out of the riverbank entrance and down toward the water. Risking giving their position away, he raised his voice for the others around him to hear. "Look alive. Someone opened the hatch."

A long stream of CS gas drifted out, mixed with the fresh air and rain, and quickly dissipated within five yards of the hole.

A figure hesitated at the entrance, coughed and gagged, then fell out of the hole and into the river.

Before Deming could say anything, there was a second splash. PFC Jimmy Ray Smith had grabbed his sling rope off his rucksack and leaped into the water and begun swimming toward the pajama-clad swimmer.

The gassed swimmer thrashed around in the water. Out of control and desperate to clear the CS gas from his eyes and throat, he kept spitting and dunking his head under the water.

Jimmy Ray didn't even need to pursue the swimmer. He just swam to a spot downstream and let the floundering gas victim drift to him. Once the man got close enough, Jimmy Ray slipped a loop of the sling rope over his neck, tightened it, and began towing the disoriented swimmer to the Ranger side of the river.

The Rangers pulled the prisoner out of the water and into the center of their perimeter. As fast as they got the rope off his neck and sat him down next to a tree to catch his breath, Rat identified him. It was Xuan.

Rat shook his head.

"What? What is wrong?" Deming asked.

"He cannot tell you much. He is just a worker."

It was not the news Deming wanted to hear. He had hoped if his team flushed anyone, it would be someone of authority.

Deming reported the snatch to operations and pulled his team away from the riverbank to protect their catch. It didn't appear to him that any more of the residents of the tunnel were going to escape from the exit on the far bank.

He knew they would soon have to begin their move to the pickup zone. There was no use in exposing the Rangers any longer if there wasn't much chance of snatching any more prisoners.

At his team perimeter, Sergeant DeSantis reached over and tapped his radio operator. He pointed at the single figure walking up the trail toward them.

The RTO passed the message on.

Satisfied the twelve men got the word, DeSantis scooted over to Corporal Greenwood's position and grabbed him by the shirt collar.

He pulled Greenwood close and whispered into his ear, "You ready?"

Greenwood pulled his head back, made eye contact with DeSantis, and nodded vigorously. Greenwood turned to Parsons, only an arm's length away.

The two Rangers slipped free of their rucksacks and placed their rifles on top of their gear. Greenwood pulled off his floppy hat and stuffed it into his pocket. Parsons stuck his inside his shirt.

Without taking their eyes off the approaching figure, they crawled to the very edge of the brush that edged the trail. There, each man looked back at the Rangers on their flank to make sure they were ready for the snatch. The last thing any Ranger wanted was to be confused with the target by his comrades.

The figure got closer. They could hear his feet splash in the puddles formed in the trail over the plopping sounds of the rain hitting the vegetation around them.

Greenwood and Parsons each got into a runner's starting stance, staying as low as they could, below the top of the brush. Parsons kicked at the grasses under his boot until he had good contact with raw earth. The new foothold was far superior to the wet grass.

DeSantis snapped his fingers and pointed at the recovery team, made up of three more Rangers. He wanted to make absolutely sure they were watching for his signal and not watching the figure. He held his arm out, steady and parallel to the ground. Telling them to get ready.

The man walked quickly, bent over in the rain, carrying an AK-47 rifle across his chest, wiping his eyes and nose with a scrap of a rag.

Greenwood and Parsons could see the man was still suffering from the effects of the tear gas. They could count on the fact that he probably couldn't see very well and was scared.

They were also aware of the advantages and disadvantages the rain brought. They knew it would cover most of the noise they would make rushing him. But the same rain would make their footing questionable and increase the difficulty in trying to subdue the man. Anyone who had ever handled a wet or muddy prisoner knew the moisture on most Vietnamese pajamas made the fabric extremely slippery.

The lone figure came to a point directly in front of the two crouching Rangers, and Greenwood whispered one short and forceful "Go."

The two burst from the tree line; ran, full speed, across the trail; and hit the man with the hardest body blocks they could. Greenwood hit high—in the rib cage behind his right arm. Parsons went for the backs of the man's knees.

They had practiced the move several times at Tay Ninh. They wanted to completely separate the man from the ground and from his rifle, launching him sideways into the brush on the far side of the trail.

Disorientation and surprise were their main objectives. Once they did that, capturing him would be easy.

The man's body reacted to the two blows from the heavier Americans. They catapulted him up and sideways. His rifle left his fingers, and he quickly found himself turning over in the air.

He landed on the far side of the trail, shoulder first. A loud whoosh of air came from him. That was followed by a whimper as the two Rangers landed on top of him—pinning him to the ground.

DeSantis snapped his fingers at the recovery party and jerked his hand toward the trail. "Go, go, go," he said.

The three waiting Rangers dashed from the edge of the perimeter to the trail. One dropped to his knee facing up the trail, the second facing down the trail.

The third man in the recovery team kept going, sliding to a stop on his knees next to Parsons, Greenwood, and the prisoner. The third Ranger helped Parsons hold down the thrashing man while Greenwood pulled a length of parachute cord from around his neck to tie the prisoner's hands behind his back.

Parsons removed his hand from the prisoner's mouth and pulled the long strip of green fabric tape from the back of his trouser leg and covered the prisoner's mouth.

The tying, wrestling, and gagging took less than fifteen seconds, and the trio pulled the man to his feet.

"Hot damn!" Caulter said. "DeSantis bagged another one."

"Another laborer?" Hollister asked.

"No, sir. He was carryin' an AK."

"Everyone okay?" Hollister asked.

"Right as rain. They're waiting for instructions. You want them to move to their pickup zone?"

Hollister turned and walked to the door. He pushed it open with his foot and looked across the compound toward the airstrip.

The rain continued to fall. The winds had let up. But the entire area was nearly an inch deep in pooled water. He could see the crews sitting inside the cargo compartments of their choppers.

He let the door swing back closed. "Jesus, I hope this rain lets up. I hate the thought of those kids trying to get out of there in this stuff."

"Last thing you want is teams running across landing zones awash in water and ankle deep in muddy oatmeal," Michaelson said, standing to stretch.

"I'll go for that," Easy said.

"Sir?" Caulter said.

Hollister looked at Michaelson.

"It's your call, Ranger," Michaelson said.

Hollister turned back to Caulter. "Ask 'em if they can watch the trail for fifteen more minutes."

Caulter turned to Loomis, who picked up the mike and transmitted the question.

"I don't want to leave them there too long or lose that prisoner. But if they get a chance to snatch another one—"

"If they haven't seen another one in fifteen then you probably aren't going to have any more traffic on that road," Michaelson said.

Hollister nodded. "Okay. Fifteen it is if it's okay with Deming. I don't want to make any team stay there if he feels spooky about the location."

Chastain's team sat along their assigned trail. For his Rangers, the rain had been a more severe problem—the tall savannas. The rain had been beating down on them since just after they moved into the position. The ground was flat and didn't drain well. It soon became soft, muddy ground that held a wash of five inches of standing water above it. What had started out as dry grasses with good concealment and adequate views of the trail soon became a marshy bog.

Every Ranger in Chastain's team did his best to avoid moving. Each change in position only stirred up the muddy bottom and caused the Ranger to sink deeper into it.

Chastain checked his watch. It was time for him to call in a sitrep. He turned to his radio operator, only to find him crouched and pointing out of the grass toward the trail.

There, walking and half jogging, a man approached the section of trail covered by Chastain's team.

CHAPTER 30

"Bingo!" Loomis yelled.

"What?" Easy said.

"Got another one. Chastain's folks grabbed an unarmed male running by their location."

"Soldier or a laborer?" Hollister asked.

Loomis finished writing down the text of the transmission. "Said he had no weapons or equipment."

"Okay. That's enough. Put the word out to all three teams to begin their moves to their PZs if they haven't already. We'll pick them up in the original order—Georgia, Alabama, and then Colorado. Unless someone makes contact."

"Roger that," Loomis said. He jotted down Hollister's instructions before picking up the radio mike.

Sergeant Young entered operations. "The old man looking for me?" he asked Caulter.

"He just left to pull the teams. He wants you to collect the prisoners we picked up out in the AO and hustle them over to province headquarters for interrogation," Caulter said.

"Count on us never seein' 'em again," Young said.

Caulter leaned back in his chair and pulled a pack of cigarettes from his pocket. "Not our problem. We were out there to find a source of intel—not to exploit it."

"If they turn some good stuff and then send in some worthless American or Viet unit, it'll all go to hell in a handbasket," Young said.

"The job was to disrupt and spoil the NVA operations just across the border," Colonel Michaelson said, having just stepped into operations.

Young turned and flushed a bit—as if he had spoken out of turn. "Oh, sorry, sir. I wasn't really bad-mouthin'—"

"No. You're right. A maneuver unit in that area probably won't turn much by the time they get in there. Their move'll be telegraphed or even expected after the snatches."

"Don't sound too slick to me, sir," Young said.

"Doesn't need to be slick to be effective."

"Damn, I couldn't be a leg," Young said.

"They wouldn't want you. Your parents are married," Caulter kidded.

The gunships flew ahead and below the flight of slicks. At the tail end of the slick flight, Chief Adams jockeyed to avoid the prop wash of the larger Huey helicopters.

Hollister tried to get comfortable in the wet seat inside the loach.

"Sorry, sir," Chief Adams said. "The poncho blew off in the rain. Not much chance it's gonna dry out while you're sitting on it."

"Great," Hollister said. He adjusted the lip mike and shrugged. "Hey, could be worse, I guess."

"Yes, sir. So, where do you want us?"

"Just stay above and behind the formation. I want to be available if the shit hits the fan." He pointed down toward the Huey that held the C & C party. "We'll just let Captain Thomas run the show for now."

Adams laid the cyclic up against his knee and put the tiny chopper into an ascending right turn. He looked out and up to make sure there was no one above him. "Third floor coming up."

The rain pounded against the windscreen of the loach. Hollister tried to orient himself by looking out the open left door and matching the terrain below to the plastic-cased map in his lap.

Adams looked over at Hollister. "You guys sure do earn yer pay."

Hollister laughed. "Ever notice how the grass is always greener in your own job?"

"Sir?"

"Pilots would rather not be grunts. Grunts would rather not be Rangers. Rangers would rather not be door gunners—and so on."

Adams chuckled into the intercom. "I guess you're right." He looked out his door and down at the rain-soaked terrain below them. "But, damn, I just couldn't see living in that kind of crap while yer surrounded by folks who would like to do really bad things to your body."

"This coming from a man who is about three hundred horse-power away from being down there himself?"

"I try never, ever to run out of airspeed, altitude, and ideas, Captain," Adams said—flashing a big grin.

"I'm real glad to hear that, Chief. Let's just hold that thought until we get back to Tay Ninh."

"Then what?"

"I imagine we can count all the noses—unload weapons and find a cold beer for both of us."

"Good deal! I'll go for that."

Hollister ran his fingers down the seam of the plastic map case and looked out ahead of the chopper through the ripples caused by the rain. He wanted to get the extraction over as fast and as safely as he could, but had to stand by and watch Thomas supervise the pickups.

He reached down and adjusted the volume to his headset. He could hear Thomas's side of the conversations, but Deming's voice was weak.

He pointed toward Deming's pickup zone. "Let's hold our orbit high and north of the pickup."

The responsive little chopper rolled over and took up a new heading. The compass on the instrument panel spun through three hundred and ten degrees and kept moving.

Hollister looked down and ahead of the loach. The flight of ten choppers flew higher than normal altitudes, above possible ground fire, and fast to avoid the antiaircraft artillery.

He realized the efforts were probably not as necessary with the bad weather, limited visibility, and gusting winds that served to cover their approach and reduce the effectiveness of enemy gunners.

The weather over the landing zones was a random pattern of low clouds, ground fog, and occasional clear patches.

They flew for another twelve minutes, taking a long, arcing route to the landing zone.

"What did you call it, sir?"

Hollister looked over at Adams. He was reaching down for the small knob on the tape recorder. "What did I call what?"

"Loach music?"

Hollister smiled. "Yeah, loach music. You got some more, Chief?"

"You bet. Check this out." Adams clicked the tape recorder to life.

The popping of the record that the recording was taken from was the first thing Hollister heard in his headset.

"It might be a bit different. It's ancient, it's classic—written before the first one of these babies ever took to the skies. But I think it's loach music," the pilot said. He leaned back and paused for the intro to the song to start.

Hollister didn't recognize the first few notes. It began with an Indian drumbeat followed by the distinctive strumming of California beach music. "Who is that?"

Adams kicked the loach into an ascending spiral and punched the intercom button. "That, sir, is Hank B. Marvin of the Shadows. It's ten years old." He wiggled the cyclic a fraction of an inch from side to side with the beat of the music, and the loach became part of the rock instrumental. "But it's flyin' music."

Hollister laughed. He looked out and down and saw the gloved hand of the front seater in the lead Cobra come up in a wave. Then the gunship's rotor disk tilted to the music.

"What the hell are they listening to?" Hollister asked.

"Same thing," Adams said. "I'm pumping it over our company alternate freq."

Hollister gave Adams a look of disapproval.

"Don't worry, sir. I'll shut it down before we get near the pickup."

"Just make sure we don't confuse Ranger operations and disc jockeying."

Chastain was the last patrol leader to report arrival at his pickup zone. Hollister rolled his wrist over and noted the time. He was impatient with the process. Waiting for Thomas to go through the steps to extract teams on the ground made him anxious. Still, he was pleased with the ease with which Thomas was setting up the teams and the choppers for three coordinated pickups.

He looked out at the continuing bad weather and then waited

until Adams came around to check the approaching weather again.

The clouds were layered and varied. The ones closest to the ground were thready and fragile looking, while the layers above them were full, dark, and threatening.

"Some lightning headed our way—over the South China Sea."

Adams smiled. "Sir, I can fly around and between the lightning strikes in this baby."

"I'm not as worried about you as I am the slicks and gunships."

"Hell, they'll be okay."

"Hope you're right."

"Lemme tell you, sir. If I was worried about getting my ass knocked outta the air by weather or ground fire . . ." He raised his left hand and pointed his finger out over the instruments at the other choppers. ". . . I'd sure like to have those guys around me. They can just about get me out of 'bout any trouble I could get into."

Hollister relaxed a bit and nodded. "Guess you're right, Chief. They're getting pretty good at what they do."

"Too bad though."

"What?"

"We all know when they finally slap the padlock on this war, we're gonna see pink slips like confetti in aviation units."

"That the rumor?"

"That's the promise. They been postcarding lots of us," Adams said, adjusting the size of his orbit above the first pickup zone.

"Postcarding?"

"The puzzle palace has been sending selected warrant officers postcards asking if they want to become RLOs—real live officers. All they have to do is sign the card and send it back, and they get their lieutenant's or captain's bars in the mail."

"What do you make of that?"

"Cockpit scuttlebutt is they're going to slim down army aviation, and if you're going to stay, you better be a commissioned officer and not just a warrant."

"Why?"

"They can't have everyone flying. So they'll be alternating pilots from cockpit jobs to regular officer jobs and back. They can put an RLO into more ground assignments than they can a warrant officer."

"So who gets the postcards?"

"We figure they are using a dartboard because of some a the assholes who got them."

"And?"

"And we all know if we don't get our postcard, we'd better start looking for jobs flying traffic choppers back in the World."

The conversation reminded Hollister about his own vulnerability. He still hadn't found much security in the fact that he had been selected early for major. They could still let him go when the war ended.

"Stand by. Your ride's on short final," Thomas said over the tactical frequency.

Chastain's voice came back without a pause. "Roger. We're ready."

Hollister leaned out of the open door to see the two pickup choppers pull their noses up, slow, and settle onto the grassy PZ two thousand feet below the loach. Through the rain, it was hard to see details as small as Rangers running to their choppers. But he could see the gusts of winds blowing the grasses in wave after wave.

He knew the buffeting would be heavy, but the choppers would benefit from heading into the wind. The added lift would help get them out of the landing zone and away from the crosshairs of any enemy gunners trained on them.

"Coming up." The voice was the lead chopper pilot's.

"Two coming up," the trailing pilot announced.

"We're above and behind you five hundred feet in both directions," said the pilot of the chase aircraft, empty except for its crew and First Sergeant Easy, riding belly man.

The two pickup choppers looked as if they were going over on their noses as their pilots sucked all the lift they could into their rotor blades to regain the airspeed they had lost touching down.

Their momentum and altitude increased rapidly, and the lead chopper crossed the margin of trees at the far limit of the clearing.

The second chopper did the same, and Hollister let himself relax a bit. They were up. A little more altitude and airspeed, and their safety would be all but guaranteed back to Tay Ninh.

"Ever get casual with this?" Adams asked.

"Never."

"I'm not sure I'd take a commission as an RLO if they offered it. I'd rather fly than make the decisions you all have to make."

"I don't know, Chief. If I were a Ranger on the ground, I just might like the idea of having the decisions made by an infantry officer who had already logged in thousands of hours of stick time."

Adams nodded. "You got a point. Maybe some other guy. I don't know if I got whatever it takes to be down there in the dirt."

Hollister looked back at the pilot, his shaggy mustache half hanging over his lip mike. "My gut tells me you probably have it."

The flight of two that picked up Chastain's team was reporting their landing back at the launch site just as the next two lift ships were approaching DeSantis's difficult PZ.

Unlike Chastain's PZ, which was an oval of tall grasses in double canopy, DeSantis's was a series of several overlapping bomb craters. During the early flyovers, it had picked up a nickname—Olympic. It came from its similarity to the interlocking ringed logo for the Olympic games.

From above, the craters were distinguished from one another by the blue-green water pooled in their bottoms. The raw earth margins of the craters overlapped, blurring the distinction between them.

As Adams brought the loach to a high orbit over the Olympic PZ, Hollister sat up and looked quickly at his map and then out and down at the PZ again. "Mud," he said.

"What?"

"The muddy water has drained into the craters and changed the colors."

"That bad?"

"Just tells you how wet it is for those Rangers down there."

As the pickup ships lined up to pluck DeSantis's patrol and his prisoner from the craters, Hollister could feel a sense of discomfort. He had no reason to think that the pickup would be any different except for the tight and irregular size of the PZ.

"Chief," he said. "Let's drop out of this orbit and take a look along the route out for the slicks."

"Roger that. Let me find out which way they are breaking, first."

While Adams checked with the lead pickup ship, Hollister reached down and pulled the set of binoculars from his claymore bag. He took one long look at the moderately forested area in front of DeSantis's PZ. The trees were clumped in tight knots, with grassy patches between them and an occasional foot trail, reminding him it was very much a well-traveled area.

"Got it," Adams said. And without warning, he jerked the small craft over into a fast, descending right spiral that dumped altitude and picked up airspeed.

The maneuver of the chopper made it impossible for Hollister to use the field glasses. He dropped them to his lap and held on to the leading edge of the open doorway for the ride down.

"This is where we need loach music," Adams said. He pulled in some collective to stop the extreme descent of the chopper.

"I think good flying is all we need lots of right now." Hollister watched Adams skillfully maneuver the falling chopper into a terrain-hugging overflight of the exit route selected by the slick pilots.

"Can you help me count the snakes?"

"What?"

"I need your eyes. These guys are watching the trees, and we are watching the trees. If we don't keep an eye on the gunships, we could mesh rotors and fuck up our whole day."

Hollister looked out and behind the chopper. The Cobras were prowling the margins of the pickup zone, looking for any threat to DeSantis or the slicks. Each run ended on the far end of the PZ where they would jerk their choppers up and back for another loop over the PZ. "They're about six hundred meters behind us and getting farther away."

"I just want to know where they are all the time."

"Don't blame you. I'd hate to have to explain bumping into one of those guys."

"Is there something special down here you want to look at?" Adams asked.

"Just a hunch. I can't put my finger on it. Just don't want to lose a Ranger or a chopper because you and I were up in the stratosphere listening to rock and roll."

"Roger. I'll just poke around down here—along the route out," Adams said, pulling the chopper into what would almost be a hover.

"Short final," a voice announced over the radio.

Hollister looked back in the direction of the PZ. He could see the Cobras prowling and the lead chopper clearing the trees to settle into the PZ. Above and behind that, he could make out the chase ship and Thomas's C & C.

He leaned back into his seat and looked out and up. The rain was still falling. He pressed the transmit button and called Thomas on the Ranger freq. "You got us down here in the loach?"

"Roger that. You find something?"

"Negative. Just want to make sure you don't."

"We'd all be happy not to have any surprises. Thanks," Thomas said.

"We'll be out of your way in a second here," Hollister said, looking over to Adams for an acknowledgment of his statement.

Adams nodded and came to a dead hover over a large tree. He moved the cyclic in a tiny circle, which translated to a wide sweeping and fanning motion that caused the branches of the tree to thrash violently. It allowed Hollister and Adams to look through the tree at the ground below—normally hidden by the large, lush growth.

"Anything?" Hollister asked.

"Negative," Adams said. "It was just a great place to hide a whole NVA football team."

"Got to agree with you. You could hide a lot under there."

"Coming out," the lead slick pilot announced. It was the signal to all that DeSantis's patrol was loaded without complication and the choppers were lifting off of the Olympic PZ.

Hollister looked back over his shoulder to see the first rotor disk tilting out of the pickup zone, several hundred meters behind the loach.

Adams rolled out of the hover and crept along the edge of an earthen ridge that formed the steep bank of a small, intermittent stream.

"Hold it!" Hollister yelled. "Come back around."

Adams looked over at what Hollister was looking at and snapped the chopper into a maneuver to overfly the area he had just covered.

"What you got?"

"Footprints," Hollister said.

"There," Hollister said, pointing out the open door at a raw spot in the grasses where the earth had eroded through from the rains. In the center of the red-brown split in the earth two long footprints clearly marked a spot where someone had lost his footing on the slippery slope and slid for several inches. The edges of the muddy skid mark were still sharp and distinct—not yet smoothed by the rain and runoff.

"Got it. Let's get the snakes over here," Adams said. He reached for the radio toggle switch.

Hollister and Adams saw the enemy gunner at the same moment—just as he steadied the large bull's-eye front sight on his antiaircraft gun on the nose of the chopper.

Plexiglas, metal, and debris showered the inside of the loach. The unmistakable klunking sounds of machine-gun rounds hitting the fuselage of the tiny chopper drowned out any other sounds.

"Hold on!" Adams yelled—unaided by the intercom.

Suddenly the trees in front of the chopper and the enemy gunner disappeared in a blur as the chopper began to violently spin to the right and lose altitude.

Hollister heard the first few words of Adams's Mayday call, telling the others they were going down, when several feet of tree branches came through the open door of the chopper. He heard the sharp cracking of large tree limbs shearing off under the falling chopper.

From somewhere in the chaos, Adams's left hand came across the chopper to grab for Hollister. The kind of move a parent would make for a child in the midst of a car crash.

Hollister looked to his left and saw the tree branches give way, exposing the ground below. The chopper was on its left side and falling through a large tree, heading for the slope of a grassy hillside below.

The impact was so violent that Hollister temporarily lost his orientation, sight, and hearing. He pulled his right hand toward his face, away from the large, leafy branch still inside the cockpit, and slid it down his chest to search for the quick release on the four-point seat-belt assembly.

CHAPTER 31

As quick as it happened—it was silent. The only thing Hollister could hear was something dripping and the ticking of hot metal cooling and changing shape. He could only guess it was somewhere in the turbine engine only inches behind his head.

"Chief?" he said, unsure if he was whispering or yelling. All he knew was his breathing was restricted by the tightened grip the safety belts had taken during the fall. And all he could think of was fire. He had seen choppers burn before and wanted to be as far away from the crashed loach as he could before something ignited the aviation fuel.

"Chief? You okay?"

There was no answer. Hollister found the release and yanked at it. The belts gave up their grip on him, and he fell from his seat. The chopper had come to rest on its nose, what was left of the tail up in the crotch of a tree.

His fall was only three feet, awkward and out of control. He landed on his back, light rain falling in his face, and fuel from the chopper dripping from the fuselage above him. He rolled over onto his stomach to try to crawl up and away from the risk of fire. The grasses were too slippery, and his boots could find no purchase.

He was aware of the continuing gunfire around them but couldn't tell who was firing. He tried to sit up and suddenly realized he was actually leaning over and rolled down the hillside—out from under the chopper.

A small stand of brush kept him from sliding into the stream at the bottom of the slope. The stop made him realize he hurt. And that he was still wearing his flight helmet.

He reached up and pulled the helmet off of his head. Spent, he let it roll down the hill.

His chest and ribs felt the pain of the impact with each small move he made. He felt for broken bones but found none.

As Hollister's focus broadened, he remembered Adams. He tried to call out his name and heard only a faint whisper coming from his own lips. He had not yet caught his breath. He laid his head back down in the wet grasses and forced himself to inhale. As his chest swelled, he felt more pain where his ribs connected to his breastbone.

He tried again. "Chief? You okay?"

No answer. A Cobra flew low and fast over the top of the crash site, firing his rockets into the enemy gunner's position—blocking out any other sounds near Hollister.

As soon as the chopper cleared the area, Hollister heard metallic noises. He flinched, worried that the precariously perched chopper might fall from its place, slide down the hill, and onto him.

He rolled over onto his stomach and tried to get to his knees. Again, the ground was too slippery, and he was too weak. He settled for falling back onto his heels in a squat.

"Sir?"

Hollister heard the weak voice of his pilot. "Chief? You okay? Where are you?"

"Over here."

A few feet in front of the downed chopper the brush moved. Hollister grabbed for his belt to find the pistol holstered somewhere on it.

A hand came up from the thicket. "Here. I'm here," Adams said.

Hollister took another deep breath, grabbed on to a root sticking from the muddy slope, and pulled himself up to a crouch. Everything seemed to hurt, and nothing wanted to work right. His knees felt as if they were about to buckle, and his head pounded. He worked his way to the waist-high bush that concealed the pilot and looked over it. "Chief? You hurt?"

Adams was on his side, his uniform ripped down the entire length of his back, his helmet missing. His face was covered with streaks of blood and mud. His left foot pointed away from his lower leg at an unnatural angle. From the top of his boot, blood dripped slowly to the ground below.

"Sorry, sir."

"What?"

"I shoulda been able to sideslip that fucker," he said. He coughed, and pain registered across his face.

Hollister moved around the bush and squatted to help Adams. "I wouldn't worry about it. I think the Cobra jocks evened the score for you."

Adams laughed and coughed again. "That's worse. I'm gonna have to take a ration of shit from those guys for the rest of my tour."

"If that's your only problem, I'd say you're okay."

"I think I broke my leg, sir," Adams said, pointing his gloved finger toward his ankle.

"You won't be doing any flying for a while."

The air suddenly filled with the sounds and the shadow of a slick. Hollister tried to shield his eyes with his forearm and still see the air crew.

His first sight was the beaming grin of First Sergeant Easy. He gave Hollister a wave and then threw out a bag of emergency gear. The pilot maneuvered the chopper to a low hover and Easy leaped out.

It looked to Hollister like Easy avoided a direct downward impact on his artificial leg by using a good parachute-landing fall. The old soldier landed on his good leg in a well-practiced roll that took advantage of the small slope.

"Airborne," Easy yelled as he hit the ground.

The chopper quickly pulled up and out of the small break in the trees to allow the first sergeant to get to his feet and move back toward Hollister and Adams.

"Damn, Top, you never know when to quit. Do you?"

Easy tried to cover the fact he was still trying to catch his breath when he crawled over to Hollister. "Hell, sir, without me you'd be in really deep shit."

"This isn't deep enough?" Adams asked.

"We been in deeper than this," Easy said, giving the pilot a reassuring wink.

"This is plenty deep for me," Adams said.

Easy examined his injuries. "Hell, Chief, you're about three good shots of Irish whiskey from being okay."

Adams looked up the hill at the wreckage of his loach. "I sure fucked that up. I never put one down before."

"You keep flyin' those things, and you'll park plenty of 'em where they don't belong," Easy said, pulling first-aid gear out of the bag he had dropped.

"We in trouble here?" Hollister asked.

"Don't look too bad, sir. The gunships got that zip machine gunner, and nobody's taken any more fire since then. If he had any friends, they've hauled ass outta here."

"The teams on the ground?"

"Chastain's home. DeSantis's about to land now, and Deming's on hold 'til we get you two out."

"Let's get the hell out of here before we end up causing some fucking international incident."

Easy held the syringe up to eye level and squeezed the plunger to force any air out of it.

"What are you doing?" the chief asked.

"We're gonna take some of the pain out of that leg so we can move it and you. This stuff'll let you travel."

"I never saw a first sergeant with a hypodermic needle," Adams said.

"You never been in Special Forces, either. Have you?"

Adams shook his head and let Easy inject the painkiller into his leg.

Easy bent the needle on the syringe against his plastic leg and threw the apparatus back into the bag. "We'll throw a quick splint on that leg so we won't tear anything up while we move."

"Where we going?" Hollister asked.

Easy jerked his head toward the other side of the stream. "There's a small clearing over there—'bout two hundred meters. Can you walk?"

Hollister got to his feet and tested his legs. "Seems like I can." He looked around. "Hell, two hundred meters, I can crawl."

The flight to the clearing station gave Hollister a chance to get caught up. Easy had a radio lashed to the legs of one of the jump seats. Once they got out of the clearing and to altitude, Hollister was able to contact the flight and the launch site.

"We're tight here. We've already sent the three folks you picked up out there over to province headquarters for interrogation. The few documents they had with them have also been sent to G-2 at field force," Michaelson said.

"Great. Everyone else okay?"

"A couple of minor scrapes. Aside from that and the trashed

loach, I guess you could mark it up in the plus column. How's the chief?"

"He'll only be flying a desk for a coupla months." Hollister turned so Adams could hear him. "And he's going to have to figure out how to pay for that aircraft out of his paycheck."

"We've got it under control here. Hope we can get some good information out of the three they brought in. Do what you got to do, and we'll see you back here."

"Roger," Hollister said. "One other thing . . . thanks for being there."

"Well, well, well . . . Ranger Six."

Hollister turned around and saw Doctor Plummer entering the curtained-off examining area of the clearing station.

"Hey, Doc. How are you?"

"I'm fine. But it looks to me like you've busted up another chopper pilot," he said, pointing a rubber-gloved finger toward Adams, who was lying on an examining table.

"No, sir," Adams said. "If I could blame it on Captain Hollister, I would, just to keep the other aviators off my ass. I have to take credit for this one."

Two of the medics had already cut off Adams's flight suit. Doctor Plummer stood at the end of the table and tried to take a long view of the angle formed by the break in Adams's lower leg.

The area around the exposed bone was already very swollen and discolored in patches of raspberry and yellow-gray.

"How's it look, Doc?" Adams asked.

"Looks like we're going to have to set and cast you before we can do anything else with you. You up for this?"

"I don't have much choice. You think there's gonna be a problem with this break?"

"Will you be able to fly again?" Plummer walked over to a portable light box and looked at the two X rays on it. Both bones were broken just two inches above the ankle. "If you do what I tell you and try not to be a tough guy, you have a better than even chance of getting back into the cockpit."

"How bad is it?"

Plummer looked at Adams's leg, then at the X ray again. "You're going to need some wire sutures and a cast to midthigh. You're fixable. But you're going to have to help me."

"Count on it, sir," Adams said, reassured by the news.

Hollister made eye contact with Plummer, throwing a question into his look. Plummer nodded and gave Hollister an encouraging wink. He'd be okay.

"I have to get back to Tay Ninh. You take it easy. I'll try to smooth things over with your boss," Hollister said, kidding Adams.

"Sorry I messed things up for you, sir," Adams said as he reached out to try an awkward handshake.

"You did a good job of getting us to the ground, Chief."

Hollister waved and turned to leave. "Take care of him, Doc."

Plummer looked up from his patient to reply when Hollister made what looked like a misstep on the plywood floor. "Hey, Ranger. Wait a sec."

Plummer motioned to the medic on the other side of the examining table to finish the cleanup he had started with an antiseptic solution, and stepped over to Hollister. "Look at me."

Hollister held up his hands in surrender. "Hey, I'm okay. It's just been a long day, and I could use some sleep and a cold beer."

Plummer pulled a penlight from his shirtsleeve pocket and held Hollister's head steady. He looked into his eyes and watched for the reaction of his pupils to the light. "Did you take a bump on the head in the crash?"

"I don't know. There was a hell of a lot happening on the way to the ground."

"Did you lose consciousness at any time?"

"I, um . . . not really *out* out. I got my bell rung. But I wouldn't use the word unconscious."

The doctor snapped the light off and put it back in his pocket. He then picked up an instrument from the tray next to the examining table, clicked on its tiny light, and looked first in Hollister's left ear and then his right.

"You're staying the night."

"No way, Doc. I've got a shitpot full of things to do and a company to run."

"You know, you have a real bad habit of pissing off doctors in their own little kingdoms," Plummer said.

Hollister pulled his beret from his pocket and unrolled it.

"Unless you are going to wear that to bed, you'd better stuff it back in your pocket. I'm admitting you and that's that."

Easy stepped in and tried to break up the argument. "Cap'n, we can probably make it through tonight without you. Why don't you take the downtime and catch up on some of that rest you need?"

"Top, there's too much to do."

"And the teams are all in. Colonel Michaelson's in town, and we're about as close to being in a stand-down as I've seen in a long while."

"See?" Plummer said. "They'll survive without you for a night."

Hollister hung his head. "Okay. Okay. But I need to get to a field phone to make a few calls."

The sheets felt so good and so heavy. He had been sleeping under a featherlight nylon poncho liner for so long that the weight of real bedcovers took some readjusting to.

Plummer had dropped in to see Hollister, but only told him they were just walking on the side of caution. There were no obvious signs he might have a head injury. Prudence and an otherwise empty hospital ward prompted Plummer to admit him.

Hollister had called operations, spoken with Michaelson again, taken a long shower, and eaten a hospital meal. After an hour in bed, he was bored. Plummer had left him some APC for the pain he predicted from the trauma, and two red capsules the doctor said would help him sleep.

Knowing that there were no teams out on the ground and little chance that there would be any activity in operations, Hollister elected to stop into the orderly room first.

Just as soon as he stepped through the door he was met with yelling and cross talk that quickly told him something was seriously wrong.

"Hey! Hey!" Hollister yelled over the sounds of Easy screaming into one phone and Captain Browning into another. "What the hell is going on?"

Easy slammed down his field phone receiver and looked at Hollister with a characteristically flushed red face—a clear sign of trouble. "That fucking dickhead has kidnapped our girl," he said.

"What?" Hollister asked. "What the hell are you talking about?"

Easy took a deep breath and started again. "Valentine. He decided the prisoners we turned over from the snatch had more to offer than his guys were getting out of them. He sweated the other two and got squat. When he got to the Montagnard laborer he got a stone wall. The guy musta told him he didn't speak no Viet."

"So? I'm not following you."

Browning raised his hand to the first soldier. "Let me fill in the blanks, Top.

"General Valentine turned the prisoners over to his provincial recon unit and told them to take the POWs back to the tunnel complex and root out some more folks or turn up some better intelligence. Apparently, he's convinced there's more going on than they were able to get out of the prisoners."

"Shit. What an asshole. Does field force or MACV know he sent Viet units across the line?"

Easy interrupted. "Colonel Michaelson's over at operations now talking to General Quinn by secure radio."

"What the hell is he trying to do and what does it have to do with us?" Hollister asked, more frustrated by his confusion.

"Well, it gets lots worse, Cap'n," Easy said.

"Jrae," Browning said.

"Jrae?" Hollister repeated. "What about her?"

"Seems she went by the darkroom to see Young's photos of her and saw the photos Deming's team had turned in for the after-action report. They had taken several photos of the Montagnard with the busted arm."

"So?" Hollister said.

"He's her brother."

"What?"

"The guy's her brother. His name is Pek. He was taken from their village some years ago by the VC."

"Go on," Hollister said, suspecting it was going to get worse.

"She split. She hopped a ride over to province headquarters to find him."

"Okay. So what's the fucking problem?"

Browning looked at Easy and they both braced for Hollister's reaction. "Valentine found out who she was, her connection to the Montagnard prisoner, and choppered her out to the river junction to act as interpreter."

"What!" Hollister yelled. He pointed toward Cambodia. "You mean she's on the ground out there?"

"Yes, sir," they both replied.

"What are they doing?"

"From what I can piece together from the folks over at Valentine's headquarters, his people have her with them. They're sweeping through the tunnel complex area and hoping she can get her brother to tell them where to look for the bad guy pot of gold," Browning said.

"Where are you going?" Hollister asked Easy, decked out in his combat gear and carrying a pump shotgun.

"I'm riding belly in the chase again."

"Why?"

"Anybody better at it?"

"No," Hollister said.

"She's my clerk, and I should have done something to keep her from gettin' into this fix."

"Like what?"

"I don't know. But I'm going with you to get her the fuck out of there—now."

"Okay, Top. You'll do just about anything to get away from the paperwork. Won't you?"

"Can't get that paperwork done without my gal Friday, now, can I?"

"Okay, okay. How we going to do this?"

"If you and Top go out there to find out just what the hell's going on, we can figure out our next steps to get her, and I guess her brother, the hell out of Cambodia before we start some international flap," Browning said.

Hollister looked outside his chopper, back toward Easy's chase ship. The first sergeant saw him and waved. Hollister turned back to Tennant, up front, and pointed down at a wide spot in the trail complex. "There!" he yelled.

Tennant nodded and put the chopper into a steep turning descent.

Hollister pulled his signal instructions out of his pocket and flipped to the advisory unit frequencies and call signs. He quickly found the line for Captain Depplemeier's job—PRU adviser. He picked up the radio he had brought along, set the frequency. "Autumn Notion Five-Six, this is Campus Killer Six. Over."

He got no answer and tried again. While he waited for a reply, he held the SOI up for Moody, flying copilot, to read the frequency and dial it into one of the chopper radios.

"This is Five-Six. Over." Captain Depplemeier's voice had a ring of irritation to it.

"I'd like you to find a place for me to land. Over," Hollister said.

"Stand by," Depplemeier said.

Tennant held the chopper into a tight turn, allowing Hollister to see Depplemeier below. The adviser-captain spun his radio operator around and appeared to Hollister to be changing the frequency on the radio.

"Betcha he's calling his boss," Tennant said.

"Looks that way," Hollister said. "Let's just hope Michaelson or General Quinn has Valentine too busy to wind his ass or scratch his watch."

Depplemeier appeared to be unsuccessful in his attempts. He switched the frequency back and looked around. "Killer Six, this is Five-Six. I've got a clearing over to the northeast."

Hollister could see Depplemeier pointing toward a small landing zone.

"It'll take me about zero five to secure it. But I have to tell you this is *very* inconvenient for me."

Hollister caught Tennant's eye. "He's got his fucking nerve," Tennant said over the intercom.

"Okay. I'll just orbit 'til you get it secured," Hollister said, a clear wash of sarcasm in his voice.

"Can you tell me the nature of your visit?" Depplemeier asked.

"Sure can. Once I'm on the ground," Hollister said. "Let me know when I can land. Out."

"Cut the crap," Hollister said. "I don't care to hear the reasons. That woman is a local national—not a combatant and not a POW. On top of that you fuckers kidnapped her—"

"I resent that, Captain," Depplemeier said.

Hollister leaned closer to Depplemeier—his face only inches from the sweating adviser. "I'm gonna kick your ass all over this fucking landing zone if I'm not putting her on my chopper in three minutes. You got that?"

Depplemeier pulled back from Hollister and turned. "She's over here. But I am telling you, right now, I will report this intrusion and your threat to the general."

Hollister fell in behind Depplemeier as he walked off the landing zone. "Depplemeier—shut the fuck up!"

* * *

The trail led to a small clearing under a large tree that had somehow survived years of bombing. There, Hollister saw the interrogation team. A Vietnamese sergeant and two other soldiers stood over Jrae, her brother, Pek, and one of the other prisoners snatched by the Rangers. The three squatted, their arms tied behind them—their elbows pulled together painfully by a piece of twine.

As Hollister got closer he could tell the two men had been beaten. Their faces were bruised and swollen. He was unable to tell if Jrae had been hurt. She sat with her head dropped, her hair falling across her face.

Hollister rushed up to Jrae. He dropped to his knees and pulled his demo knife from his belt to cut the line holding her elbows together. She whimpered and slumped forward, crying.

Hollister grabbed her gently and helped her to sit up. He brushed her hair from her face and saw the trails of tears and evidence of the punishment she must have taken from the Vietnamese sergeant and his assistants. Her lower lip was split, her right eyebrow had another cut through it, and her cheeks were red and swollen.

Hollister didn't telegraph his move. He simply rose and came around at the same time, catching the Vietnamese sergeant in the side of his jaw with his open palm—his full weight behind the blow. Every man on the ground heard the report of the slap. As the soldier reeled back Hollister stepped forward and brought his leg up, kicking the sergeant in the crotch—doubling him over in pain.

The other two soldiers reacted by spinning their weapons to point them at Hollister.

Hollister stepped toward the first soldier—making clear and promising eye contact. "I'll shove that fucking rifle up your ass and break it off!"

The soldier got the message and quickly dropped his weapon and his confrontational attitude.

The other did the same.

Hollister waved his hand at the other prisoners. "Untie these men."

"I'll see you are court-martialed for this!" Depplemeier yelled, still keeping his distance.

Hollister ignored the hysterical captain and dropped back to his knees to look at Jrae. "You okay? Can you walk?"

Jrae whispered a barely audible, "Yes, Captain. Yes, I think so."

He helped her to her feet and steadied her, then turned to Pek and motioned toward the landing zone. "Tell him to come with us," he said.

Jrae looked at Pek. He got to his feet, having understood Hollister's instructions.

"Depplemeier . . . get your ass over to that landing zone and set up something that looks like real security. Your goddamn people look like they are waiting for a fucking bus."

Depplemeier spoke in hushed tones over his radio and glared at Hollister, but made no moves.

"Now!" Hollister pulled the radio handset off his harness. Dropping all radio procedure, he called Tennant in the chopper. "Dale. Come get us."

Tennant responded by pulling out of orbit to set up his landing.

Depplemeier stood his ground as Hollister moved in his direction, helping Jrae along the path.

"I'll see you are raked over the coals for this. I'll make sure your ass is in as big a sling as I can find," Depplemeier babbled.

Hollister jerked his pistol from its holster and pulled the hammer back. He pointed the weapon at Depplemeier. "Last chance, asshole. Get some security on that PZ, or I promise you I'll call in a medevac for a friendly-fire casualty."

Depplemeier gave in and yelled some instructions to the ARVNs in very bad Vietnamese. They made a pretense of security by doubling the number of men on the PZ and getting them down into prone firing positions.

His radio operator rushed to his side and thrust the handset toward his face.

Depplemeier turned away from Hollister and answered the radio call. Again, he spoke in heated but hushed tones to keep Hollister from hearing him.

Hollister led Jrae and Pek to the side of the PZ to wait for Tennant to bring the pickup chopper in.

Depplemeier ran over to Hollister and waved his hands in the air. "General Valentine said you are to immediately release my prisoners and leave this area. You are interfering with our operations and jeopardizing the lives of the people we advise."

"He knows you have this woman and her brother out here?" Hollister asked.

"Of course he does. And he wants you to get the hell out of here and leave us to our business."

"Great. Now that I know for sure he's behind this, you can get him back on the radio and tell him to start packing."

"What the hell does that mean?"

"You figure it out."

Tennant lined his slick up with the landing zone and began his approach-descent.

Hollister raised the handset to his face and spoke above the chopper's blade noise. "We're on the east side of the Papa Zulu. Over."

"Rog. I got an eyeball on you. Can you give me a little smoke?" Tennant said. "The winds have gotten a little squirrelly since I put you in."

"Stand by," Hollister said. He pulled a smoke grenade off the packtray holding his radio. With one firm pull, Hollister yanked the cotter pin from the striker on the smoke grenade. He tossed it into an off-center spot in the clearing and watched the spring-mounted spoon fly in another direction. The grenade hit the ground, and brilliant purple smoke spread from it.

"Killer Six. Got goofy grape," Tennant announced more for the benefit of the circling pilots than himself and Hollister.

Hollister spoke into the mouthpiece of his handset. "Roger. Goofy grape. That's us. Anytime you're ready."

"Inbound. Out."

Hollister turned to Jrae and Pek. They squatted timidly under the overhang of a tree bordering the landing zone.

"You have really gone too far. You Rangers think that your shit's so hot. Well, you're going to find out screwing with my ARVNs was a stupid move," Depplemeier said, careful to keep his distance from Hollister.

Hollister raised his hand and pointed at the few soldiers standing on the margin of the landing zone. "Listen, asshole. You get your fucking ARVNs organized and put somebody outside this circle—now! There isn't a bad guy inside of five miles that doesn't know we're here and just how many of us there are. So, try to do something right and get some fucking security out."

Tennant slipped the nose of the C & C over the end of the landing zone, flared it to slow his forward airspeed, and settled.

Hollister waved for Jrae and Pek to join him—on the way to the spot on the ground where he guessed Tennant would put it down.

The trio began to run, at a crouch, toward the landing chopper. Hollister hesitated long enough to look up and check out the location of the two circling Cobras and Easy's chase ship.

Hollister slid to a stop at the side of the chopper and waited for Jrae to catch up. Without letting her lose momentum, he grabbed her by the waist and arm and lifted her up and shoved her into the chopper.

He turned to help Pek and found him already crawling over the lip of the cargo deck. Hollister put his hand on the deck and vaulted up into the chopper. Without a break in his motion, he reached up and slapped Moody on the helmet and yelled, "Go! Go! Go!"

Hollister rolled farther inside the chopper and began to settle in for the ride when he heard the whoosh and then saw the impact and detonation of an RPG. It came from the tree line on the far side of the landing zone. The round hit the skin of the chopper behind the left door gunner's seat and just above the skids and the fuel cell. The gunner's face and shoulder disappeared in a froth of blood and bone, and the blast threw Jrae and Pek into Hollister.

Before he could right himself, the chopper began to lose the few feet of altitude it had gained. Hollister looked up from the floor of the chopper at Tennant, who was trying to control the chopper—headed for the trees at the end of the LZ.

Hollister reached out to steady Jrae with one hand while his other automatically searched for something to hold on to. His fingers found the left rear leg of the peter pilot's seat and locked on to it.

The chopper continued to float toward the trees until Tennant finally yelled out for everyone to brace themselves. The chopper seemed to collapse into a large thicket with a sigh.

At the last moment before the chopper sank into the fifteen-foot-tall mesh of barbed nettles, Hollister caught sight of Depplemeier's soldiers behind the chopper. They were almost a hundred meters away and firing furiously in all directions, some of their small-arms fire passing over the chopper.

He tried to find his radio to tell Depplemeier to stop the

firing and realized it was all the way back under the other door gunner's seat.

Tennant kept repeating his Mayday call as long as the radio would transmit and then popped the quick release on his seat restraints. "Get out! Get out!"

CHAPTER 32

Hollister heard the unmistakable sound of another RPG firing at something or someone several dozen meters behind the chopper.

The chopper leaned toward the left, and it was all Hollister could do to hold himself and Jrae on the slanted cargo deck. With Tennant's instructions clear, he let go of the seat and grabbed Jrae.

They slid out of the chopper and fell into the thicket. The dense growth acted to break their fall. Hollister pulled Jrae close to his chest as their momentum caused them to roll off the cushion of impenetrable growth. Followed by Pek, they landed on the hard ground, unable to see anything more than a foot away from them.

"Dale?" Hollister said.

"Over here," Tennant said. He waved his hands and shook the brush.

"You and Moody okay?"

"Yeah," Tennant replied.

"Where's your crew chief?"

"I'm over here," the crew chief said.

Hollister turned to find the soldier barely three feet away. His face was covered with little scratches—all bleeding. But through it, he smiled broadly and held up Hollister's handset to let him know he had grabbed the radio on exit. "Great! Good man."

The firing around them continued. Enough of it was coming toward the crash site to make Hollister even more concerned about their safety. "Listen up," he yelled, loud enough for the others to hear. "It doesn't make much difference who's shooting at us. Good guys or bad, we're going to take some hits if we stand up. So stay tight to the dirt until I can do something about it."

Hollister reached out for Jrae and pressed down on her

shoulder—emphasizing the danger for her. She understood and stayed close to the ground. He then found the coiled cord to his handset and followed it from the radio connector out to the handset.

Pressing it to his face, he tried to reach the gunships orbiting above. "Raider Three-Six, this is Killer Six. You got a visual on us?"

"Rog. That you stacked up to the November Echo of the Lima Zulu?"

"Affirm. We need to get this incoming off our back to get out of here."

"Lemme come in there and see if I can tell who's doing what to who. Stand by."

Joe Raymond slipped sideways into a rapid descent. Just above the trees, he jerked it back level and skimmed across the landing zone and over Hollister's position. "Hot dog," Raymond said. "I got a bunch a little fuckers in uniform carrying weapons just west of you."

"Can you lay some fire on them so we can get back to the landing zone?"

"Negative. Negative. They are dead-on centered between you and the perimeter. If I try to get in there, I'm going to be too close to you or to the other friendlies," Raymond said.

"Shit! Got any suggestions, Joe?"

"Stand by a sec." Raymond rolled into a turn and headed back. He prowled the right side of the landing zone. Two green tracers leaped from the nearby tree line, searching for the underside of the Cobra. The shots were unsuccessful, but confirmed Joe's location of some of the enemy forces. At the southern end of the landing zone, Raymond pulled up and headed north again.

"You're goin' ta have to go east, then south to hook back around to link up with the friendlies," he said.

"I was afraid you were going to say that. Okay, thanks. Break. Autumn Notion Five-Six. This is Campus Killer Six."

Depplemeier answered the radio call, a trace of panic in his voice. "This is Five-Six."

"Did you copy mine with Raider Three-Six?"

"Affirm. Over."

"I'm going to try to work my way back to your location. I've got the survivors from the chopper with me. Make sure your people know we are coming your way. I don't want to take any friendly fire. You got that?"

"Roger. I'll pass the word."

"And you'd better tighten up your perimeter so that we can put some fire on the targets the guns can identify."

"Roger."

"Expect me in four-five to an hour. It's going to take a while to pick my way back."

"It's going to be dark by then."

"Yeah. I know. Out," Hollister said.

Hollister moved to a point with some concealment and pulled Jrae close. He motioned for the others—Pek, Tennant, Moody, and the crew chief—to join him in a tight knot.

"Listen. We have a few problems here." He raised his hand and pointed to a spot along the line between them and the ARVNs. "We've got bad guys to get around before we can get back to the inside of the perimeter."

Tennant looked up at the horizon.

"I know. I know. It's gonna be dark pretty soon."

Jrae explained Hollister's words to Pek. He waved his hand in the direction of a game path. She turned to Hollister. "My brother knows this area well. He said he will take us to the ARVNs. He says it will be safe. He knows where to go."

Hollister nodded to recognize the gesture. "Tell him we can't walk the trails. If we do, we will surely be ambushed."

They conferred again in their native dialect. Jrae turned again to Hollister. "He said he will stay away from the trails. But it will be slow."

"Tell him that is good," Hollister said.

He turned to the others. "Okay, folks, you are grunts now. What have we got?" Hollister raised his M-16.

The crew chief raised his machine gun. He had pulled it off the chopper mount. That left him with a nearly unmanageable weapon with no bipod to rest it on while firing it. It also had no rear stock or butt to place up against the shooter's shoulder. Instead, there were a pair of handgrips and a butterfly thumb-trigger, designed for firing from a chopper.

"How much ammo do you have?" Hollister asked.

" 'Bout five hundred rounds," the crew chief said.

"Okay. You're going to have to hold what you've got until we get in a world of shit. If it gets to needing that machine gun, I want you to wedge it into the crotch of a tree or prop it up on something that'll keep it from walking across Cambodia, and press that barrel toward the ground. Shoot dirt. You got me?"

"Sir?"

"You won't have shit for accuracy. So let's take advantage of what we know. All of your targets will be standing, squatting, kneeling, or lying down. Try to spray the area between you and them. A ricochet is more likely to hit them than trying to aim at them and watch the tracers jump up over their heads."

The crew chief nodded and clutched his machine gun close to his chest.

Hollister turned to the two pilots.

Tennant pulled out his .45 pistol.

"Ammo?" Hollister asked.

"Got two eight-round clips."

"Great. Shoot only if you have a target and only if he's within twenty-five feet of you. Anything else is wasted ammo."

Moody held up his .38 revolver. "Just got six rounds in the weapon."

Hollister shook his head. "Okay. Same deal with you. Don't shoot unless you can make it worth your effort."

Jrae translated again while Hollister outlined the order of march. He wanted the small party to move in three elements. Pek out front—on point. Then Hollister, Jrae, and Moody. The rear element would be Tennant and the crew chief to cover their rear.

Hollister made one last transmission. "Raider Three-Six. This is Killer Six. We are moving. Have you notified Campus Killer base of our *problem*?"

"Roger your move. And affirm on the relay. We're all starting to run a little short on fuel. What's your pleasure?"

"Get some replacements for your gun team to fly cover in case we get into more shooting. Take your team and the slicks back, refuel, and stand by. I'll call for the slicks in enough time for you to get out here to pick us up."

"Anything else?"

"Keep something up over us. I need someone to relay commo back to Tango November. I can't rely on the other friendlies' commo," Hollister said, not caring if Depplemeier heard his declaration of no confidence.

"Got it. Keep your head down, Jim," Joe Raymond said.

"No problem there."

*   *   *

Darkness closed in before Hollister's small group had moved twenty meters. The going was very slow, and Hollister worried the unskilled in the file were making too much noise. Twice he had to stop and work his way back. First to Moody, who was breaking the small branches instead of sidestepping them. The second time to tell the crew chief he could hear his belted ammunition clanking against the metal on the machine gun as he walked.

The delays to correct the problems were added to the delays for caution on the move. This in spite of the fact that Pek was skilled at moving at night—quietly, without wasted motion.

Hollister watched him pick his way through the brush, taking care to know where he was stepping and what was around him. He tried to copy each move Pek made. He also tried to keep track of Jrae.

The fact that she was a woman and unaccustomed to moving tactically in a hostile environment was overcome by her familiarity with forested terrain. He regretted having to put Tennant and the crew chief in the tail of the file—but he had no choice. He needed the firepower back there and didn't want the only other captain too close to him. Should he get killed or wounded, he wanted Tennant to make the decisions and pick up control. He may have been a little rusty on the ground, but he was a sharp thinker and a cool head. With Hollister's radio, he could get things done no one else in their small group could.

After another hundred meters of moving, Hollister held up the small group. He felt something was wrong and wanted to pull off their line of march and sit. He turned their direction ninety degrees and set up a small perimeter. He took Pek back to where they changed their direction and made an effort to trample some vegetation to make it appear as if they had turned into a nearby clearing. On the way back to the perimeter, he and Pek stood the vegetation they had disturbed back up.

They then sat and waited.

After only ten minutes, Hollister and the others heard someone approaching—using the same route they had taken. He was right. They were being followed.

Sixteen North Vietnamese soldiers—uniformed and well armed—moved down the trail made by the passing Americans.

Hollister reached over and put his hand on the top of the crew chief's machine gun—to make sure he knew to hold his fire.

They all watched as the enemy soldiers stopped near the point Hollister had changed their direction and then moved on—toward the clearing that Hollister had hoped to lead them to.

In five minutes they were out of sight. Hollister was the first to move. He looked around at the others to see if the close call had made an impression on them. All appeared to be very motivated by the nearness of the enemy patrol and the danger they were in.

He was sure they would move more quietly and do damage to less vegetation on the move once they continued their route to the landing zone.

Hollister cupped the mouthpiece of his handset with his hands. "Five-Six. This is Killer Six. Be advised, there is a one-six man November Victor Alpha patrol moving in your direction from your east."

Depplemeier came back immediately. "Roger, enemy patrol."

They continued to move through the thick brush, only occasionally able to see where they were from the in-and-out moonlight between the clouds.

After several more minutes of movement, the cloud cover thickened, and it began to rain again. The circling gunships were forced to gain altitude to get above the clouds. Then they were forced to fly back to Tay Ninh. The worsening weather left Hollister with only the few weapons they had to defend themselves.

Artillery would be out of the question because he couldn't be sure where the ARVNs were. Air strikes wouldn't be possible for that reason and because of the lack of visibility.

Their situation had seriously worsened.

Hollister kept them moving toward the landing zone. Their pace had slowed because of the visibility and the unknown location of the passing enemy patrol.

As they got close to the LZ, they heard some noise. Hollister stopped and called Depplemeier. "I've got some movement at what I guess to be five hundred meters southeast of your position. Are those your folks?"

"Negative. Negative," Depplemeier said. "I don't have anyone in that area."

"Are you sure?" Hollister asked. "I don't want to fire only to find out there's a misunderstanding."

"I just finished counting noses. All accounted for, and no one in the area you described," Depplemeier said.

"Okay. If you hear any shooting, you'll know what it's about."

*   *   *

The darkness became so complete it was impossible to see anything more than an arm's length away. And the enemy soldiers seemed to become bolder. The noises became muffled voices. The pattern indicated to Hollister that they had spread out and were searching the area. He could hear the sounds of equipment clanking and brush being crushed underfoot.

It became clear to Hollister that he had enemy soldiers behind him and in front of him. Beyond the ones to his front were the ARVNs. He was less sure about their location than the enemy's.

Hollister looked back where they had just come from. He knew he had to get his small group away from the searching enemy soldiers. That meant cutting across a small clearing.

He reached forward and grabbed Pek by the shoulder. The others stopped and waited for his instructions. Hollister motioned to Tennant, Moody, and the crew chief to stay put while he gathered Pek and Jrae around him.

"We have to change direction, across that clearing. We will go first. Then we will wait while the others cross. Okay?"

Jrae translated to Pek, and they both nodded.

Hollister worked his way back and explained the same thing to the pilots and the crew chief. He positioned each of them where they could cover Hollister's, Jrae's, and Pek's movement across the clearing.

Hollister pulled the red-filtered flashlight off his web gear and cupped the lens with his hand. He turned it on and off quickly. The light barely illuminated a margin of skin around the lens. "Okay. When we're in position, I'll give you two very quick shots of light. You move carefully. I'll try to cover your move."

The three started toward the clearing. With Hollister in the lead, Jrae and Pek moved quietly behind him.

Hollister knew if the enemy didn't see them, they surely wouldn't hear them. He had never moved in the bush with anyone who could be as quiet as the two Montagnards. He was encouraged by their skills, overcoming some of the shortcomings of having two unarmed people in tow.

Halfway across the clearing, Jrae stopped Hollister and turned him around. There, west of them, the noises and searching enemy soldiers had grown even more aggressive. They could see the flickering of several flashlights through the thick vegetation. The talking grew louder, and there was even some shouting.

To Hollister that meant they either knew they had the Americans and the ARVNs outnumbered or they didn't know the ARVNs were nearby. Either way, it wasn't a good sign. And he'd have to assume there were more enemy soldiers searching for them than they had seen pass by earlier.

Hollister grabbed Jrae's wrist and hurried her across the small clearing. Trading safety for speed, he took the chance they wouldn't hit any mines or booby traps getting to the far side before they were seen.

Once inside the far tree line, Hollister stopped, grabbed the others, and pulled them to the concealment of a large hedgerow. They watched the enemy flashlights move closer and tried to control their breathing to keep from being heard.

Some of the enemy soldiers used their rifles to search. They fired random shots into the trees in hopes of flushing out the intruders.

Three or four of the approaching soldiers sprayed long bursts of automatic rifle fire across the clearing. Again, their aim was probing fire—not aimed fire.

Hollister still decided not to return fire and hoped Tennant and the others were smart enough to do the same on the other side of the clearing.

No one needed to speak to understand things had turned much worse. The enemy flashlights broke out into the clearing and began to work their way across it—separating Hollister, Jrae, and Pek from the downed chopper crew.

Hollister knew the reality of their situation. They had no choice. They had to move away from the edge of the clearing without the pilots or risk being discovered by the searching enemy soldiers.

He turned to Jrae and pulled her ear to his face. He whispered, "We need someplace to hide. We can't keep moving. Ask your brother where we can go."

Jrae passed the question on to Pek, who immediately pointed in the direction of a stream.

Before they left, Hollister could see the spot where Tennant, Moody, and the crew chief had been waiting being searched by the soldiers. He had to assume that they too had moved to avoid being discovered.

Pek stopped them a dozen steps short of a stream bank. The move had taken them another hour—picking their way through the brush, stopping frequently to listen. After the first half hour, they could no longer see or hear the enemy soldiers searching the clearing.

The problem facing them was to find a place to hole up until first light. Only then could Hollister hope to get the choppers and air cover in to help them get out of their fix.

Pek motioned to Jrae and Hollister to stay put. He walked toward the stream and out of sight of the other two.

After several minutes, he came back and waved for them to follow him.

Less than fifty meters upstream the terrain and vegetation overhung the stream. Pek sat on the bank and slid quietly into the rushing water. Hollister and Jrae did the same.

They waded, armpit deep, along the bank and up under the overhang. There, Pek pointed them to a hard-to-make-out pocket in the bank. It had been undercut by the flow of the stream.

Hollister waited for his eyes to adjust a little more to the even darker world and then pulled his flashlight off his harness. Allowing only a sliver of light, he looked around the pocket in the earthen bank. It was less than three feet high, but was long enough for all three of them to get up on the ledge above the waterline.

Pek and Hollister climbed out of the stream, onto the ledge, and then reached back to help Jrae up. They had not even stopped dripping water from their clothes when they heard the sounds of automatic weapons fire. First AK-47s and then M-16s. The bursts seemed to alternate twice, then went silent only to be followed by one more combined burst of fire and what sounded like two hand grenades.

There was no way to tell the direction of the shooting from their burrow. Hollister knew it didn't involve Tennant's party since they carried no M-16s.

Hollister, Jrae, and Pek sat quietly for almost an hour before speaking or moving about. Finally, satisfied they hadn't been followed, Hollister set up his radio and tried to extend the whip antenna toward the opening.

"Campus Killer Control, this is Killer Six. Over."

He waited for a reply and heard what sounded like a squelch break. But he was not able to recognize anything. He tried again. Still no answer, just the sound of an attempt.

Hollister gave up on the launch site and tried to call Depple-

meier. He got no answer there, either. After two tries, he decided
to save the battery and wait until something was flying overhead
to make another attempt.

Outside the hole, the sky must have cleared somewhat because the
water reflected a bit more light back up onto the ledge. He could
see the outlines of Jrae and Pek. He checked his watch and saw it
was nearly two A.M.

He tried to decide what to do with the time until first light. He
considered getting some sleep but felt too responsible for the
Montagnards' safety.

Instead, he checked and rechecked his weapon to make sure it
was still in working order, and did the same with his ammo. He
thanked the NCOs along the way who had made him assemble
and disassemble weapons blindfolded. They had promised him if
he needed to do it in combat he would be glad he mastered the
skill.

He pulled his claymore bag around and slipped his hand in to
inventory the contents. He was sure he had a signal mirror inside,
but hadn't seen it in days. His fingers found the smoothed-off
edges of the machined glass mirror and worked to the string
attached to the hole in the end of the mirror.

Pulling it out of the bag, he slipped the cord around his neck
and tucked the small mirror into his shirt. It would be as vital to
them in the morning as the radio. He could call the choppers, but
he needed some way to signal their location. With no smoke
grenades, he had to put his faith in the signal mirror. The last thing
he wanted to do was get separated from the claymore bag with the
mirror in it. Around his neck was a better place.

Another hour went by. Hollister checked his watch and tried to
dismiss his impatience. Jrae shifted her position on the ledge and
her leg brushed up against Hollister's hip. She was shivering from
the wet, cold, and dampness of the wet earth.

Hollister reached over and slipped his arm around her. Without
waking, Jrae rolled over into Hollister's arms. He pulled her
closer, her head resting on his chest, her knees curled up against
his thighs.

It had been so long since Hollister had even touched a woman.
Her hair smelled of the fresh vegetation they had traveled through.

He soon found himself rubbing her back. He wished he had

something to cover her with to take the chill away. He moved her so the small of her back was off the ground and against his hip. The added warmth would help her fight the cold. Soon, her shivering diminished, and he could feel the warmth of her body.

After a few minutes Jrae reached out and took Hollister's hand. She pulled it to the hollow of her neck and held it there.

He wondered if she was even conscious she had done it. He suspected not.

Hollister listened to her breathe and continued to gently stroke her back and her hair. He was surprised at how comfortable he felt with a woman from another culture and almost another era of time. The mountain woman had only taken on some of the trappings of modern women. He had realized how much of her primitive skills and instincts still lived within her as he watched her move through the bush that day.

Just before dawn, Hollister woke Jrae and Pek. Pek slipped off the ledge into the water. He swam to a point under the overhang where he could stay concealed by the vegetation but still see out. After several minutes, he came back to Hollister and shook his head—telling Hollister that he saw nothing alarming.

Hollister knew it only meant there was no one moving in the small slice of the outside world Pek could see. It was not a guarantee of safety for the trio.

Jrae looked at Hollister.

He pointed up. "We wait until we hear something flying, and then we will try to contact them by radio. After that, we'll work out a way to get out of here."

The heat of the day quickly turned the hollow in the stream bank into a steamy, fly-infested cavern, making the wait even more uncomfortable than the night had been.

Hollister checked his watch and looked out at the water. The dullness of the surface told him the cloud cover still hung over them. He had to assume the absence of chopper noises was due to the weather.

Another hour went by, and the water began to sparkle with the reflections of the sun. No one needed to speak to know it was a good sign.

Hollister heard the radio handset before he heard the sounds of chopper blades.

"This is Six. Go," Hollister said.

Michaelson's voice was clear and strong over the radio. "What's your situation?"

Hollister shorthanded the problems of being separated from the pilots and unable to work their way back to either the pilots or the ARVNs and Depplemeier.

Michaelson asked if he had a pickup zone nearby.

"We haven't seen what this place looks like in the daylight. How far out are you?"

"At least ten minutes away from where you might be. My guess it's the same stream we are familiar with. I'm going to turn north and hold in a high orbit until you know more and want us to come in," Michaelson said.

"Roger that. If I lose commo, look for a shiny. It will be me or the two folks with me if something happens to me. I don't have much confidence in my battery."

"Got it. Be careful," Michaelson said.

Hollister didn't need to explain what was happening to Jrae or Pek. He simply motioned for them to stay put. He pulled the mirror from his shirt and placed it on the ledge. He took the side of the radio handset and placed it under the centerline of the mirror and pressed down on it. The mirror cracked into two usable pieces. He handed one to Jrae.

"If you have to signal Colonel Michaelson, use this. He will know it's you."

Hollister rubbed his hands along the wall side of the earthen bank and picked up some of the slippery mosses and mud. He used the remaining piece of mirror to break up the skin tone and features of his face, turning highlights into darker spots. It wasn't his best camouflage job, but it would help. He wiped the rest of the mud over the backs of his hands and on his neck.

"I won't be long," he said. Then, after checking the radio and his weapon, he slipped off the ledge and into the cool water. He held his weapon high and bent over to get out from under the overhang.

Reaching the grasses and brush that trailed in the stream, Hollister stopped and peered out across the water. From his limited vantage point, he could see an otherwise calm and untroubled stream wandering through a peaceful meadow that might have been someone's farm had there not been one war or another near there for over a hundred years.

The absence of enemy soldiers only meant he couldn't see any.

It didn't mean there weren't any. Hollister moved out from under the overhang and hugged the bank. He wanted to find a pickup zone on their side of the stream. He wanted to avoid having to cross the stream to find one, and again to pick up Jrae and Pek, and a final time to go back to the PZ. That many crossings in the daylight was a sure invitation to trouble.

The footing under the water was uncertain. Roots and rocks made it difficult for Hollister to move along the bank and keep his head and his weapon above water. He had doubts about taking the radio with him and how much more water it could take before giving out on him. He knew if he got into trouble looking for the landing zone, he might be able to get out of it by calling for air support. Without the radio, he'd give up that possibility.

At a point where the stream began to make a gentle bend there was a stand of reeds on the inside of the turn—where the water moved more slowly. It was the perfect place for him to climb up from the water to the stream bank. The reeds hid his outline and allowed him to look quite a distance up and down the stream as well as back from the turn.

From somewhere back where they had been the night before there came three rifle shots followed by what was surely a pistol. Hollister pulled out his compass and shot an azimuth toward the shooting. He ducked back down and pulled the handset off his harness. "Golf Mike, this is Killer Six. Over," he whispered, using Michaelson's initials.

"This is Mike," Michaelson replied.

"I think we need to worry about Detroit Two-Six and two crew members with him. I want to send some guns over there to check them out. Can you help me out?"

"Roger. I'm going to let Easy direct the guns to your last known, and you can work from there. Stand by."

In what seemed like less than three minutes, the Cobras flew over at max speed.

"Mark, mark, mark," Hollister yelled over the chopper sounds to let them know they had just overflown his position.

Joe Raymond pulled up hard and reversed his direction.

Hollister pulled the scrap of mirror out of his pocket and found the sun. As best he could guess the angle, he reflected the sun back toward the lead gunship.

"Roger. Got your shiny," Raymond said.

Hollister looked at the orbiting gunship and pointed to the southwest, just in case Raymond could see him standing in the reeds. "Detroit Two-Six's element is about six hundred mikes from mine at two six five degrees. Over."

"Got it. We'll take a look," Raymond said as he rolled the gunship out of the orbit and headed to where Hollister thought Tennant, Moody, and the crew chief might still be.

Raymond was over the position in a matter of seconds. He and his wing man prowled the area in tight, low orbits. Before they made the first complete circle the sounds of ground fire were added to the chopper noises.

Hollister couldn't see the firing at first. He watched Raymond roll out away from the ground fire and pick up speed and altitude to set up for a firing run.

Raymond's Cobra dove for a target. The minigun on the nose of the chopper spit out an interrupted rope of red tracers. As soon as Raymond got to the bottom of his run, his wingman replaced him to keep the pressure on the enemy positions.

Hollister lost sight of the gunship. The trees between him and the target area blocked much of the gun run.

"Six, this is Golf Mike. You might want to move in the same direction you would from the mess hall to the orderly room for a few hundred mikes to look for that Papa Zulu," Michaelson said, trying to not give away the direction over the radio.

The mess hall–orderly room reference meant he should move northwest—the same direction he would move between those buildings back at Tay Ninh.

Hollister knew he had to move. Had the enemy been monitoring his earlier radio transmission to Raymond, they would have been able to figure out the back azimuth and the distance from the firing to Hollister's position.

The sounds of the gunship and ground firing helped Hollister. He knew enemy soldiers were not so disciplined that the contact would not distract their attention. It gave him the best chance to move without being detected. Any sounds he would make would be covered by the prowling choppers. Chances were everyone near him would be watching them.

He stepped up out of the marshy water and onto the bank. Gallons of water fell from his uniform and equipment as he took his first few clumsy strides to the nearby tree line.

Inside the trees, Hollister was able to survey the area near the bank and still stay concealed. He moved up the tree line, looking for a spot large enough to bring in one chopper to get them out. As he moved, he was still concerned by the amount of fire being exchanged between the enemy gunners and the Cobras. He knew it had to be frightening and disorienting for the pilots trapped on the ground—if they were still alive.

Hollister began to worry about his distance from Jrae and Pek. The farther he had to travel to find a pickup zone, the more chance they had of getting ambushed moving back to it.

The gunships stopped firing and pulled up into a high orbit. Then two of the three orbiting slicks dropped out of their orbit and set up for a landing in the contact area. Hollister hoped the shift to the slicks meant the enemy firing had been suppressed, and they had some friendlies on the ground to pick up.

Hollister continued to search for his landing zone while keeping an eye on the progress of the slick only eight hundred meters away from his location. For a moment, he considered asking Michaelson if he should think about using that same landing zone. But then he realized it would be nearly a fourteen-hundred-meter hump for them from the hollow in the stream bank.

He stepped around a thick stand of bamboo and suddenly found himself looking out onto the landing zone Michaelson had directed him to. It was large enough to land two or possibly three slicks, and the height of the trees surrounding it wouldn't pose much of a problem for choppers.

Hollister tried to study the PZ and commit its features to memory before he returned for Jrae and Pek. He didn't want to have any difficulty finding it again. He noted the major landmarks in the area and figured its proximity to the stream. He then looked around for any signs of enemy traffic. The trails seemed to be undisturbed, and there were no signs of broken branches or twisted limbs of bushes.

He turned to start back to the stream overhang when he caught sight of a slick coming to a hover over the contact site. He saw two sandbags fly out the cargo door just as the chopper flew over the site.

What he saw concerned him. He hoped his earlier insistence on cross training the pilots and crews would help Tennant and the others. They were going to have to come out on a McGuire rig.

He remembered how he had insisted the pilots get a ride at the end of those ropes. He knew the familiarization would help Tennant. But being extracted at the end of 120-foot nylon climbing ropes was difficult even for experienced Rangers. And doing it for real, under fire, was a tricky stunt to pull off.

The bags thrown to Tennant contained the harnesses they would need to attach themselves to the end of the ropes that would later be thrown from the choppers.

CHAPTER 33

Hollister began to work his way back to Jrae and Pek. His route was just under the widest of the orbits of the circling helicopters. He shielded his eyes from the sun and looked up. Above him, he saw the numbers had grown to four gunships, three slicks, and another lone chopper. He assumed it was an ARVN aircraft.

He was careful not to take the same route back to the streamside hideout. If he had been seen on the way out by enemy troops, they might have moved into position to fire on him on his return.

Hollister wanted to make sure his route back would still leave him a way to make his third trip along the same general route once he picked up Jrae and Pek. The repeated travel, the randomness of the enemy elements, and the unpredictable nature of the ARVN soldiers somewhere nearby troubled Hollister. Still, he had no options. He didn't want to look for a hole in the trees to try a McGuire rig extraction with two Montagnards who had never seen the technique. He had to get them to the PZ he had found and hope to be able to get a chopper in to pick them up—and not be discovered.

It was a long shot. He put the risks out of his mind and tried to focus on how to tilt the weight of the advantage the enemy had. He knew if he could get to the PZ with Jrae and Pek, he could call on the choppers and gunships to improve his odds of making it out. And they would be available if the weather held.

He looked up at those parts of the horizon he could see through the trees. The sky was blue and clear of threatening cloud formations.

* * *

Hollister stopped and slipped into a thick stand of bamboo to look back over the route he had taken. He wanted to have as much of the area committed to memory as he could. He didn't want to waste any time or hesitate or to be forced to stop to check his map on the final trip back.

The sounds of the pilots' pickup chopper grew. Hollister looked over to the area where he heard the pistol shots and had seen the first chopper drop the McGuire rig harnesses.

A chopper came to a high hover over the spot. Three climbing ropes flew out of the cargo compartment, thrown by the belly man. Hollister could tell by the sudden tension pulled into the whipping ropes that someone on the ground had grabbed the snap links tied to them.

Arrival of the chopper was the best time for Hollister to make the last dash to the stream. Attention would be focused on the chopper again, and the sounds would help cover his move. He left the bamboo and grabbed the shoulder straps to his radio backpack. Breaking into a trot, he only had a hundred and fifty more meters to go.

He reached the stream bank, and leaped over it and into the rushing water. As he hit bottom, he reached out and grabbed a handful of edge grasses to keep him close to the bank.

He turned and saw the chopper, some six hundred meters away, rising straight up. Two of the air crew members dangled under the chopper, holding on to the limp body of a third—connected to the ropes, but unable to hold himself upright.

He couldn't tell who each outlined figure was because he was looking into the sun. But he was sure the third figure was seriously wounded or dead.

The three dangling crew members hung helplessly beneath the chopper as its pilot tried to gain enough altitude to clear the trees while he rolled forward.

Hollister caught the thin green line made by a tracer from somewhere to the south of the chopper. They were taking fire. And the pilot's options were severely limited by the fact that he had three live Americans hanging under his aircraft while he was taking fire from the same direction he was trying to fly his chopper.

Hollister raised the handset to his ear to listen to the cross talk. The net was filled with competing message traffic from the gunships, the pilot in command, and the C & C chopper.

More fire leaped from the ground, reaching for the chopper and the passengers swinging beneath its belly. Hollister saw DeSantis step out onto the skid of the chopper, flame spitting from the muzzle of his M-16 as he tried to help the door gunners suppress the ground fire. He leaned over at the waist, held in the chopper by a nylon monkey strap that allowed him the freedom to work out on the skid.

"Killer Six, are you clear of this?" a voice asked over the radio.

Hollister couldn't make out the voice over the din, but didn't care. "That's affirm. I'm clear. Don't worry about me."

Tracers defined the web of fire aimed at the pilots—in and under the chopper. Some of the fire found the thin skin of the chopper. Hollister couldn't tell if both sets of crew members were surviving the heavy fire.

Once the chopper gained enough altitude to make the move, the pilot put the craft into a hard right turn to avoid the intense ground fire. The maneuver pitched DeSantis backward into the chopper and swung the crew members dangling below in a wide, out-of-control arc, nearing the horizontal.

As fast as the pickup chopper rolled out, Joe Raymond led his Cobras in on the enemy firing positions. He let loose with three pairs of rockets.

The rockets found their mark in the dense bamboo, exploding with sharp cracks, little flame, and lots of smoke. Joe's wingman fired off two more pairs of rockets and flew blind through the huge clouds of smoke, while Joe came around for a second pass.

Hollister looked for the pickup chopper with the string riders below it, but they were masked by the horizon.

Inside the overhang, Hollister explained the plan to Jrae while he waited for his eyes to adjust to the dark. They had no option. They would have to move overland in the daylight to the clearing he had found, signal the chopper, and wait for an extraction.

He waited for Jrae to translate to Pek and then explained he would point out a rally point halfway to the PZ. If they were separated on the way before he picked it, they were to meet back in the overhang. If they were broken up after he identified the rally point, they would meet there.

Expecting the greatest need for air support would come near the PZ, Hollister called Michaelson and asked him to send all but a pair of gunships back to refuel. He wanted them on standby while the trio moved to the PZ.

*   *   *

Their move was slow and deliberate. Hollister decided to point out intermediate landmarks that would take them to the PZ and then let Pek move to them first. Pek could pick the best route for noise and concealment. He was also more familiar with the enemy markings for mines or booby traps. And he was likely to avoid being fired upon if they made a chance contact with enemy patrols. His native features, familiar clothing, and lack of a weapon might cause the enemy to assume he was an ally or an unarmed mountain man.

They were held up twice by what they thought was enemy movement. In each case it proved to be a false alarm. By midafternoon, Hollister held the Montagnards up and edged forward to see if the clearing was still void of enemy soldiers.

He found a place on the east side of the PZ and crawled under the bushes to look out across the clearing.

Seeing nothing alarming, he closed his eyes and listened. The wind was soft and made a slight swishing sound as it blew through the waist-high grasses in the clearing. The trees rustled. The sounds of birds were positive noises. They hadn't been spooked.

He opened his eyes again and noted the prevailing wind was out of the south at no more than three knots. It was perfect for the pickup.

The sound of the arriving choppers gave Hollister some hope of being able to pull off the extraction. He looked to Pek and Jrae to see if they recognized the presence of the two pickup ships that fell into orbit with the gunships and the C & C.

"Anytime you are ready," Hollister told Michaelson over his fading radio.

"We are going to come in from north to south. Our guess is any trouble might be on the west side of the Papa Zulu. Joe's going to check it out," Michaelson said.

"Roger. Put some fire in here, and we'll get on board. We don't have much in the way of options."

"Stand by. They are five out," Michaelson said.

Hollister passed the word to the others and looked around the PZ and then behind them—away from the clearing. He felt his gut tighten and tried to focus his senses on being as alert as he could to anything out of place. The effort was complicated by the

long hours without sleep and the high level of vigilance he had
sustained.

He fought off the impulse to be angry. He tried to convince
himself he would postpone it until he got back inside Vietnam.
Focusing on how incensed he was over Valentine's actions was
wasted energy. They were there, and God only knew how many
others had already been killed and wounded by Valentine's grab
for glory. Hollister needed his strength and tried to divert his anger
to getting them out of that hole in the Cambodian jungle and back
to safety. There he would make sure he settled the score.

The momentum picked up after the arrival of the other choppers.
Michaelson counted down the minutes to touchdown, and Hollister relayed the information to Jrae and Pek.

They all held their breath as the nose of the pickup ship peeked
over the north edge of the clearing and exposed its belly to slow
and settle into the grassy field.

Hollister pointed at Pek—launching him from his ready position into a flat-out run in spite of his casted arm toward the landing
chopper. Pek reached a point half the twenty meters to the
chopper's side door when Hollister got himself and Jrae up to
follow.

As he took his first step, Hollister heard the gunship passing
behind him belch out an angry burst of minigun fire somewhere to
his left rear.

He saw Pek leap up and into the chopper and then slump to the
floor—spread-eagle. The chopper jerked and bucked as the
window next to the command pilot's seat blew out from enemy
fire that had crossed through the cockpit of the chopper from the
far side of the PZ.

Suddenly the chopper rolled forward and up, not waiting for
Hollister and Jrae. Hollister reached out and grabbed Jrae, who
was running toward her wounded brother more than for the
chopper as a means of escape. One hand firmly wrapped around
her ankle, Hollister tripped her up and fell next to her in the tall
grass.

Her eyes were wide and showed the terror of her reality. She
had just seen her brother take gunshots in his back and legs. Hollister guessed she was anticipating the chopper might also crash in
its attempt to get out of the line of fire—crippled and unstable.

He pressed the radio mouthpiece to his lips. "Tell me what we are doing," he yelled, hoping Michaelson could hear him in the C & C and see him and Jrae faceup in the grass—ten meters from the tree line.

"Stay! Stay put!" Michaelson yelled. "The chase is inbound to the same spot. Get ready to move."

It was all Hollister needed to hear. He rolled over on his belly and raised up enough to see the second chopper coming in hotter, more deliberately than the first.

Hollister grabbed Jrae by the shirt and pulled her to her knees while he tried to juggle his handset and his rifle with his other hand.

Sporadic enemy fire crossed the PZ from two opposing directions. He couldn't raise his head enough to see without giving away their location and giving them something to fire at.

The chopper's shadow fell across their womblike depression in the tall grass. Unable to make a more informed decision, Hollister had to trust his instinct and his ears. "Now! Now!" he yelled as he helped Jrae to her feet.

He shoved her forward—toward the chopper—and raised his rifle to his shoulder. He spun, searching for any threat to her dash to the chopper, and spotted two uniformed NVA soldiers standing, full-length, directly in front of the chopper, aiming two AKs at Jrae. The first soldier fired and Hollister opened up on automatic. He heard himself speaking out loud—to himself. "Shoot low. Shoot low!"

His eight-round burst skipped off the dirt beneath the grasses and popped back up—taking the first soldier out. The second soldier got a few rounds off, then he, too, was cut down by Hollister's next short burst, which caught him in the legs and torso.

Hollister spun to the chopper, searching for Jrae. All he could see was Easy almost filling the open door, firing a submachine gun at something behind Hollister in the tree line.

Easy saw Hollister's expression and pulled one hand from the short stock of his weapon. He pointed at a spot half the distance between them.

Hollister ran to the depression in the grass and found Jrae collapsed on her side. An enemy AK-47 round had found her neck and a second her collarbone just below her chin. She lay near death on the ground, blood spurting freely from the wound in her neck. He fell to his knees and slid into her. He shrugged off his radio in order to scoop her up. As he slipped his arms under her, he bent forward, putting his cheek near the center of her torso, and heard her gurgle, struggling for air—even over the choppers and gunfire.

He was able to summon up the strength and manage his momentum to get to his feet and make a wobbly run to the waiting chopper, Jrae cradled in his arms.

Hollister could hear rockets exploding in the tree line he had just left and the jingle of expended minigun shells falling from the gunships and onto the decking near the slick door gunner. His eyes burned with salt as his sweat flooded them.

He kept repeating, "Hold on. Hold on. We're okay. Hold on," as much to Jrae as to reassure himself that he could get them out of the hell that had replaced the tranquil clearing.

He shook his head to clear the tears and sweat from his eyes and could see Easy reaching out of the chopper to help him. His best guess in the distorted world was that four more steps would get them to the first soldier's grasp in the door of the chopper.

One. Then the next. His foot slid in the grasses, and he shifted his weight to recover and keep from falling. Then all of his senses registered a silent, blinding explosion of black, red, and yellow.

He had no idea what hit them. He was thrown forward— toward the chopper. His center of gravity got out in front of him, and he felt himself losing the strength in his legs. A flash of panic registered in his head. He worried about going down carrying Jrae. He had to get her to some help. He couldn't see. He couldn't hear. It was like being underwater. Sounds were muffled and time accordioned—first fast and then almost motionless.

He felt no real pain, but became aware of the fact that his legs had left the ground and then remade contact.

"Here! Over here!" he thought he heard Easy yelling—from a great distance.

Hollister became more confused and, unsure of his orientation, he leaned forward—toward the chopper, his legs still pumping in the unseen grass. He collided with the deck of the chopper and fell down between the skid and the belly of the aircraft.

The next few minutes were even more confusing. Hollister was unsure if he was inside the chopper or out. He felt hands grabbing at his web gear. He heard the muzzle of his rifle clank against something metal. But he couldn't hear the chopper or voices or firing. He saw nothing. He felt nausea and unconsciousness coming on. He gritted his teeth and tightened his stomach muscles trying to will blood back up into his head.

He reached for the metallic sound, afraid he had lost his rifle, and heard someone say, "Okay. I got it. Okay." But the words were as if on a record played at far too slow a speed.

He could feel Easy rocking back and forth on his knees putting all of his weight into crushing Jrae's chest, forcing her lungs to work—trying to hold back death while he administered CPR.

Then there was the air. He felt the cool air on his wet face. It was altitude. The air was cooler. The chopper was flying. Or he was falling. He tried to wipe the blood from his eyes. It didn't help.

He could see nothing.

He knew he had been out—but not for how long. He knew that he would not see Juliet Company again. But he didn't know if they were still flying or even what country he was in. He reached out for Jrae and found her left forearm. He grabbed it and began to pray. He was very afraid.

He lost consciousness again.

EPILOGUE

1972

The investigating officer's questions went on for almost three hours. Though Hollister was tired and felt light-headed, he forced himself to concentrate on the colonel's words and to answer as accurately as he could. He owed it to Jrae and the others killed and crippled as a result of Valentine's misuse of his authority. He fought the urge to let the anger in his belly color his answers. The justice would come from the completeness of the investigation, and he would have to provide much of the details.

Once finished, he was wheeled back to his hospital bed. On the way, he again listened to his wheelchair as it traveled the hollow-sounding ramps between hospital wings.

The *New York Times* characterized the small action on the Cambodian border as still another outrageous incursion designed to widen the war and lock the United States into civil-turned-regional war. They claimed Phnom Penh filed complaints with the White House and with the Vietnamese government.

A month later, Juliet Company was added to the list of units to be deactivated. America's longest war was over for the Rangers.

First Sergeant Evan-Clark tried to remain in Vietnam but was placed on a medical profile that severely restricted his duties. He submitted his retirement papers and spent his last two years at the Florida Ranger Camp at Eglin Air Force Base. Two decades later, they still tell the stories of the one-legged Ranger first sergeant who ran patrols with the students—his prosthetic leg clanking against the cyprus knees in the swamps along the Yellow River.

General Valentine was forced to retire early at the rank of colonel. His name was purged from the brigadier generals' promotion list. But no further action was taken.

Susan Hollister became a writer for *Time* magazine and was posted in Oslo for three years. She never bothered to tell Jim Hollister.

Grady Michaelson rose to the rank of lieutenant general and then was loaned to the CIA by the Department of Defense.

Corporal Greenwood became the command sergeant major of the 101st Airborne Division and retired after the Persian Gulf War.

Estlin was killed in Desert One—trying to rescue the American hostages in Tehran.

After sixteen months of hospitalization, surgeries, and physical therapy, Major James Hollister was released from Letterman Army Medical Center. The vision returned to one eye. He would have to endure many future operations on the other in attempts to restore its sight.

Authorized ninety days of convalescent leave, he declined. Instead, he picked up his reassignment orders and his travel voucher and flew directly to Bangkok.

He spent the next three years with the Joint Casualty Resolution Center, searching the jungles of Southeast Asia looking for the missing in action and the prisoners of war left behind after the American departure.

It was what he wanted to do—to be busy, to be useful. And to never forget.

For more astounding tales of life in war, look for

SPECIAL MEN: A LRP's Recollections
by Dennis Foley

For a glimpse of this true story, please read on. . . .

I was just eighteen and only four days into basic training at Fort Dix, New Jersey, when my platoon was called out of our aging World War II barracks for the third formation of the morning. A cadreman, a young acting corporal, formed up the platoon with an uncharacteristic smirk on his face. Once he was satisfied that we were all there, had handed out a moderate number of push-ups for various infractions that we didn't really understand, and once he had our attention, he told us that we were going to a briefing. He made sure that we understood it was a briefing we were not ready for, and one that the army was wasting time and money on.

He told us we were worthless, and that it was highly unlikely that we could hack it. In his opinion—formed in the six months he had been in the army—the army would be better off sending us to the regimental headquarters to police the area.

We were joined by the other platoons, double-timed to a small battalion theater, and hustled into seats. My platoon was lucky to get seats in the front rows. None among us knew the subject of the briefing, and the late-June heat was almost unbearable in the tiny theater as we sat there waiting.

We waited for the longest time, reminded to sit still and be happy that we weren't out in the sun. In only a few minutes we were getting sleepy and the fight to stay awake was on. Getting caught dozing off would be worth an easy twenty push-ups.

Finally, from the back of the room someone yelled, "On your feet!" and we jumped up, having learned the multiple-push-up penalties for anything less than an instant response. We couldn't see them, but two sets of boots clumped down the aisle, approaching the chin-high stage.

"Gentlemen, please take your seats," another voice said.

Gentlemen? It was the first time anyone had called us "gentlemen" since our arrival at the reception center on the other side of the post almost two weeks earlier. We'd not been in the army very long, but we knew something was up. And that something mounted the stage in the persona of two sergeants, one a sergeant first class and the other a master sergeant.

Since our induction we had rarely seen NCOs of that rank. Our days had been controlled by privates first class (PFCs), acting corporals, and an occasional three-stripe sergeant. A couple of times a day we would stand a formation led by our field first sergeant—himself a sergeant first class.

But those two sergeants on the stage were nothing like the sergeants we had all met in recruiting stations, induction centers, and the reception station. They were both tall, lean, and hard looking—yet they were younger than any NCOs we'd seen of comparable rank.

They radiated a sense of self-confidence that would have shown up on an X ray. But most apparent were their uniforms: spit-shined paratrooper boots, bloused trousers with razor-sharp creases, highly polished brass, and badges that we would come to respect—parachute wings, the Ranger tab, and the Airborne tab over the Special Forces arrowhead patch. To us, they were truly men of iron.

They were there to recruit us into Airborne training and to set the hook for Special Forces. Before the briefing was over, we began to think of those men as much larger than we could ever be. As we listened to them tell us how difficult Airborne training was and how selective Special Forces was, we all were sure that the corporal was right. We were not made of the same stuff that those two soldiers were.

The two NCOs spoke with confidence and authority. Each word was carefully measured for its impact on us and each pause was well rehearsed to let the point that followed sink in.

They showed us a film about parachute training. We sat there in the dark watching soldiers—paratroopers—hurl themselves from aircraft at what seemed like incredible speeds and frightening heights.

No one spoke, and no one in the room missed any parachutes deploying from the pack trays of the jumpers, who seemed to us to be totally out of control as they exited the small doors of the large, silver C-119 Flying Boxcars.

A thought entered my mind for only a fleeting second, and then I quickly wished it away. Hell, I had never even *been* in an airplane. Stepping out of one at over twelve hundred feet above the ground was more than I could imagine, even though I was watching it happen in that steamy little theater.

The mass jumps were interspersed with scenes from training. It seemed every clip had one of three things in it: soldiers jumping from aircraft, soldiers running in formation, or soldiers practicing landings or exits. Nowhere in the film was there a moment where soldiers were sitting or listening or taking notes or relaxing.

It was very clear that anyone who volunteered for parachute training was in for a month of dawn-to-dusk PT, followed by an evening of spit shining and polishing.

While we were all impressed with the tales of derring-do and the promise of challenges and danger far beyond our imagination, not many of us were interested in falling out to the designated area to fill out the application forms to go to Airborne school at Fort Benning.

I walked out of that briefing unaware of how my life had been changed by the remote possibilities suggested by those two sergeants. Little did I know then that men like the two who had stood on that stage would be such a large part of my life—eventually finding a permanent place in my heart.

SPECIAL MEN
by Dennis Foley

Published by Ivy Books.
Available wherever books are sold.